Modern Confucian Entrepreneur

Biography of Steve Tsai

The legendary life of the founder of the United Pacific Hotel Group

Written with Kaiping Liu
Translated by Jonathan Brody and Wang Shuang-chiu

Published by
CHUNG HWA BOOK COMPANY, LTD
2022

This book is dedicated to the joys of my life, my darling wife Tina, and my dear family. My life has been made rich through the guidance and help of many friends, and by faith in the Lord.

Steve Tsai / Tsai Shiding

San Francisco, July 16, 2014

Steve at age 90.

Steve's smoothly flowing calligraphy.

"Seek Truth From Facts", "Promises Are Precious as Gold":
Calligraphy by Steve.

Formal portraits of Steve and Hung by famed painter Li Quanwu.

Li Quanwu graduated from China's Hubei Academy of Fine Arts in Hubei and Central Arts Academy before moving to New York in 1985 where he now serves as Art Director for NBC Universal, Inc. He has executed portraits for many famous people. The portrait of former US president George H. W. Bush at the George H.W. Bush Presidential Library and Museum was executed by Li Quanwu.

We Make Our Own Path

— Steve Tsai, founder of the United Pacific Hotel Group

I have experienced many things in my life: Some difficult and some complicated, but I overcame them one by one. Thinking back, I sometimes ask myself: Who am I? Where did I find the strength to face these challenges?

I think this strength mainly comes from four sources:

First, I learned a great deal from my parents. My father died suddenly at age 49. I was nine years old at the time. I remember the shock that reverberated through our community at his death, and the sudden outpouring of public grief. It impressed on me that a person's contribution to society extends beyond his own lifetime. Although my parents' lives were unfortunately short, they lived well and left a lasting legacy. In contrast, a mediocre person lives and dies quietly. Even if one is not blessed to live to one hundred years old, those who take responsibility for the well-being of their community will surely enjoy a full and meaningful life.

Although my parents left me long ago, my father's compassion and enthusiasm for public welfare, and my mother's virtues of diligence, thrift and knowledge have always stayed with me. Their virtues and good deeds continue to flourish in the world through my own life.

The second source of my strength comes from my religious faith in the Lord Jesus Christ. I came to Christianity at the age of thirteen at the century-old Quanzhou Puyuan Middle School, turning from Buddhism to a new faith. But at the time, I considered myself unworthy to call myself a Christian, and refused to accept baptism in part because I had not been able to give up cigarettes. I would often sneak outside to smoke and kept this habit up through the 1970s. Finally, I confessed this "sin" to Pastor Yeh Wen-yuan in San Francisco. He laughed and said, "Smoking is a bad habit, but it's certainly not a sin in the eyes of the Lord." He told me, "Being a believer takes a different kind of discipline. Let me baptize you, and I have confidence that you'll be a good believer, even if you continue to smoke."

Thus, that Sunday, after believing for more than 40 years, I finally became the last person in my family to be baptized, and gave up this unhealthy habit I'd had for over half a century.

In my family, our children and grandchildren are enthusiastic churchgoers, and their faith moves past the church doors and into greater society. My faith has grown in my heart, driven by love of family, country and humanity. When facing any difficulties, I put my trust in the omnipotent and omnipresent creator of the universe. This faith brings a vibrant confidence into my life, creates harmony in my family, and gives us invincible strength. If you ask me how to face difficulties in life, I will say: Do everything you can, and leave the ultimate outcome to God.

Third, I have drawn inspiration from my study of classic literature. In my teens, I had to drop out of school due to the war, but my desire for knowledge remained undiminished. After the war, I read all the books I could find. I also took copious notes on my readings and submitted book reviews to newspapers. I found new books at friends' houses, but sometimes they were reluctant to let me take them. I'd occasionally resort to "borrowing" these books, and quickly take copious notes before returning them with apologies. I took absolution from the words of Lu Xun: "Books taken by a scholar should not be seen as stolen."

My favorite book at the time was Ba Jin's Torrents Trilogy: Home, Spring, and Autumn. Sometimes I imagined myself as the protagonist, Juehui. Decades later, I traveled to Shanghai, hoping to meet and learn from Ba Jin, but at the time, he was recuperating from illness in the hospital and couldn't be disturbed.

The preface to Ba Jin's Torrents Trilogy includes the following passage:

"Some people say that there is no road at first, but rather a road gradually emerges through the footsteps of travelers. Others say the road exists from the steps of that first traveler. It is not for me to judge right and wrong. I am still young; I have to live, to conquer life. I know that the torrent of life will never stop. I will see where it takes me!"

I copied this passage out with a calligraphy brush, and then framed it and hung it on my wall where I would read it every day.

"I want to conquer life." "The torrent of life will never stop." When I look back, these words now remind me of my youthful struggle and vision for the future.

Wang Rensheng was once the general manager of my factory and is now known as the "King of Henan". When he was preparing his own memoir, he asked me to suggest a title. Thinking of Ba Jin, I replied, "We Make Our Own Path," and he took this as the title for his book. Had he not, I might have used it as the title for my own book.

I was also an avid reader of Lu Xun's essays. Although these could be a bit difficult to understand, he shone a light on mendacity and his prose was full of passion. I was young and wanted to transform society, and I found these sentiments deeply appealing. As I grew older, I came to better understand objective criticism, to better appreciate underlying causes and effects, and developed a deeper appreciation for more moderate characters. Over time, my devotion to Lu Xun gradually faded.

Upon returning to the mainland for the first time, I took my wife and children to Suzhou to visit the Hanshan Temple. This temple has achieved worldwide fame because of the poetry of the Tang Dynasty poet Zhang Ji. Situated outside Gusu City, the Hanshan Temple attracts countless Chinese and foreign tourists and is particularly popular with Japanese worshippers. The temple has a powerful cultural impact that travels through time and space.

In the past, when I was in Mainland China, I worked as a teacher, a freelance writer, a newspaper editor and later as editor-in-chief. I never intended to go into business. When I first arrived in Taiwan, I first served as the editor-in-chief of a publishing house and wrote "*A New Free China.*" I served as the Taiwan correspondent to a Philippine overseas Chinese newspaper, mostly focusing on cultural and educational work. I encouraged overseas Chinese in the Philippines to actively invest in Taiwan. They felt I had a strong understanding of Taiwan and sought my advice on many investment projects. These discussions gradually brought me into the world of business. However, having grown up steeped in Confucian culture, care for the nation and society were never far from my heart.

Whenever I had the opportunity to write an article or give a speech, I would emphasize the social responsibility of entrepreneurs.

Mencius said: "We are born in sorrow and die in peace." The educator Tao Hsing-chih said: "Life is education, and society is a school." These words inspired me to make the most of my learning and to choose my own path in life."

The fourth source of my strength has been the help from my beloved friends. If you deal with others with sincerity, then all men are your brothers. Friends relieve loneliness and make life more colorful. When facing adversity, one must first count on oneself, and then appeal to friends for help. I've known two kinds of close friends: the wise ones who offer sage advice, and the bold ones who bring great strength to bear. Friends can offer both spiritual encouragement and practical assistance, providing solutions that turn adversity into prosperity. Friends are also an important source of strength in life.

These four influences have deeply affected my outlook on life and have given me great strength to face various difficult and complex challenges.

Let me turn to how we achieve self-cultivation, contentment, joy, and health. To be healthy, we must maintain joy, and to be joyful we must maintain a mentality of contentment. To put it more plainly: Spend more time eating sweet potatoes and less time dreaming.

As the Chinese linguist Mr. Ji Hsien-lin said: Don't tell only lies, but also don't only tell the whole truth. Throughout my life, I have constantly improved my values in terms of "being what people need," which led me to realize that "to help others is actually to help oneself, and showing respect is the key to being respected."

Opportunities to help others come along by chance. But helping others is actually helping oneself and going out of one's way to benefit others ultimately comes back to you.

I do not see old age as a "magnificent sunset just before dusk". I hope to live to be quite old, and to always live with grace and vigor.

Who am I? This year, I'm 90 years old, and my life is gradually entering the evening stage. Looking back on the past, my happiness has been based on the feeling of being "needed," and this will always be my nature.

Steve Tsai

San Francisco, April 2014

Foreword

For as long as I can remember, my grandfather Steve Tsai has been a larger-than-life figure. When I was born in 1986, he at 61 had established himself as a successful businessman, instrumental in cultivating post-war investment in Taiwan. He was a proud father who raised and educated his four children on two continents. He, along with my grandmother Tina Tsai Hung, possessed a love of life that made for legendary evenings, filling their home with singing, eating, and dancing.

Contrast the confidence, dedication, and glamor of this man with a childhood that was fractured by loss, poverty, and conflict. My grandfather came of age during the turbulent and deadly times of the Sino-Japanese War and Chinese Civil War. Four of his six sisters died in childhood; he was only nine years old when his father passed away. Food at times became so scarce that a lone yam, found in the forest, would be the day's great blessing. Young adulthood would not come any easier. The Civil War in China scattered and separated his brothers and sisters across Asia. Only decades later would they be able to reunite.

For me and my cousins, such challenges can seem nearly unrecognizable amidst the modern comforts and peace that our grandparents and parents have tirelessly worked to provide us. That history has been shared with us in fragments: stories shared around the dinner table, life lessons written onto red envelopes, the tastes and sights of Gulangyu, where he and my grandmother fell in love.

My grandfather's memoir pieces those experiences together, allowing me—through this translation—to see anew the portrait of the man who has inspired, sometimes intimidated, but always cared for my generation. He made the best of a childhood and adolescence shaped by the brutality of war, using his talents to make life better for his family, his community, and his country. But no matter where opportunity and success have taken him—Xiamen, Taipei, Manila, San Francisco—"home" has remained my grandfather's deepest ambition and greatest joy.

Hold still, his memoir suggests. We have travelled far, been separated by war and oceans for too long. But let us be together again: can you see the rivers and mountains that surround our village, Tangdong? Can you hear the waves washing over the golden beaches I loved so much as a young man? The moon is shining. There are voices singing in the distance.

I am transported there. I can hear the music. It is the sweetest sound.

Garrett Eng
San Francisco, April 2022

Garrett Eng is the son of Steve's eldest child Tenny Tsai. He received his BA in English Literature and BMus in Musicology from Northwestern University, an MPhil in English Studies from Cambridge University, and an MBA from New York University's Stern School of Business. He works in Real Estate Development in the San Francisco Bay Area.

Modern Confucian Entrepreneur

{{ Part 2: Beginning of Wisdom }}

Chapter Three
Crossing a Shallow Strait

Chapter Four
From Journalist to Entrepreneur

Chapter Five
Solving Two Crimes with Wisdom

{{ Part 3: Beginning of Justice }}

Chapter Six
An Inch of Land, an Inch of Blood

Chapter Seven
Playing a Part in Taiwan's Economic Miracle

Chapter Eight
A Crosswalk in the Real Estate Market

Chapter Nine
Responsibility for the Nation

{{ Part 4: Beginning of Trustworthiness }}

Chapter Ten
Recalling Highlights of a Career in Journalism

Chapter Eleven
Across the Deep Pacific Ocean

Chapter Twelve
Dr. Tsai 's Business Philosophy

{{ Part 5: Converging to Benevolence }}

Chapter Thirteen
Behind the Success

Chapter Fourteen
Homecoming

Afterward

Appendix

— The Life of Steve Tsai —

Rising from Poverty to Serve the World

Vincent Siew
12th Vice President of the Republic of China

I met Mr. Steve and his wife Tina in Kuala Lumpur, Malaysia in 1969 when I was serving as representative of the Republic of China in that city. Consul General Chang Chung-jen and Mr. Tsai are old acquaintances. He told me that Mr. Tsai and his wife came to Malaysia to explore business opportunities and asked me for assistance. While the trip did not produce any significant business opportunities, I was deeply impressed by Mr. Tsai, who was gentle and bookish, and Mrs. Tsai, who is beautiful and generous.

In 1972, I was transferred from the Ministry of Foreign Affairs to the Ministry of Economic Affairs. In 1982, I was transferred to the post of Director of International Trade and Economic Cooperation. During the same period, while serving as the Taiwan correspondent to the Philippine Xinmin Daily News, Mr. Tsai vigorously advocated for overseas Chinese to invest in Taiwan. He also actively developed his connections in the corporate world. At the same time, he was elected as the standing supervisor and chairman of the board of directors by many national business organizations.

During his tenure as Chairman of the Taiwan Decoration Bulbs & Light-Set Exporters Association, he had more official contacts with the International Trade Bureau. When I was the President of the Executive Yuan, he participated in a delegation I led to multiple countries as a standing director of the National Chamber of Commerce, and this gave us a chance to better understand each other.

Steve has enjoyed a rich and wonderful life. Before he came to Taiwan at the age of 24, he was the principal of a primary school in Fujian, editor-in-chief of the Hsing-chuan Anti-Japanese Command, a judicial police officer and the editor-in-chief of a newspaper. After coming to Taiwan, he served as the Taiwan special correspondent to the Philippine Xinmin Daily News, the managing director of OCBC Bank, the general manager of OCBC Life Insurance Company, chairman of Taishan Electric Industrial Company, standing director of the Taiwan Paper Company, chairman of the Chiaofu Construction Management Company, chairman of the National Association of Construction Managers, executive director of the National Chamber of Commerce and the National Arbitration Association, and chairman of the Taiwan Decorative Light Exporters Association.

Mr. Tsai arrived in Taiwan in 1949, fleeing the oppression of the Communist Party. At the time, Taiwan faced existential national security and economic challenges and had dire need for investment from overseas Chinese. The overseas Chinese in the Philippines were active in this regard. Mr. Tsai had close connections in both the Philippines and Taiwan and was able to gain trust on both sides. As a journalist, he reported on Free China's new development, with business opportunities particularly in the construction industry, and encouraged overseas Chinese to come to Taiwan. He actively promoted Philippine Chinese investment projects, including multiple major tourist hotels, as well as in the financial and manufacturing sectors, and was also active in bringing in overseas Chinese investment from other places in the world. For example, he was instrumental in the establishment of the Taipei Hilton Hotel, the OCBC Life Insurance Company and the OCBC Bank.

Of particular note, the government had originally intended to give overseas Chinese priority approval to establish insurance companies before fully liberalizing the market at a later date. Mr. Tsai, however, went against his own self-interest in promoting full market opening to both overseas Chinese and Taiwanese capital to compete openly and fairly. As a result, insurance companies have sprung up like bamboo shoots after a rain, creating an insurance industry that played a crucial role in the development of Taiwan's economic prosperity. In the early days, Taiwan's economy relied heavily on labor-intensive industries to earn foreign exchange. To help employment, many handicraft producers depended on piece work with production occurring in people's homes rather than in centralized workshops or factories, and this provided an important source of supplemental income for many families. The government began to promote the slogan "The living room as factory" to encourage everyone to work hard for economic development. At this time, Mr. Tsai founded the Taishan Electric Industrial Company with overseas Chinese leaders in the Philippines, providing job opportunities for families in rural and exurban areas.

To rationalize otherwise voracious industrial competition, Mr. Tsai lobbied enterprises to establish the Taiwan Decoration Bulbs & Light-Set Exporters Association. Under the Association's guidance, Taiwan quickly emerged as the world's third most important producer of Christmas lights, after Italy and Japan, directly creating about 150,000 jobs. Mr. Tsai served as the chairman of the Association for three terms and was named the Association's permanent honorary chairman as a reflection of his tremendous contribution.

He also actively promoted the Association's development of the "Export Price Verification Seal" under the International Trade Bureau. At that time, Taiwan's foreign trade was growing rapidly; and every year, hundreds of thousands of import and export applications were being filed with the Bureau of International Trade. The Export Price Verification Seal helped reduce the processing time for each case from three days to one day.

In addition, Taiwan's successive applications to join the General Agreement on Tariffs and Trade and the World Trade Organization required the government to undertake timely measures to promote the liberalization, internationalization and institutionalization of trade policies. On behalf of the Association, Mr. Tsai actively promoted the authorization of the Export Price Verification Seal to help rationalize Taiwan's export operations.

After more than two years of hard work, he obtained unanimous support from the Association's 600-plus members, and the policy was subsequently approved by the International Trade Bureau, making it the first of many trade associations to obtain such approval.

Beginning in 1973, the Tsai family's children one by one went to study in the United States, and Mrs. Tsai went along to watch over them. However, Mr. Tsai did not give up his career in Taiwan. After the children finished their studies, the Tsai family began to invest in hotels in the United States. They bought their first home in America in San Francisco and subsequently developed their Bay Area hotel operation into a large-scale group with six hotels that is still expanding.

On December 15, 1978, US President Jimmy Carter announced that the US would establish diplomatic relations with Beijing on January 1 of the following year. The next day, the president of the Executive Yuan instructed the National Chamber of Commerce of the Republic of China to immediately send personnel to establish an office in the United States to prepare for the maintenance of business exchanges with the United States. As the executive director of the Republic of China Chamber of Commerce and the director of the Liaison Center of the Foreign Chamber of Commerce, Mr. Tsai traveled to California to establish the Republic of China National Chamber of Commerce office in the United States. The severance of diplomatic relations between the US and ROC raised tensions and challenges; but, working closely with his legal counsel, Mr. Tsai was able to accomplish the task.

Later, Mr. Tsai was dispatched to set up a Canadian office for the Republic of China Chamber of Commerce in Toronto, which also became an important platform for communication and relationship building between private enterprises in Taiwan and Canada. From 1973 until 2014, Mr. Tsai served as executive director of the Chamber of Commerce, enthusiastically promoting Taiwan's interests through commercial diplomacy for 41 years and making countless significant contributions.

In addition to their extraordinary professional achievements, Mr. Tsai and his wife are to be commended for the education they provided for their children. The four children are all very filial and spared no effort in the care for their grandmother, as she spent more than a decade suffering from Alzheimer's disease, taking turns to care for her night and day. Following on his professional success, he and his children extended this love to remote areas of the United States and overseas through charitable works and donations to the disadvantaged and infirm.

Mr. Tsai was inspired by his father's enthusiasm and willingness to help others, and he has passed these traits on to his children. Mencius advocated that "the poor strive to be good, and the good care for the world," an aphorism that truly reflects the Tsai family's dedication to charitable causes.

I think that readers of this book will find that Mr. Tsai has the following characteristics. First, he is a dutiful son who inherited his parents' virtues of benevolence and justice, values he has passed on to his own children who live these values in their dedication to social welfare. Second, he is a patriot. Particularly after the United States broke off diplomatic relations with the ROC, he went to the ends of the earth, tirelessly promoting Taiwan's commercial diplomacy.

Third, he has a deep sense of social responsibility. For over forty years, he labored unceasingly in positions of great responsibility in multiple civic organizations, working with a practical and dedicated approach to serving his community. Fourth, he has a rich sense of justice. He has demonstrated great personal courage many times. Falsely arrested with many others on a spurious murder charge, he refused to accept release until all those arrested with him were freed as well. Fifth, he has dedicated himself to the greater good, emphasizing the public welfare above his private interests, insisting for example that Taiwan's insurance market be opened to all potential entrants with full and fair competition, despite the challenges that such competition would bring to OCBC.

In May of this year, Mr. Tsai returned to Taiwan after celebrating his ninetieth birthday in the United States. Upon arrival, he came to see me, and we delighted in each other's company. Our conversation confirmed that Mr. Tsai's deep concern for the future development of the country is a strong as ever.

This book was written with the assistance of a senior American journalist, Mr. Kaiping Liu. It portrays the brilliant life of Steve and his devotion to charity. It is a rich and rewarding story, and young people today should find inspiration in it.

Mr. Vincent Siew was the 12th Vice President of the Republic of China, President of the Executive Yuan, legislator, Chairman of the Mainland Affairs Council, Minister of Economy Affairs, and Vice Chairman of the Chinese Kuomintang.

In July 1998, former Vice President Vincent Siew, who was ROC Premier at the time, led a delegation from the ROC to friendly foreign nations, with Steve attending as a representative of the ROC Chamber of Commerce. This picture was taken in Guam while they were on their way back to Taiwan.

A Man Must Be Caring and Resolute

Wang Chien-shien
President of the Control Yuan, Republic of China

A man went to see an orthopedist who asked him where he felt discomfort. The man said he was perfectly comfortable. So, asked the doctor, why are you here? The man responded that his wife wanted him to come to an orthopedist because she said he'd lost his backbone.

A person with no backbone lives in vain. Mr. Steve Tsai, however, is a man of strong backbone and loyalty. I met him when I was the undersecretary of the Ministry of Economic Affairs. At the time, we were merely acquaintances, but I was already aware of his reputation as an able and principled businessman. But now that I have read his biography, I am thoroughly impressed by this man, and feel that one can learn many worthwhile lessons from his life.

What I admire most about him is his fierce sense of loyalty.

When I served at the Control Yuan, I sought to encourage a dedication to fairness and justice, qualities apparent in Mr. Tsai and his father.

When Mr. Tsai was a child, life was difficult, but his father was a kind-hearted, philanthropic man who went into debt to support good works. Clearly Mr. Tsai inherited his sense of justice from his father, along with his backbone.

For example, during the War of Resistance Against Japan, the Kuomintang government was notorious for pressing civilian men into the military. In one instance, angry villagers fought back and beat several officers who had come to take their young men. In the resulting crackdown, over 200 people were arrested and charged with rebellion. The youngest of these was Mr. Tsai, who was only 19 years old at the time.

Mr. Tsai went to the press to explain the truth and sent letters to villagers everywhere. Under the resulting public pressure, an official decided to release Mr. Tsai and one other prisoner. But Mr. Tsai insisted that all prisoners should be released and refused to leave the prison otherwise. Later it emerged that the people who had actually committed the beatings were ruffians who had escaped the scene before the crackdown. All 200 of the arrestees were thus released, and Mr. Tsai's insistence on their release at his own expense showed that he was a man of righteousness, justice, and backbone even at a young age.

Today, Taiwan is in chaos, and many people, thinking to protect themselves, are afraid to speak truth to power. I hope everyone can learn a lesson from the backbone that Mr. Tsai has always shown.

Mr. Tsai has continued his father's commitment to public philanthropy. He leads a household of good Christians devoted to the teachings of Christ. He is full of the love of Christ and has glorified God throughout his life. He is a good example for all of us, especially for Christians. Mr. Tsai has also led a very successful career in business management. There are many great Chinese entrepreneurs, some of whom rival Bill Gates and Warren Buffett. But great entrepreneurs only know how to make money, but don't know how to use money to the betterment of society. Mr. Tsai, however, is both a great entrepreneur and a great philanthropist.

The early years were a difficult time in Taiwan. Mr. Tsai had an opportunity to secure a lucrative official license in a restricted market for insurance from President Chiang Kai-shek, but he politely declined, suggesting that the country would benefit more from open competition in the insurance industry. This showed his deep commitment to the country, placing the public interest ahead of his own.

May God bless your family with peace and happiness.

░ Mr. Wang Chien-hsien served as President of Control Yuan, Minister of Finance, legislator, and leader of the New Party.

Steve (far left, then Executive Director of the ROC Chamber of Commerce), Wang Chien-shien (far right), Tsai Neng (second from the right, Chairman of the Eel Exporters Association), and Mr. Hsiung (second from the left) a counselor at the Revolutionary Practice Research Institute.

22nd Class of the Revolutionary Practice Research Institute, including Steve (far left, second row) and Wang Chien-shien (fifth from left, second row).

Chivalry and Confucianism
Heroism Reaching to the Clouds

Chen Mu-tsai
Former Deputy Minister of Finance of the Republic of China

Brother Steve and I have a strong karmic relationship, and while he is older than I, he graciously and joyously spends time with the younger generations.

Brother Steve and I were both students in the 22nd Revolution Practice Workshop of the Revolutionary Practice Research Institute. We lived together for a month in late winter at Chunghsing Villa in Yangmingshan. The class had 58 students from all walks of life including trade associations and government agencies, with legislators and officials from the Ministry of Finance and the Ministry of Economic Affairs, along with directors of many industry associations, and high-level executives from financial institutions. For decades, we have maintained close contact and see each other frequently. The eldest person in our group was Mr. Tsai Neng, born in 1918 and who was once the chairman of the Taiwanese Eel Export Industry Association (known as the "Eel King"). Brother Steve was the second oldest, born in 1925. I was born in 1945, making him 20 years older than me. At that time, I was the director of the Economic Research Office of Taipei City Bank. During our training, in addition to serving as the chairman of two companies, Steve also served as the chairman of the Taiwan Decoration Bulbs & Light-Set Exporters Association and the executive director of the National Chamber of Commerce. Also, from 1982 to 1999, he served as the executive director of OCBC Bank.

Our group included many officials and prominent business executives, leading Mr. Kwoh-Ting Li, our lecturer, to refer humorously to the group as the "Government-Business Collusion Class" but noted that coordination between officialdom and private enterprise was not necessarily improper if it was done in the interests of the public. Mr. Li's words made a big impression on everyone there. The two Mr. Tsais were both cheerful and enthusiastic people, charming everyone who met them. Each night after dinner, they would take the group to the nearby hot springs, which was particularly enjoyable in the cold winter nights. These informal and friendly gatherings were very conducive to the development of revolutionary fervor! It's certainly difficult to find a modern equivalent!

I have always had great curiosity about and taken a keen interest in Taiwan's financial development and financial reforms. At that time, I was studying issues related to the establishment of a private banking sector. So on July 9, 1982, I visited Steve and his brother Tsai Youhui (who, at the time, served as director and deputy general manager of the OCBC Bank). They explained how the OCBC Bank was established in March 1961 at a time when the establishment of new banks was prohibited. Brother Steve told me that, for various reasons, OCBC Bank should not be seen as a model for local private bank operations. Another institution, the World China United Commercial Bank, was a domestic public bank with similar style and effective business support, but it was not a private bank and had low qualifications, and thus applications to establish new private banks were rejected. Brother Steve's life is colorful and eventful. He was very well informed about the development of the OCBC Bank and the many challenges it had overcome. But of these events, only Tsai Chennan's stock manipulation is discussed in Chapter 7, and there are many aspects of the development of OCBC Bank that could be explained in greater detail. Perhaps a separate book is in order.

Brother Steve not only witnessed a very important period of modern social and economic history, but also participated in many controversial public and enterprise policy decisions, providing excellent solutions and leadership for the country and society.

In the 50th year of the Republic of China, due to the foresight of Brother Steve in persuading President Chiang Kai-shek, the government fully liberalized the domestic markets for property and life insurance to both domestic and overseas Chinese entrants. This is well described in Chapter 7 of this book. Starting out as a teacher and journalist, Brother Steve spent years of hard work to emerge as a virtuous businessman. The story of his adventure along this road is full of fascinating insights and adventures. A graduate of the school of life, Brother Steve developed broad and deep expertise through his talent and hard work. These years of training laid a solid foundation for all his later achievements.

This story of the life of Brother Steve is a biography that reads like a novel, revolving around a chivalrous, heroic and admirable protagonist in the Confucian tradition. Dictated by Brother Steve to the journalist Kaiping Liu of the San Francisco World Journal, Sing Tao Daily, and China Daily, it is a brilliant narrative which will amuse and astound readers.

Chen Mu-tsai

July 26, 2014

Chen Mu-tsai was formerly Executive Deputy Chief of the Ministry of Finance of the Republic of China, Chairman of the Farmers Bank, Chairman of the Bank of Taiwan, and Chairman of the Banking Association of the Republic of China. He currently serves as Chairman of the China Development Finance Holding Company.

{{ **Part 1: Beginning of Propriety** }}
Chapter One

Lovely Home, Lovely Hometown

I Am from Quanzhou

Steve was born in Tangdong Village, Jinjing Township, Jinjiang City, Quanzhou, Fujian, China on April 29th of the 14th year of the Republic of China (1925). Tangdong was more elegantly referred to as Jindong.

Quanzhou is famous as the hometown of many overseas Chinese, with more than seven million descendants living in more than 90 countries around the world . The people of Quanzhou are colorful, hospitable, loyal and persistent.

Starting from Tangdong Village

As you might guess, Tangdong ("East of the pond") Village has a large pond named Longguang Pond. Tsai Wodong, the founder of the Tsai family moved here from Dalun Township (commonly known as Beitsai), first settling in the east of Fushi, which is now Dongjing to the east of Tangdong Village. Later he moved to the east side of the pond.

The Tsai family traces its origins back to the Yellow Emperor, with a lineage through the fifth son of Zhou King Wen (born Ji Chang), Shudu, the younger brother of King Wu. Shudu was put in charge of Tsai State (now Shangcai County, Henan), where he founded the house of Tsai.

Beginning with Tsai Wodong more than 700 years ago (i.e., since the Southern Song Dynasty), the Tsai family has lived in Tangdong Village.

According to 2008 records, the village had 986 households with 4,679 individuals, most of whom early on shared the common surname of "Tsai". The village is home to the magnificent Tsai family ancestral hall (Eastern Tsai Family Temple). At the time, among the villagers, it was stipulated that only ancestral halls of families in which a man had achieved the civil service examination rank of "jinshi" can be called a family temple. The Tsai ancestral hall was built in 1548, just a few years after Tsai Zuan had achieved the rank of "jinshi" in 1541, but the gall was badly damaged by fire in the late Qing Dynasty, and rebuilt in 1912. It subsequently fell into disrepair and was completely rebuilt using funds raised from abroad in 1985.

To the east and north of Tangdong Village is mostly farmland leading up to mountains (including the Baogai, Fengzhi, Mo, and Zhuowang mountains), with the Pacific Ocean to the southwest, fronted by the golden sandy coast stretching more than 2,000 meters. Here, between the mountains and the sea, Tangdong is situated in a beautiful setting with a pleasant climate. The Tsai clan has thrived here for generations, working in agriculture and fishery.

Traversing the Ocean, Chasing a Better Life

While Tangdong today has fewer than 5,000 rural residents, tens of thousands of Tangdong expatriates moved to live overseas in the Philippines, Myanmar, Vietnam, the United States, Australia, Taiwan, Hong Kong, Macau, and some European countries. Overseas Chinese associations play a prominent role in the expatriate Chinese populations of many countries, especially in the Philippines, where they exert a strong economic and social influence. Jindong Associations can be found in the Philippines, Hong Kong, Macao and elsewhere. For over a century, these Associations have helped maintain ties between Tangdong expatriates and their hometown, actively channeling support for education, culture and infrastructure development back home, providing funds for primary and secondary schools, kindergartens, libraries, science education halls, and gymnasiums.

Less than 20 kilometers off the southwest coast of Tangdong Village lies Kinmen (Quemoy), and further to the east is Taiwan. While the climate in Tangdong Village is mild and well suited for agriculture, the quality of the soil is poor, and there's insufficient arable land to support the population. With only 0.3 mu (about 2200 square feet) of land per person, most villagers depend on the sea for their livelihood. Located on China's southeast coast, southern Fujian has for centuries sent its sons abroad to Southeast Asia to seek their fortune, sending money home to support their extended families. The local clan associations would assist locals in seeking a new life abroad.

While some of these young men would have an elementary school education, many did not. They left with tattered clothes on their backs, many shoeless, with a few copper coins in their pockets. Leaving their parents and families behind, they crossed the ocean and wandered the world with empty hands.

When you arrive in a foreign country, you are not only empty handed, but you also have to face a completely unfamiliar environment - a stranger in a strange land. You must work hard to survive and endure more hardships than ordinary people. You must endure the unbearable suffering of life. Most of these people were reluctant to spend money on renting a place to live. If you're working in a vegetable market, you close the door at night, spread some newspapers on the counter and sleep there. If there is no counter, then make do with the floor.

These young men from Tangdong Village worked tirelessly throughout Southeast Asia, saving every penny they earned for the day they would return home to their families to marry and start families of their own. But this was a daunting prospect. First you'd need to pay for your passage back to Fujian. Once you arrived home, there were gifts to distribute to your family and neighbors, sometimes a clutch of eggs or a chicken. Returning wanderers would also prepare gifts they bought overseas.

The Indominable Spirit of the Southern Fujianese

At the age of 11 or 12, they would leave home. At 16 or 17, their parents would arrange a marriage with a matchmaker, but this would require money, for which the boys would then go abroad to earn with their bare hands, toiling incessantly every day to save the sum needed to return home.

Steve said, "Wandering around the world is not easy. Generally speaking, the life of an apprentice is very difficult. They need to be able to survive by adapting quickly to their new environment."

Once they'd saved the required funds, they'd return home to be married, staying home for a year before leaving again to return to their jobs overseas. They needed the income from these jobs and would weep as they left their new brides. At the time, communications were very primitive, and these young couples could only keep in touch through sporadic letters.

Why wouldn't these young men take their wives with them? It simply wasn't done at the time, mainly because the living conditions of the men were so spartan, having their wives abroad with them would make life even more difficult. Also, he would need his wife to stay behind and care for his parents.

Today, the descendants of these migrants from Fujian are scattered throughout Southeast Asia. Their ability to survive, adapt, and endure hardships in pursuit of a better life formed a strong tradition of entrepreneurialism.

The legacy of this spirit is readily apparent in today's Taiwanese, who are clever and hardworking, and continually strive for self-improvement. Nearly half of Taiwan's 23 million people are descended from south Fujian, and a great affinity still exists between the people on both sides of the Taiwan Strait - after all, blood is thicker than water.

Quanzhou: The Departure Point of the Maritime Silk Road

Tangdong Village is located in Jinjing Town, Jinjiang City, Quanzhou City. Steve studied in Quanzhou Peiyuan Middle School. During the War of Resistance against Japan, Steve, who was then less than 20 years old, came to Quanzhou and served as an editor at the Xingquan area's Anti-Japanese Command. He also worked at the Quanzhou Times Evening News. After the war, he spent several years in Xiamen. The quaintness of Quanzhou and the vibrance of Xiamen left a deep mark on Steve, and Tangdong Village, Quanzhou and Xiamen can all be considered to be Steve's hometowns.

Quanzhou has a long history and was home to the Minyue people during the Zhou and Qin Dynasties. During the Song and Yuan Dynasties, Quanzhou became the first of China's four major ports, and later emerged as the largest port city in the East, known as "Citong (Erythrina Tree) Port." Marco Polo visited Quanzhou Port, noting it was more magnificent than Alexandria. At the time, Quanzhou was a major maritime transportation hub between China and the wider world. Over time, the legendary overland Silk Road had faded due to sporadic warfare, giving way to a new Maritime Silk Road that originated at Quanzhou. Surrounded by eight mountains, Quanzhou is a broad plain bisected by a river which flows to the sea. At the time, Kinmen and Penghu also fell under Quanzhou's jurisdiction. In 1982, Quanzhou was included in a list of 24 Chinese cities with historical and cultural significance published by China's State Council. Later that year, the Fujian Provincial Government established a Special Economic Zone on the West Coast of the Taiwan Straits, made up of five cities: Quanzhou, Fuzhou, Xiamen, Wenzhou, and Shantou.

Quanzhou is home to Qingjing Temple, built during the Northern Song Dynasty (1009 AD) and Anping Bridge, built during the Southern Song Dynasty (1138 AD), one of the world's oldest and longest existing stone bridges measuring a remarkable 2.5km in length. Quanzhou is known as a living museum of the world religions, with places of worship dedicated to Taoism, Chinese Buddhism, Catholicism, Nestorianism, Islam, Manichaeism, Hinduism, and Judaism. In addition, Quanzhou is also the birthplace of Southern Shaolin.

Quanzhou was also an important source of high-ranking members of the imperial civil service. Only 18 counties in all of China have been home to more than one thousand scholars who achieved the "jinshi" rank in the imperial examinations. Jinjiang County in Quanzhou was one of them and alone was home to 1,610 notable scholars and 13 prime ministers during the Song Dynasty.

Zhu Xi, a great scholar of the Southern Song Dynasty, came to Quanzhou as a young official, and later returned many times, leaving behind more than 100 poems, along with couplets and inscriptions too numerous to mention, creating a rich literary legacy that had a huge influence on ancient education in Quanzhou. An influential monk of his generation, Hong Yi, passed away in Quanzhou in 1940. The great writer Ba Jin once taught in Quanzhou and wrote several novels based on the area, including "Autumn in Spring" and "Electricity."

Nanguan, an early form of vernacular music, originated in Quanzhou during the Tang Dynasty and was later further developed in the Song Dynasty, and is still highly popular in Fujian, Taiwan and Southeast Asia. In addition, Quanzhou is also home to many traditional cultural and art forms including Gaojia Opera, Taiwanese Opera, Liyuan Opera, and marionette theater.

The founding father of the Philippines, José Rizal, the mother of former Indonesian President Wahid, and former Singaporean Prime Minister Lee Kuan Yew all have one thing in common: they all hail originally from Jinjiang, Quanzhou. Former Singapore Prime Minister Goh Chok Tong was born in Yongchun, Quanzhou, while the father of former Philippine President Ferdinand Marcos came from Hongjian Village, Tong'an County, Quanzhou (now Longhai City, Zhangzhou).

Quanzhou is famous for its global diaspora. According to statistics compiled in 2012, over seven million people in over 90 countries and territories around the world trace their roots to Quanzhou, along with about nine million Taiwanese.

Steve left Fujian for Taiwan with his family in 1949. For the next six decades, memories of his hometown stayed with himl and every time he spoke of it, his face lit up in a smile. He often said, "Sometimes, when I'd take a break from my work on a rainy day, I'd look out the window and sing a favorite song: *My hometown, my hometown, is the place in my dreams.*

One particularly vivid memory is of an old building in Quanzhou: the Ruyuan Pavilion was a western-style building built by his father, but was destroyed by the Japanese army during World War II. In 1989, Steve returned home and rebuilt the Ruyuan Pavilion, renaming it "Huaixianglou" (Nostalgia House).

In his mind, his hometowns of Tangdong Village and Quanzhou

were a kind of Shangri-La. This was the cradle of his lifetime. On reaching advanced age, he still often returned to his hometown to visit kneel in mourning at his ancestors' graves during the Ching Ming Festival.

He often encouraged the villagers in saying, "There are two important things in life, one is not to forget the parents who gave birth to me; the other is not to forget the place where I was born, my homeland and motherland."

Steve began life in Tangdong Village, and then followed his path to Quanzhou, Xiamen, Taiwan, and the United States. Compared with his predecessors who sought their fortunes in Southeast Asia, Steve embarked on a completely different path in life.

A Benevolent Father

Honor your parents so that you can be blessed and live a long life.
-- Ephesians 6:23

Steve did not follow in the footsteps of many boys from Tangdong Village who went to the Philippines or other countries in Southeast Asia to seek their fortunes. Steve's father, Mr. Tsai Zhique (October 25, 1884 - February 15, 1933) never left his hometown. Unfortunately, Steve's father passed away at the age of 49, when the boy was only nine years old. However, his father's words, deeds, image, and his selfless and enthusiastic dedication to his hometown during his lifetime made a deep impression on Steve and guided the rest of his life.

The elder Mr. Tsai was a notable philanthropist in Quanzhou and Shishi. This period, the late Qing Dynasty and the early Republican period, was marked by frequent fighting in the local countryside. Tangdong and its coastal neighbor Weitou were two commercial ports critical for the operations of overseas Chinese merchants. The two ports fell into a pattern of sporadic but intractable conflict, competing for an advantage serving the shipping and operations needs of the Chinese diaspora. This mutual antagonism resulted in frequent violence, retribution, and vendettas, with each village receiving firearms and other support from its local clan members overseas.

The root of the conflict lay in the poor economic conditions of the surrounding countryside, making the competition for port traffic and revenues an existential struggle that was difficult to resolve. As the conflict wore on, it was reinforced by personal grudges. The elder Mr. Tsai came forward to seek to mediate a truce between the villages, working earnestly and tirelessly to calm tensions.

Going to Tangdong to Find "Uncle Que"

The Shishi district lies just outside Quanzhou's south gate, and when tempers flared between the ports, messengers would run here to find Mr. Tsai Zhique. Each of these villages had their own local leaders, but these were often so embroiled in their own petty squabbles that they could not be seen as honest brokers. These situations required a defter hand.

Tsai Zhique was younger than the local bigwigs, but he enjoyed high status due to his reputation for righteousness. Whenever facing a difficult dispute, the locals knew to send to Tangdong for "Uncle Que".

What special traits did Mr. Tsai Zhique have that others lacked? Steve said that his father had no particular magic at his disposal. Rather, he approached problems with a strong sense of public spiritedness, and that his integrity and genuine concern could resolve problems that defied money or force. "It sounds very cliche," he said, "but integrity and positivity were my father's watchwords." In his short 49 years, he made a huge contribution to his community and is fondly remembered for his public service. "I seek to emulate my father's sense of self sacrifice and perseverance, even though this may sometimes lead me to strain my financial resources."

In engaging in public service, Mr. Tsai Zhique cultivated a spirit of boldness. Arriving in a sedan chair at the mediation site, he would be welcomed by an adoring crowd. Approaching each dispute, he first sought to develop a comprehensive and objective understanding of the facts of the case. While some disputes seemed to be caused by personal conflicts and feelings, in the last analysis, most of these problems came down to an issue of money.

In engaging in mediation, he sought to restore a just and lasting peace that could be wholeheartedly accepted by all sides. He would interview both sides of the dispute, and quickly cut to the heart of the matter, proposing a clear and logical resolution, seeking to reconcile the parties and bring them to agreement. In cases where one party refused to be swayed, he would launch into a spirited negotiation, gently but insistently coaxing the parties to find an acceptable common ground.

If the parties still could not come to an agreed figure, Uncle Que would volunteer: "I'll make up the difference."

Through such methods and approaches, Uncle Que resolved all manner of disputes, from simple disagreements between neighbors to potentially disastrous conflicts between the rival villages. His success in this lay in his willingness to put the welfare of the community ahead of his own interest.

Uncle Que lived simply in Tangdong Village, in an ordinary house. His income from his property and business was supplemented by remittances from his son Shirong working in the Philippines. In cases where Uncle Que was obligated to make up the difference between disputing parties, his obligations often exceeded his resources, forcing him to borrow funds, a growing debt he shouldered for many years. But his actions brought him prestige, trust and a priceless reputation for integrity, and his ability to command the support of the populace was critical to resolving these disputes.

Uncle Que was very particular about issues of ethics and morality. His brother had passed away, childless, at a young age, and Uncle Que took in the man's widow, bringing her a boy named Shishang to adopt as her son. Shishang grew up and married, but also had no children, so Uncle Que helped her to adopt a grandson named Jipin, who went on to become a Chinese language teacher in his hometown, esteemed for his broad literary knowledge. Shishang was one or two years older than Uncle Que's eldest son Shirong, and Uncle Que raised them as brothers.

Uncle Que took responsibility for managing all aspects of household life of his brother's widow and her adopted grandson. Because Shishang had gone to the Philippines, Uncle Que also gave his own youngest son, Youcong, to his sister-in-law to raise. Thus, Youcong grew up calling his aunt "mother", and his mother "auntie".

Mutual Aid Association, Aiding the Living and Consoling Death

Uncle Que was also intimately involved in two other initiatives that had a great impact on Tangdong Village. He established a "Parents Mutual Aid Association," collecting funds from the whole community to cover the funeral expenses of poor villagers, preventing their children from going into debt or even selling their own children to buy a burial plot. He also was a central figure in the establishment of the village's first school, trading on his prestige and reputation to raise funds from his fellow villagers, with particular support from the Tangdong Village Association in the Philippines. The establishment of the school provided a first opportunity for local children to receive an education, and it was later followed by the establishment of a secondary school, kindergartens, nurseries, science and technology centers, and an indoor gymnasium, mostly from funds raised by the overseas sons of Tangdong Village.

The Village Mourns

The memory of his father's death has remained clear in Steve's mind his whole life. He and his mother normally slept in the same room. Just before dawn, he remembered waking to the sound of his older brother Youhui calling out, "Mother, what's the matter with father?"

Youhui and his father shared the room across the hall. Steve and his mother immediately rushed over. "My father was sleeping peacefully, it seemed. There was no sense of struggle or discomfort. He seemed perfectly normal. I called out to him, but he didn't answer. He just continued to sleep."

"My father would start every morning with a cigarette and would wake up Youhui to strike a match for him. This morning, Youhui woke up on his own and wondered why father hadn't awakened him. He shook father, but he didn't respond, so he called out to us for help. My father was only 49 years old when he left us. My mother was 40 at the time, and I was only 9."

He died peacefully in his sleep, without any signs of illness. Today, 80 years later, his cause of death is still something of a mystery, and there's speculation he suffered a sudden heart attack.

"My mother recalled that, the night before he died, my father did not get home until very late. There had been a dispute about an unjust killing in the countryside outside Tangdong Village, and there was a great deal of tension between the two sides. This was not a normal financial dispute. Despite the hour, my father would feel obligated to mediate and seek to prevent violence. It was already after one o'clock in the morning by the time he came home, which is really very late for country folks."

"By the time he returned, we were all asleep, except for mother who had stayed up waiting for him to return. Upon arriving home, he said to her, 'This was a serious matter, and it could have resulted in further killing. Now it has finally been resolved.' He also mentioned to her that he felt a bit of stomach upset. We didn't have any medicine at home, so mother brought him a cup of hot water, and said they should visit the doctor the following day. Father dismissed her concerns and changed the topic to talk about their second son who was 14 or 15 at the time, and that they should start making arrangements for his marriage in the coming year or two. Mother protested that he was so young, and that there was no hurry, to which father told her not to worry. After talking for a bit about this, father went to his room to sleep. It was the last time they would speak."

The news of the sudden death of Uncle Que spread quickly. That day, villagers in Tangdong and the surrounding towns and villages came to express their condolences. Some said it seemed as if a giant star had fallen from the sky. The people involved in the dispute the day before also put aside their differences out of respect, coming to offer their condolences on bent knee, bewailing their role in his untimely demise.

Over the course of the day, more than 200 destitute beggars began to arrive at the Tsai's house to attend the funeral, kneeling and prostrating themselves outside the front door. In those times, beggars would often attend funerals in expectation of receiving alms from the grieving family. The family thus made arrangements to distribute alms, but none of the beggars would accept it. "Normally, we mourn for money," they said. "But not for Mr. Tsai. He was so generous in life, and we mourn his passing. We will never find his like again in this life." Uncle Que had indeed been known for his compassion for the poor and marginalized, and any beggar that approached him never went away empty-handed. He spent his life standing up for the downtrodden and persecuted.

Paying a Father's Debt

On news of his father's death, the eldest brother Shirong rushed home from the Philippines for the funeral, followed by forty-nine days of mourning.

During his lifetime, Uncle Que had tirelessly struggled for justice and righteousness. But, in his devotion to resolving disputes in his community, he had run up considerable debts. The mourning period was still underway as the creditors came calling. Shirong met them with an account book, and each arriving creditor would carefully write down each item, gradually filling up the pages with thousands of yuan of obligations.

At the time, you could build a palatial home in Tangdong Village for less than a thousand yuan. At the age of eleven, Shirong had crossed the ocean to make a living in the Philippines, gradually building his trade as a fabric merchant. He was hardly a man of means at this time, but he said, "My father was a man of his word, and I will honor his debts." Seeing that Shirong was cut from the same cloth as his father, the creditors felt reassured of Shirong's integrity, and assured him that he could take his time to repay.

At that time, Steve and his younger brothers were still very young, leaving Shirong to shoulder their father's debts alone. This he did without complaint or regret, successfully repaying all of his father's debts to the cent, certainly an impressive feat for such a young man.

Brothers

While he was back for the funeral, Shirong took the nine-year-old Steve aside. "First, you must remember that our father is different from other people's fathers," he said. "Like him, we have to strive for justice all our lives. Second, you must receive the best education and fulfill your potential. I am fated to a life of toil, so our hopes lie in your achievement through learning."

Uncle Que left behind another mark on his hometown: The three-story western-style Ruyuan Pavilion, was easily the most striking and modern building in the entire village of old traditional houses. Situated at the shore, facing a broad sandy beach, the Pavilion came under artillery fire from Japanese warships following the fall of Xiamen. An artillery shell passed through the Pavilion's south gate and exploded, causing extensive damage. Fortunately, Steve and his mother had fled minutes before. Had they tarried but a few more minutes, the history of the Tsai family would have to be rewritten. As it is, the family lost all their poultry, livestock, and family dogs.

Later, after the war, Steve restored the building. But, following the conclusion of the civil war between the Kuomintang and the Communist Party, the building sat neglected for decades. Finally, in 1987, Steve returned to his hometown and rebuilt it a second time, renaming it the Huaixianglou.

An Illiterate but Sophisticated Mother

Steve is particularly fond of white tofu without seasoning, as it evokes the love of his mother,

Hongxiang. She was a simple rural woman, raised in a traditional family. Her marriage took her far from home, and her husband's busy public life left her in charge of child-rearing and discipline. While she doted on all her children and grandchildren, Steve felt a particular affinity for his mother. When he was young, he and his mother would sleep in the same room. Every night, she would tuck him in before going back to her housework. Often, however, he would lie awake in bed until his mother could come to lie down with him.

Her eldest son had gone to the Philippines at the age of 11, and then came back to marry at 16, soon blessing her with a grandchild, and later two more grandsons and a granddaughter, and earning her praise throughout the village as "the youngest, most fortunate, and most admired grandmother."

Uncle Que's public generosity often put the family finances under strain, but his wife bore up without complaint. "Mother never

Steve with his loving mother, returning to Xiamen following training at the Fuzhou Police Academy.

spoke out about this. She had a kind heart and supported father's benevolence and righteousness." But the death of Uncle Que in 1933 left the family in a difficult situation. Mr. Tsai's brother told his wife "Father dominated family life while he was alive, but now mother is the head of the family. Please turn over the money I send home to our mother to care for our brothers and sisters, and she will give you an allowance to cover your expenses."

Following the period of mourning, Mrs. Tsai would rise before sunup to visit her husband's grave and weep. She often said that, if not for her responsibilities to care for the children and grandchildren, she would have gladly followed her husband to the next world.

Surviving through Calamity, Dying in a Time of Ease

The Japanese invasion of China disrupted the remittance system by which overseas Chinese sent money back home to support their families, leaving entire communities in dire straits. In the Tsai family, the burden of supporting the household fell on Mrs. Tsai and Steve's sister-in-law.

Without money, the family's diet quickly became overly reliant on yams, eaten dried or roasted, supplemented by fermented soybeans and pickled vegetables. Soon, they were eating yam leaves and seaweed, which had previously been used to feed the pigs. Chicken, duck, fish - these were virtually unknown and white rice was reserved for the rites of ancestor worship. After class, children would go to the shore to try to catch a handful of shrimp or a couple of fish. With what food was available, the adult women let the children eat first, after which they would encourage each other to take a larger share of what little remained. For eight long years, Mrs. Tsai subsisted on leftovers, always going to bed hungry.

After the end of the War of Resistance against Japan, Steve continued to work in Xiamen, where his fourth brother continued to study. Their mother, sister-in-law and her four children came to join them. Their eldest brother and sister and their families also came to Xiamen from the Philippines. Thus, the family was finally reunited.

The children hoped that this would allow their mother to put down some of her burden and lead a more peaceful relaxing life. They bought her a good quality, comfortable wicker chair to rest in every day, and bought her a lot of new clothes. Her children and grandchildren spared no effort in making her comfortable and making up for her past sufferings. Surrounded by her large family, Mrs. Tsai was very happy, though she found it difficult to adjust to this new idleness after a lifetime of hard work.

Later, the Tsai family moved to Taiwan. At first, Mrs. Tsai did not want to leave the familiar confines of their hometown, but the children were gently insistent. But after arriving in Taiwan, she found herself lying awake each night, dreaming of returning home, and was found frequently looking west towards Fujian.

In 1950, two years after arriving in Taiwan, Mrs. Tsai was hospitalized for six months for treatment for liver cancer, with Steve staying with her at the hospital nearly the entire time, making himself a bunk beside her hospital bed. The sight of his mother's suffering left him terribly distressed, and he ran to the home of a physician named Dr. Kuo, begging on his knees for the man to save his mother's life. When she finally passed, nearly all her children and grandchildren were at her side. She was 57 years old at the time of her death, and Steve was 26.

"My mother was finally enjoying a peaceful life when she passed away, but she wasn't accustomed to such a lack of strife," he said. "Once, she told me, 'I have spent my whole life serving my husband, my children and my grandchildren. I get up at five or six o'clock every morning and stay busy until midnight. Now I've abandoned my whole life and my hometown. Here in Taiwan, I have nothing to do. Every day, you take me out to eat, but I don't feel useful. I want to go back.'"

It's possible that this homesickness and feelings of displacement may have led to depression, which may have left her body more susceptible to the cancer that took her life.

Steve noted: "Mother was exhausted. For years, she ate nothing but leftovers. There was no refrigerator, and she was eating leftovers off dirty dishes. It must have had an effect on her liver. Later, when we left for Taiwan, she wasn't emotionally prepared for the move. Her eldest son left again for the Philippines, splitting up the family again, which made her sad. There is a reason my mother died at such a young age. Without these difficulties, she would have lived a long life. Otherwise, I can hardly ever remember her being sick."

Later, when Steve eventually returned to his hometown, he specially built a pavilion to commemorate his loving mother and engraved an elegy on a stone tablet before it.

His mother's ashes were interred at the Fazang Temple in Beitou. For three years, without fail, whenever he was in Taipei Steve would climb

For three years of mourning, Steve visited the Fa-tsang Temple daily to pay respects to his mother.

the three hundred steps to the temple to pay his respects to his mother. To show his devotion, he waited through the entire three-year mourning period before marrying in 1953.

As an elementary school student, Steve would return home from school to a snack lovingly prepared by his mother, sometimes a zongzi (glutenous rice dumpling), but more often a couple of pieces of plain white tofu without seasoning. "To this day," he says, "this plain unseasoned tofu is one of my favorite dishes. I still eat it just like this. For me, it not only tastes like tofu, but also of my mother's love."

Long-Lasting Brotherly
Affection, Stronger as Time Passed

*The man who says he loves God but hates his brother is a liar. If you
don't love the brother you can see, how can you love an invisible God?*

-- 1 hohn 4:20

The Tsai family was a large one, with the parents raising four sons
and six daughters. Steve was the third son. Four of the six sisters
died before Steve was born. When, as previously mentioned, the
fourth son Youcong was given away, it left only four children in the
house at the time: Steve, his older brother Youhui, the eldest sister
Shuqiong and the second sister Binying.

As mentioned earlier, like many other local boys, the eldest
brother Tsai Shirong (1909-1996) went to the Philippines at the age
of 11 but came home to get married at the age of 16 or 17. Today, a
boy of this age might be home playing video games, getting ready to
apply to university. but in Tangdong Village at that time, boys of this
age were already mature beyond their years.

The eldest brother had an important position in the Philippines,
and he was worried about staying away too long for fear of losing
it. Thus, he returned to the Philippines less than a week after the

wedding. Not long after, his wife gave birth to the Tsai family's first grandson. However, the boy's father would not return home to see him for the first time for nearly 20 years, during which time his wife lived as a virtual widow. Even then, it was just a fleeting visit before he returned to the Philippines. During this time, the boy was essentially raised by his uncle Steve. He later remembered, "I had a father, though I never saw him." Thus, despite the Tsai family being one of the most well off in Tangdong Village, he grew up with strong feelings of inferiority.

The arrival of the eldest brother's son brought another big change to the Tsai family: the matriarch was honored as a venerated grandmother at the tender age of 35. "My mother married into the Tsai family at the age of 15 and had her first son the following year," Steve remembers. That son married at 16 or 17, thus making his mother a grandmother at 35, bringing her honor and blessings in Tangdong Village.

Steve was sixteen years younger than his eldest brother. By the time he was twelve or thirteen years old, the situation of the Chinese diaspora in southeast Asia had begun to change. The younger generation was more resistant to leaving home for years on end and was especially reluctant to leave their young wives and children behind. They began to look for a new future.

In 2007, Steve poses with his second sister, five years his senior, in front of his Gulangyu residence.

Steve's second brother, Tsai Youhui (1921 to 1993) went to the Philippines but returned soon thereafter. Steve himself went to the Philippines but was also unwilling to stay away from home. In this way, they resisted the conventions and old customs, using their own initiative to seek a new path.

The sixth child, Binying did not live with the family very long. When she was young, she was given to a friend, who adopted her. Soon after Binying was born, a fortune-teller noted that after one son, the family had six daughters, four of whom had died, and warned that another son would only come if the youngest girl left the house. At the time, such predictions held considerable sway. Thus, the Tsais appealed to a friend who had no daughters to take their girl into their family. Mrs. Tsai was heartbroken but was ultimately persuaded by her husband. Thus, the girl went to live in Yangxia Village, about fifty minutes' walk from the Tsai home. Later, she married into a family in Liujiang Village and then moved to the Philippines with her husband who worked there in the timber business. Later, when her husband retired, they both returned home. At the time of this writing, she is 96 years old, still living in Liujiang Township, Fujian Province, surrounded by generations of descendants.

A Happy Time for the Siblings

Steve still recalls a happy time with his second brother and his two younger brothers and two older sisters about 80 years ago. At that time, Tangdong Village held an annual festival on August 21. The locals called it "Holy Father's Day," and this was the day every year when the sisters would return from their husband's families to visit their mother's house. "Before my eldest sister got married, she and my second sister all had a wonderful time at the festival, along with my second brother." The festival commemorates the martyrdom of Shenggong Ye (born Ni Guozhong), a native of Jinjiang in Quanzhou in the Southern Song Dynasty. In the second year of Xiangxing (1279), this civil and military official was executed for his efforts to protect the emperor against the Yuan army. He was first commemorated at Nanyue Temple in Jinjiang. Later, given Jinjiang's coastal location, Shenggong Ye also became the patron saint of sailors and seafarers. In 1995, Tangdong Village built the Zhaofuhou Shenggong Palace in his honor.

After his eldest sister got married, "Holy Father's Day" also provided Steve and his second brother with an opportunity to earn some extra income. Mother would send him and second brother to the neighboring villages to bring their sisters home. Fourth brother was still too young to make the trip. Early that morning, the two sisters would happily prepare gifts and red envelopes for their younger brothers. "Eldest sister is very generous and very sincere," Steve recalls. "When we arrived, she was very happy to see us. She asked us to go to her room, while her in-laws waited outside. She closed the door and give us red envelopes and filled our pockets with sweets." They then went to pick up their second sister who had not yet married and still lived with her adoptive parents. Seeing her two younger brothers arriving, her heart leapt. All year, she waited for this day, and couldn't sleep well the night before. Despite the years she'd spent growing up in her adoptive parents' home, she was still homesick for her birth mother. When the brothers arrived, she also called them into the room and closed the door. "I'm so happy you're here," she said. "But I can't show my true feelings in front of my adoptive parents. Open your hands and I'll give you your red envelopes."

With the two brothers carrying the luggage, the two sisters followed, and all four sang songs together all the way back to their mother's house. "The two sisters would spend at least three days at home. Over the past year, my sisters have been counting the days to August 21."

Holy Father's Day is one of the liveliest local festivals, and all households, rich or poor, will serve up a feast at home, even if they have to borrow the necessary funds. Anyone who passes by the house is welcome to come in and join the meal of various seafood, fried oysters, fried meatballs, and fried rice, washed down with wine. After the meal, the residents of Tangdong Village would wander the streets from one public performance to another, including Gaojia opera, marionette shows, and puppet theater. All night long, the town filled with the sounds of gongs and drums, barely drowning out the cries of peddlers hawking their wares, and the endless laughter of children.

The three days of the festival pass quickly, however. "All good things come to an end, and after the festival came a tearful farewell. Of course, we could go to visit them at their in-laws' homes, but it's not so easy to do so. My mother always felt so guilty for having given up our second sister for adoption. As she left, mother would stand at the edge of the field and watch her go until she disappeared in the distance. Second sister knew the circumstances of her adoption, and that it broke mother's heart to let her go. But still, she carried resentment in her heart, but only for mother. She didn't dare stand against father. Every time she came back, this resentment was plain and caused mother no end of suffering. As she walked away from home, she didn't look back at mother. It was truly a tragic situation. Mother told me that she felt she had wronged her daughter and thinking about it still made her weep."

The eldest brother made a living in the Philippines and came home to marry a wife and have children. Generally speaking, married Fujianese who work hard in the Philippines will not have a second wife in the Philippines. However, after the Japanese war of aggression began, they were cut off from their hometown. Many overseas Chinese in the Philippines did not know the situation of their families in their hometowns, nor could they return home, let alone know when the war might end, so many men chose to either marry or live together with Filipino women. The eldest brother also lived with a Filipino female colleague, and they had nine children.

Victory Celebration and Reunion, Civil War and Separation

After the war, the eldest brother returned to Xiamen with his Filipino wife and their children born in the Philippines. In addition, the eldest sister, her husband and five children also returned from the Philippines. Since the Japanese occupation of the Philippines had brought great hardship to the families of the eldest brother and elder sister, they all hoped that the whole family could reunite in Xiamen and begin a new life there. Mother and Steve came to the pier repeatedly to meet their family members as they disembarked, welcoming them home and helping them to find and furnish lodgings. The victory over the Japanese was celebrated all over China, and the Tsai family celebrated their reunion. But their happiness was tinged with sorrow: Jizhi, the second son of the eldest brother with his first wife, had died of plague in Jinjiang in his early teens.

Mr. And Mrs. Tsai in the Philippines with his eldest sister (far left, first row) and her family.

The four Tsai brothers make music together in the Philippines. Clockwise from lower right: eldest brother Shirong, second brother Youhui, third brother Steve, and fourth brother Youcong.

Later, with the continued civil war between the Kuomintang and the Communist Party, many members of the Tsai family moved to Taiwan. Fourth brother had gone to Hong Kong for his studies, while the eldest brother's wife and her children Yingshan and Yili stayed in their hometown to maintain the ancestral homestead. Eldest brother's eldest son Jiyang went to Taiwan with his extended family.

After arriving in Taiwan, the family first stayed with the uncle of a friend in Beitou, and later moved into a Japanese-style house on Zhongshan North Road. At the time, the road was still lined with rice paddies. The KMT troops and dependents retreating to Taiwan with the government KMT were confident that they would counter-attack and retake the mainland at any time, thus few bothered to buy a house in Taiwan despite the low prices.

The eldest brother, Shirong, was in the fabric business in the Philippines and had brought large quantities of fabric back to Xiamen after the defeat of the Japanese, planning to establish a fabric store there. However, CCP forces attacked the city, forcing him to abandon Xiamen for Taiwan. There in Taipei, he would lie on his tatami mat, listening to the radio and trying to assess the situation in Taiwan and beyond. On May 16, 1950, he listened to President Chiang Kai-shek announce that, despite the KMT's retreat to Taiwan, plans were in motion to retake the mainland in five years. For eldest brother, five years was too long to wait, and he was eager to leave Taiwan. It was during this time that the family's matriarch also passed away, and eldest brother decided to take the first opportunity to move his family back to Manila and begin again. The eldest sister's family also went to the Philippines, and thus the family, briefly reunited after the war, was forced to separate again.

On the morning when the eldest brother and eldest sister left Taipei with their families, Steve asked the whole family to kneel in front of his mother's portrait and say goodbye to her, singing a song of commemoration he'd composed for the occasion. Beset on all sides by personal and national crises, the entire family wept. The reunited family, a dream pursued through decades of crisis, split apart again.

Although the eldest brother and brother-in-law faced a daunting prospect to restart their lives in the Philippines, the eldest brother's nine children by his second wife had all received the best education available in the Philippines. Later, Steve applied for his nephew through

Steve takes his wheelchair-bound second brother to tour Beijing.

his eldest brother, Xiangzhong, to come to the United States from the Philippines, and the nephew then brought his father to the US as well, where he lived for many years, finally dying at the age of 90. Steve was in Taiwan at the time, and he rushed back to the US, as did his sister-in-law and niece who were in Hong Kong. Steve presided over the grand funeral of his eldest brother.

Steve also brought his eldest brother-in-law to Taiwan to serve as vice president in his own factory. The eldest brother-in-law spent the rest of his life in Taiwan, but later succumbed to illness. Soon after, the eldest sister unfortunately also passed away in the Philippines. When she became seriously ill, the four Tsai brothers individually made their way to Manila, all sleeping on the floor of her hospital room. For three weeks they stayed with her day and night, retelling her favorite stories, bringing her favorite foods, and accompanying her through the most painful moments of life.

"Eldest sister kept repeating her love for our parents, telling happy stories of the siblings from when she was a child. We hoped that recalling these memories could help alleviate her pain." Second brother was handsome and clever; fourth brother was industrious and thrifty, irritable, straightforward and quick with words; Steve was hard-working, prudent, simple, and honest. Their parents would reward them with New Year's red envelopes and delicious snacks. Steve would hoard his money and snacks, while second brother's disappeared almost instantly, leaving him to "borrow" some from Steve, who shared generously without complaining to their parents, who nonetheless would give him extra to make up for his generosity. Perhaps Steve absorbed the concept of "paying it forward" during his childhood. He always felt that kindness should have the last word in life.

The second and fourth brothers would often give Steve a hard time. During the Anti-Japanese War, the brothers would make salt from sea water, selling the salt to help support the family. It was hard manual labor, requiring physical strength that the young Steve lacked. Struggling under the weight of the sacks of salt, he stumbled and fell, much to the amusement of his brothers. Later, however, as they grew up, their sense of brotherhood became unshakable, and second brother would go to great lengths to care for Steve, increasingly relying on his younger brother's advice in negotiating his career.

As the brothers grew up, they increasingly recognized that Steve's kindness, seriousness, patience, and diligence would surely lead to success. Second and fourth brothers put great trust in Steve. Later, when second brother retired from Taiwan's Overseas Chinese Bank, Steve relinquished the position of general manager of the Taishan Electric Company, passing the position to second brother, and his two university graduate sons were also invited to work in the company. In the 1980s, second brother and his family immigrated to the United States. Steve often lead delegations from industrial and commercial organizations to visit Europe and America. He would often bring his second brother with him. The two brothers were very happy to travel together. Later, second brother fell ill, and his very filial son sought to have him transferred to Beijing for treatment by Traditional Chinese Medicine doctors, leading to family disputes that were only resolved when second brother announced that all important decisions should be made by Steve. Steve made arrangements for second brother to go to the Beijing Cancer Hospital, accompanied by his wife and children, along with their second sister Binying and niece Yili. There, his condition improved slightly, but relapsed upon returning to Taipei. After second brother's death, Steve asked the renowned business leader Koo Chen-fu and others to organize the funeral with him and the family.

Even as he lay dying, second brother reached out to Steve, sending a handwritten note out to him in the waiting room. "Third brother, come and save me. Hurry, hurry," written in a skewed hand that spoke of his need to survive. Second brother was relying on Steve for his life. Steve rushed to the operating room, but was stopped by the doctor. Thereafter, every time he thought of this last note from his brother, the memory cut like a knife. Before his very eyes, the members of his family were leaving him, and he could only stand by, helpless. In the space of ten years, he'd lost his dearest eldest brother, eldest sister and second brother, leaving him deep in grief.

After second brother's death, his widow spent most of her time in Qingdao, living with her two sons who were doing business there. She died there in 2009, at the age of 88. Steve, accompanied by his eldest daughter, attended the grand funeral in Qingdao from the United States, along with fourth brother from Taipei and his niece from Hong Kong.

Eldest Sister-in-Law Assumes the Role of Mother

After the patriarch passed away, the Tsai family was held together by Steve's mother and the eldest brother's wife, Xie Shushun, who was very close with Steve. After their mother died, Shushun stepped into the role of mother to the family.

When she was nearly a hundred years old, living in Hong Kong, her health began to fail. Steve immediately rushed to Hong Kong from the United States. He'd originally planned to send money for his sister-in-law's for medical treatment, but his children advised him to go and see her one last time. "You may not need to attend the funeral, but if you miss your last chance to see her alive, you'll always regret it," they said. Steve was on the next flight to Hong Kong.

She was already in a coma when he arrived, and her daughter Yili spoke to her, saying, "Third uncle is here." Sister-in-law's eyes suddenly opened, but she was unable to speak. Steve spoke to her of all that she had done to care for the family, saying, "When mother died, you became our mother. We pray for you to recover so we can all celebrate your hundredth birthday with you. Please hold on and let me do my duty to you who served as our mother."

A rare reunion at the end of World War II brought all the Tsai children together with their mother in Xiamen.

Sister-in-law's condition soon began to improve slightly, and Steve had to rush back to the United States to attend to some important matters, leaving his niece and nephew with money to cover sister-in-law's medical expenses and, eventually, her funeral.

When she did finally pass away, Steve asked his 90-year-old second sister to travel from their hometown to Hong Kong to preside over the funeral. During the service, she delivered a eulogy Steve had written for the occasion, praising her moral rectitude, and moving the attendees to tears.

The Filipino wife of eldest brother had spent more than 20 years living in the United States with her husband, but had returned to the Philippines in recent years, and she also fell ill and passed away there, not long after eldest sister-in-law's funeral.

A Celebratory Reunion

On the wall in Steve's home in California hangs an old black and white photo showing his mother with her four sons and two daughters. In the photo, mother looks young, and her six children are shown brimming with vigor. The picture was taken in Xiamen following the victory of the Anti-Japanese War, and the photo marked the family's happiest time. The caption for the photo reads "Following the end of the Second World War in 1945, our six brothers and sisters, after being scattered to the winds, had reunited. We had this picture taken in Xiamen. Today, fewer than half the people in this photo are still with us. Touching this photo, recalling the past. how can I bear this deep grief."

During the Civil War between the Kuomintang and the Communist Party, Steve paid for his fourth brother to attend a university in Hong Kong. Later, when the family left Xiamen for Taiwan, Steve made arrangements for fourth brother to meet them there, but he refused to go to Taiwan. From that time on, he was separated from the family for many years. Like many other young, idealistic Chinese people, he wanted to return to the Mainland and build a "new China" that he could see in his mind. As a result, he transferred to Sun Yat-sen University in Guangzhou, and after graduation, was assigned to work in a foreign trade unit in Beijing.

However, fourth brother's familial ties to Taiwan, and thus

association with the retreating Kuomintang, placed him under suspicion and due to his "undesirable background" he was sent to Tangshan to work as a miner. During the Cultural Revolution, he was often tortured in attempts to extract a confession of having secretly contacting his relatives in Taiwan. Fourth brother resolutely denied these charges and was forced to stand in the snow all night.

In the early 1970s, Steve had gone to great lengths to try to apply for his fourth brother's family to leave China but encountered bureaucratic obstacles. The government of China stated that it was not possible to get a travel permit to the Philippines. The only choice was to go to Hong Kong, and even that required applying for an entry permit for Hong Kong. Steve spared no expense or effort to secure an entry permit for fourth brother's family. The fourth brother, his wife and their two daughters separately made their way to Hong Kong, and lived there for seven years, during which time they relied on assistance and support from Steve, who nearly exhausted himself negotiating the bureaucratic maze and making useful connections.

Seven years later, Steve changed tactics, and hired a lawyer to assist in arranging for fourth brother's family to immigrate to the United States. Steve provided a three-bedroom house in San Francisco for them to live in.

"I spent a lot of money and effort on this," he said. "I was in Taiwan at the time, and my wife helped them in the United States. She appealed to everyone she knew and had to overcome many difficulties, but finally they were able to go." With Steve's help, fourth brother's two daughters also received the best possible education in both Hong Kong and the United States, where they resettled and raised their own families.

Fourth brother followed his youthful love of the motherland back to China for study and work. As a result, he was separated from the family for half a century during which he suffered terribly, and his family overseas had no word on his fate.

After Steve took fourth brother to Taiwan, he immediately fell in love with the place, especially its sense of freedom, saying "now this is a place where people can live freely." Despite having American citizenship, he mostly stays in Taiwan where Steve arranged for him to work as a consultant for the Taiwan Paper Company and the National Association of Construction Managers until he retired. Fourth brother was in his eighties when Steve began writing this biography and still lives in Taiwan.

Recalling the past 80 years of his parents and brothers and sisters, Steve is silent from time to time, with his eyes sometimes welling up with tears.

Following victory in WWII, the family was reunited after having been separated for years. But the family was soon split up again by the Chinese civil war.

Chapter Two

The Barefoot Student

Dreams of School, and a Lost Pair of Shoes

In 1931, Steve began studying at the Jindong Elementary School, founded by his father. His grades were consistently among the top three in the class up through 1937, when he graduated. At this time China was fighting a full-scale war of resistance, and the system of international remittances upon which the community depended had broken down. The family's eldest brother, in the Philippines, had promised to provide support for his younger brothers, but the war made it impossible to send money home. Second brother Youhui was already in high school in Quanzhou, and his mother could not afford to support another son to continue his studies. At that point, Steve's biggest concern was whether he could go to school at all.

A Cousin's Gold Ring

Steve was not alone in his plight. Many in his graduating class of about a dozen students were facing the same situation. Serving as prefect for the school, Steve visited the parents of each of his classmates, and convinced them to keep their sons home, rather than to send them to the Philippines. This generation of young people would take a new path in life. Steve also urged all students to continue to seek knowledge in order to contribute to society in the future. Deeply touched by Steve's message, nearly all parents agreed to let their children go to Quanzhou to continue their studies, determined to move heaven and earth to raise the necessary tuition funds, even if it meant selling their land.

However, the matter of Steve's own tuition had not yet been settled. The night before the students were due to leave for Quanzhou was probably the longest night of Steve's young life. After dinner, he stayed up with his mother trying to find a solution that would allow him to go to Quanzhou to study and pursue his future.

With the flow of overseas remittances stopped, the Tsai family had resorted to selling off their belongings, and credit was unavailable. Mother and son spoke late into the night, embracing and weeping. Finally, late into the night, mother looked up and said, "I have an idea. We need to talk to your cousin."

The cousin in question was a widow whose husband had made some money in Myanmar but had died on the way home when his ship was swamped by a typhoon. This cousin has always been very kind to the Tsai family and she had a special fondness for little Steve. Mother said, "Your cousin has always been very kind to you. We should tell her about our situation. Perhaps she can help." With this glimmer of hope, the two immediately left for the cousin's house.

A cold wind was blowing off the sea as the pair headed out into the moonless night. The barking of dogs followed them as they stumbled nearly blind along the road, hand in hand. When they finally arrived at the cousin's home, they woke her and told her the problem. "Why didn't you come to me earlier," she said. "I'm glad to help." She turned her to trunks and cabinets and began to pull out drawers, opening one bag after another. Finally, she found what she was looking for: she opened a tiny fabric bag and took out a gold ring, "Take it," she said.

That morning, more than a dozen classmates and their parents gathered waiting for the bus that would take them to Quanzhou. They turned as one to see Steve rushing down the street with his luggage. Everyone cheered and lifted him up. A classmate said, "The bus is about to leave - there is less than 20 minutes left, and we were so worried that you weren't here. We were afraid that you wouldn't be able to afford to go." Finally, the students boarded the bus under the forlorn gaze of their parents, and they set off to Quanzhou with pride. Sitting amidst his friends and classmates, Steve felt as if he had won a great battle.

Arriving in Quanzhou without Shoes

They arrived at Quanzhou Peiyuan Middle School and applied to take the entrance exam. This was a prestigious Jesuit school, and the tuition was relatively high. Most of the students were children of Chinese working overseas. All of the applicants stayed in a school dormitory. Despite the gold ring in his pocket, Steve entered the city barefoot, reluctant to spend money on shoes and determined to save the ring for absolute necessities to pursue his education. For the next few days, he ventured out into Quanzhou with his classmates, wandering the streets barefoot. This elicited sympathy from some of his classmates, and scorn from others. "We are all civilized people, coming from the countryside into the city," they said. "It is uncivilized to be without shoes."

Steve did not respond but kept silent. Later, a classmate took him aside and said, "Sooner or later, you'll need to buy a pair of shoes. School starts immediately after the entrance exam and, assuming you don't fail the test, you can't enter the auditorium for the opening ceremony barefoot. Just buy a pair of shoes."

Together they went to a shoe seller, dazzled by the selection. In the end, he bought the cheapest pair of cloth shoes, but continued to go barefoot, saving his new shoes for the matriculation ceremony. That night in the dormitory, he used his carefully wrapped shoes as a pillow for fear they would be stolen while he slept. The next night, feeling more confident, he left the shoes by his bed. On the third morning, he awoke to find that his shoes were missing.

While today, the loss of a pair of shoes seems trivial, at the time it was a terrible blow to his finances and his morale. The money from the gold ring had to be saved for myriad expenses including tuition, food, books, and dormitory fees. The loss of his shoes left him feeling shaken, but he pulled himself together, saying "Loss leads to change, and change leads to continuity. You must find a way."

A Sympathetic Headmaster

After much deliberation, Steve decided to seek out the headmaster. He felt he was being very presumptuous to trouble the headmaster, but he was out of options. Walking barefoot up to the headmaster's office, he summoned all his courage to walk in and bow to the headmaster.

The Headmaster, Xu Xi'an, was a very prestigious leader of the South Fujian Christian Church and a great educator. He glanced up from his work at the new boy who introduced himself as a native of Jindong Village. The headmaster listened and nodded. Having regularly preached in the four townships, he was very familiar Steve's hometown.

Then Steve asked, "Does our school offer a discount or exemption of tuition for students with good academic performance and a poor background?" The question caught the headmaster by surprise, and he carefully focused his attention on the young boy, finally noting his bare feet.

"I believe I understand your situation," he began. "And I sympathize with you. However, all of the school's expenses depend on the tuition fees from students."

At this, Steve felt embarrassed and said, "I'm very sorry. I'll find a way by myself and shouldn't have troubled you with this. I am a poor student and have always dreamed of studying here. But now I understand the situation from your point of view, and I should have tempered my expectations to match my lot in life. I'm afraid that I will not be able to pursue my education here, and I will return home." With this, Steve bowed and turned to leave.

He hadn't made it ten steps before the headmaster called him back.

"While we depend on tuition, we should seek to encourage less wealthy students to pursue an education in addition to their more fortunate counterparts. In your case, I will make an exception. If you place first on the entrance exam, I'll waive your tuition. If you place second, your tuition will be cut in half. If you place third, your tuition will be one-third off." Steve was filled with hope and excitement, and at first didn't know what to say. He immediately bowed in gratitude to the headmaster, who replied, "Don't thank me until you've earned a discount." Steve promised to work hard and not disappoint the headmaster. Then he bowed again and took his leave.

At the time, the tuition was 12 yuan per semester and 24 yuan per academic year.

Top Placement, Free Tuition

In that year's exam, about 3,000 candidates competed for 300 spaces. However, while his classmates and the other applicants feverishly prepared for the exam, Steve felt under less pressure. He was habitually a very diligent student, taking note of everything the teacher said. He put a great deal of effort into ensuring he fully understood the material and did not hesitate to ask questions or for clarification. Thus, he approached the exam with a clear mind and high confidence.

The day the exam results were posted the applicants gathered to find their names, hoping to have at least made the cut off point. Steve, however, had higher expectations.

Steve was twelve years old at the time and couldn't see over the heads of the boys in front of him. Finally, he pushed his way to the front, but still couldn't see clearly. Several of his classmates from Jindong Village had already found his name in the rankings. They lifted him up with a cheer, and Steve finally found his name, at the very top of the exam result ranks.

Steve left the crowd and, with a spring in his step, went to the headmaster's office. It was the beginning of term, and the headmaster's office was crowded with people who required his attention. Steve waited patiently for them to leave. Finally, the headmaster turned and saw Steve, standing there barefoot again, but couldn't immediately place him.

"Can I help you?" he asked.

"I'm here to thank you."

"Thank me for what? Oh, right. You were here the other day. What are you thanking me for?"

"You made an exception for me, giving me an opportunity."

"Did you place in the top three?"

"Yes."

The principal smiled, but he couldn't immediately remember the student's name. "Sit down. How did you place on the exam?"

"First place."

"Oh! You are Tsai Steve!" he exclaimed, marveling that the first-place finisher was the same barefoot boy who had come to him for help.

"Headmaster," said Steve. "You gave me this opportunity, and I will never forget it. Thank you."

"You deserve it. Tuition is free this semester. Study hard. If you need anything, please come to me again."

With this, the barefoot champion scholar turned and nearly floated out the door.

But despite the reprieve of the 12-yuan semester tuition, Steve still had considerable expenses: food, books, and dormitory fees. The money he'd made from selling the gold ring wouldn't cover all of it, and he still didn't have any shoes!

Scholar Gardener, Supply Fees Waived

To replace his stolen shoes, Steve bought the cheapest open-toe sandals he could find, despite the fast-approaching winter. With his new sandals on, he abashedly returned to see the headmaster.

The headmaster welcomed him in and asked him to sit. "Is there some problem," he asked. Steve told the truth about his financial straits. "I really can't help it, "he said. "So, I have to come to you again to see if there is a solution."

The headmaster thought for a few minutes and said, "Well, our school is very big and there are many flowers and fruit trees on campus. Can you endure hard work? The other students get up at six o'clock, but you will have to be up at five o'clock to help the gardener care for the grounds and maintain the campus. In return, I will pay you a salary and subsidize your other tuition and fees."

Steve was very moved by this generous offer, and gratefully thanked the headmaster, assuring him that he would not disappoint him. As he left and walked down the corridor, he turned and looked back to see the headmaster standing in the doorway, watching him leave like a loving father.

Steve's initial economic difficulties at Peiyuan Middle School were directly related to the fact that the family had already spent their savings to send his second brother to this school years earlier. Now, through his own efforts, his fortunes had changed. He applied himself diligently and happily immersed himself in the new school, determined to make his mother, her cousin and the headmaster proud.

Seventeen-year-old Headmaster

Life is education, and society is school. -- Tao Xingzhi

Leaving School, Returning to the Countryside

However, the serenity of the campus was not immune to the growing chaos that engulfed the country due to the Japanese war of aggression.

Xiamen fell on May 10, 1938, and the Japanese invaders stepped up their bombing of Quanzhou. Steve said, "Sometimes the Japanese bombers would fly so low that we could see the pilots from the ground," Steve recalled, "Nearly every day, our classes were interrupted by air raid warnings, forcing us to run back and forth between the classrooms and the air-raid shelters."

Due to the growing danger, the school was forced to move into the mountains in Penghu Town, Yongchun County. As the second school year started, Steve was unable to pay for the tuition. The school's relocation had put a lot of pressure on the headmaster, making it difficult to continue to subsidize Steve's tuition. Faced with the priority of allowing second brother to finish his education, Steve dropped out of school, tearfully returning home to help support the family.

Upon his return, he planted a few acres of land and devoted himself to farming and study. Plowing the fields with the family water buffalo, he would hang his book bag from the animal's horns, reminiscent of the Sui Dynasty's folk hero Li Mi. While guiding the buffalo through the fields, surrounded by bamboo forest, he would read from his books and take careful notes. Learning here in the open fields rather than the classroom, he adopted the name "Mo Nong" (Ink Farmer) for himself. Thus, Steve kept active in his studies while plowing the fields, and did not lose his educational ambitions due to the war.

In the words of the renowned educator Tao Xingzhi, "Life is education, and society is a school." Steve put this saying to practice in his daily life, as he moved from school to studying on his own. "Although I could no longer go to school," he said, "by working hard, I felt I could still make a way for myself."

When not working in the fields, Steve went hunting for books. He searched the town library, the Tangdong school libraries, and in schoolteachers' homes, collecting all the books he could find, with a particular focus on works of history, literature and art. He divided these books into different categories and made a reading plan to systematically govern what he would read each day, and for how long. Tsai Jinghe, the Jindong school headmaster, often gave Steve advice on his studies.

Steve also read newspapers every day. But without the money to buy them himself, he would pick up discarded newspapers left behind at Tangdong school. Thus, he was able to stay current with the events in China and the world.

Being out of school, Steve nonetheless threw himself into his studies and became an able and confident self-learner. He read voraciously, taking copious notes which he would then review over and over, recording his feelings and impressions of the texts he read.

He thoroughly devoured each book and found that his knowledge grew even faster than it had in class. Sometimes at night, he would fight against sleep to continue reading. But at the same time, he recognized that he couldn't stay in the countryside forever. He would have to make a new opportunity for himself.

Answering the Call of the Literacy Campaign – Admittance to Dehua Normal School

Steve began to contribute essays about his readings to the local Quanzhou newspapers: the Dazhong Daily and Times Evening News. The publication of these essays brought him recognition and some income. One of his readers was Kang Zhuang, the president of Fujian News Agency, who hired Steve as a special correspondent, marking the beginning of his journalistic career. Fujian was the origin of much of the overseas Chinese diaspora, and many overseas Chinese were eager for news from home. Paid by the piece, Steve's work focused on social current affairs, including the war. When a Japanese warship fired at Tangdong Village, destroying the Tsai's ancestral home, readers throughout southeast Asia learned of the event through Steve's pen.

"I read the newspaper every day, and saw a real opportunity there," he said. "At that time, the country was in complete turmoil, but Chairman Chiang Kai-shek was far-sighted and saw that rebuilding the country would require a serious initiative to increase literacy."

As part of this initiative, teachers schools were established for the systematic training of teachers. The graduates were then sent to implement adult literacy programs for those lacking a primary school education.

One day, sitting in the bamboo forest beside the field, Steve read an announcement in the newspaper that the Dehua Normal

School would begin enrolling students in the spring of 1940. He immediately recognized the opportunity he'd been looking for. At that time, his second brother Youhui was still studying in Peiyuan Middle School, but Steve sent word for him to come home and join him at the normal school. "After graduation, you can be a teacher," he wrote. The normal school had an important attraction for students with financial difficulties: students were not only exempt from tuition and fees, but also received a monthly living stipend of six yuan. In addition, students in normal schools were allowed to defer their compulsory military service.

The two brothers Youhui and Steve, along with their cousins Hanzhang and Zhuji, were admitted together to Dehua Normal School. Dehua is in the mountainous area of Daiyun Mountain, far away from the war zone and thus relatively safe.

The school offered an accelerated but intensive course of study, taught by highly effective instructors. The students were all highly motivated and brought a strong sense of purpose and urgency to their studies.

Student Captain

Reflecting the war raging outside the school's walls, the normal school imposed military training on the students and also sought to instill leadership skills. Students were encouraged to form their own government. Students also provided their own meals, taking turns to buy provisions, cut firewood in the mountains, and cook.

Steve served as student captain at Dehua Normal School and joined the Three Principles of the People Youth League.

At the time, the school had no cafeteria, and students took their meals together on a grassy field in groups of ten. Meals typically consisted of two dishes (usually beans and vegetables) and soup. Every few weeks, a few pieces of pork would be found floating in the soup. As soon as the teacher gave permission to begin, ten pairs of chopsticks would rush into the pot, trying to get a piece of pork. The students ate a thick brown rice porridge, but even this required strategy. Instead of filling one's bowl in the first serving, the trick was to only fill the bowl about 70%, and then go back for seconds before the pot was emptied. The competition for extra food was fierce, and students often ended up with their clothes spattered with porridge.

As the students ate their meals, they had to constantly shoo away flies. At night, sleeping on hard beds in the local Buddhist temple was made even more difficult by the constant intrusion of mosquitoes. Medicine was also hard to come by. Once Steve stayed alone in the dormitory with a serious cold, looking up at the huge feet of the Buddha statue. He suddenly felt a flash of fear and felt terribly homesick for his mother. He sang a song about wartime separation with tears running down his face: "Will I ever see you again? Even if we never see each other again, please don't forget me."

Despite his young age, Steve was selected by the instructor to be captain of the student brigade, in which capacity he was responsible for assisting in military training, including the daily 6am morning flag-raising ceremony and exercises. Steve was thus responsible for organizing three to four thousand students, standing in formation in a sea of black hemp uniforms, leading the call of patriotic slogans, and getting the students ready to listen to their principal and instructors.

Despite the honor of being selected as captain, Steve himself couldn't afford a uniform. "My cousin had served as a soldier," he recalled. "He had a yellowish uniform, but it was terribly worn. I asked him to let me have the uniform, and I bought black dye and cooked it with the dye in a big pot to make the color match that of the other students. Even then, it fit very poorly."

On Sundays, classmates all went into town, but Steve didn't have any spending money. He brought his only "uniform" to the river where he would carefully wash it and lay it out on the rocks to dry while he studied his coursebooks. In the evening, he would return to the dormitory in his freshly washed uniform, feeling contented. But within a few months, the dye began to fade, and the uniform gradually turned yellow again, making Steve stand out amidst the sea of black, and many students simply assumed that the yellow uniform was a sign of special rank for the captain.

One Year in School Is Worth Ten Years of Reading

In any case, the "uniform" did not cause major problems, and the young Steve's physique soon filled out due to the military training. The school's headmaster, Zou Youhua, was an experienced and enlightened educator who had recruited excellent teachers. Within a year of commencing his studies, absorbing the essence of knowledge integrated into the daily lessons, Steve felt that he'd made more progress than he could have achieved in ten years on his own.

Steve was greatly influenced by his Chinese literature teacher. More than 70 years after he left Dehua Normal School, he can still recite the "Farewell, My Wife" by Lin Juemin, one of the 72 martyrs of Huanghuagang, and "Funeral Oration for My Sister" by Yuan Mei.

The Chinese literature teacher's surname was Ke, but he was a widely published essayist who went by the pen name Luoye, and when he felt like it, by the name Luye. He had a particular fondness for Steve, and Steve had a great affinity for the materials he used in class. The education Steve received there not only strengthened his awareness of resistance and patriotism, but also enhanced his knowledge.

Music was taught by Ms. Shang. Under her guidance, Steve learned many anti-Japanese songs. More than 70 years later, he could still burst into song with the same passion and clarity from his youth.

17-Year-Old Headmaster Tsai

One year later, Steve graduated with honors and was assigned by the Education Bureau of Jinjiang County to serve as the headmaster of the Elementary and Adult Education School in Shangan Township, in Shishi District, not far from Steve's home. At the time, Steve was only seventeen years old, and still small for his age.

Soon after arriving at the school, a dozen village representatives came to the Jinjiang County Government in Quanzhou to protest to the Section Chief for Education: "Why are you sending a child to be the headmaster of our village school? This shows contempt for our village. Please explain, what is the rationale for sending a child to be the headmaster?"

The section chief said to the village representatives: "We have considerable trust in headmaster Tsai. He is a top student in the normal school and an excellent headmaster. Give him a chance. Come see me again in two or three months."

After the villagers had gone, the section chief called for Steve.

"Headmaster Tsai, the parents of the students are coming to complain. What do you think?"

"It's not unusual, and I understand it."

"Understand? Do you want me to fire you and replace you as the headmaster?"

"That's not what I mean. Give me a little time, one to two

months, and I will see if I can change their minds."

"What are you planning to do?"

"Please trust me. Wait and see the results."

Steve didn't take the villagers' complaints personally. After all, their displeasure was born from their concern for the quality of the education they and their children would receive. Nearly 80 of the students were adults from 18 to 40 years old, all older than the incoming headmaster. Steve took the initiative to individually visit the homes of each student, first preparing by understanding their particular needs. During the visit, he would attentively and patiently talk with the students and their families about his plans to help them receive a quality education. Some of the parents said, "We have been their parents all this time, and you already understand them better than we do."

In introducing himself to the families, he said, "I have been sent here by the government. My task is not only to promote adult education, but also to promote social harmony by helping everyone to understand our national laws and regulations. I am happy to help you find answers to any questions you have, for instance, about taxation on farmers. I will also try my best to assist you in any grievances that may arise."

The new headmaster hoped to secure the cooperation of all the parents. "If necessary, after school, the students would stay for two or three hours for after-school tutoring. From 6 to 9 o'clock, I would take turns with each student, sometimes staying late into the night. I asked the parents to agree to this." The headmaster set up a temporary dormitory in the school, large enough to sleep three students, thus allowing him to tutor at least three students every night. The school gate stood open 24 hours a day, and the headmaster welcomed villagers to bring any questions or problems they might have to him any time day or night. Soon, the headmaster had established strong ties of trust with the community. His sincerity and actions made a deep impression on the villagers, who ultimately sent a representative to the section chief to request Steve be allowed to stay in their community to work. "We were completely wrong and withdraw our complaint. We like this young man and would like for him to stay." Thus, Steve stayed as headmaster for one year, and his tenure was quite successful.

A year later, Chen Fengyuan, the headmaster of Shenhu Key School in Shenhu Town, Jinjiang City, hired the two brothers Youhui and Steve as teachers. When the time came for him to leave, the villagers sadly accompanied him on the road for several miles.

A year later, he received a letter from Tsai Jinghe, the old headmaster of their alma mater in Jindong, saying that due to the interruption of overseas remittances, the school was unable to pay salaries for teachers, and the school was facing closure. He asked that Steve and Youhui, along with their cousins Hanzhang and Zhuji, all alumni of the Jindong school, return home to take up volunteer teaching positions and help the school weather this crisis. All four immediately obeyed.

The old headmaster later became a good friend of Steve. Decades later, Steve returned to his hometown and was fortunate to meet him again. However, Steve's involvement with the headmaster did not end there. Later, the headmaster's son was smuggled out of China and ended up in the Bahamas. Trying to enter the United States, he was intercepted and detained by the US Coast Guard for repatriation to China.

The headmaster placed a desperate call to Steve, seeking assistance. Steve was in Shanghai at the time and asked his son to rescue the headmaster's son from his predicament. Later, the son came to work for Steve in his hotel, and afterwards went on to prosper in the high-tech industry.

Steve's time in Jindong marked the last time he would work in the classroom, but throughout his life he continued to have strong ties to education. In 1948, Steve was working as a police officer in Xiamen and was sent to be a member of the first class of the Fujian Provincial Police Academy. Later, after arriving in Taiwan, Steve was selected to participate in the 22nd class of the Revolutionary Practice Research Institute (the predecessor of the National Development Research Institute). This institution had been established in 1949 in Chengdu, selecting senior party, government and military cadres and social elites to study the KMT's defeat in the Chinese Civil War, conducting in-depth research to establish plans for reforms and revival that would help the KMT eventually retake the mainland. In 1953, it was re-established on Mt. Yangming.

Steve (middle, back row) with Xiamen police colleagues attending the inaugural class of police officer training at the Officers Training Facility of the Fujian Police School.

Steve at the Revolutionary Practice Research Institute with Chiao Jen-ho (right). Mr. Chiao went on to serve as secretary of the Straits Exchange Foundation and chairman of the Overseas Community Affairs Council.

Graduation of the 22nd Class of the Revolutionary Practice Research Institute.

Honorary Doctor of Laws

On March 26, 1984, Lincoln University in San Francisco (now in Oakland) awarded Steve an honorary Doctor of Laws degree. On the same day, the California Secretary of State March Kong Fong Eu, who also served on the Alameda County Board of Education, was awarded an honorary Doctor of Education degree.

The honorary degree award ceremony was held in Sacramento, the capital of California, and Yu was the highest-ranking Chinese elected official in California at the time.

Steve was awarded an Honorary Doctor of Laws degree in consideration of his contributions to promoting trade and civil diplomacy between Taiwan and the United States, as well as between Taiwan and many other countries. It also recognized his work as a judicial police officer and, following World War II, as an investigator

at the Kinmen Military Commission and the Sedition Investigation
Committee in Xiamen, and for his excellent performance in
arranging the repatriation of Japanese citizens to Japan.

In awarding the Honorary Doctor of Laws, Zhang Daoxing,
President of Lincoln University, said: "Mr. Tsai often emphasizes the
importance of business diplomacy. He believes that those countries
that do not maintain diplomatic relations with Taiwan can still
establish robust bilateral relations through the National Chamber of
Commerce of the Republic of China and their bilateral counterparts.
Over the past ten years, through his efforts, this institution has
established business organizations in the United States and Canada,
and he has participated in or led business delegations to many
European and Middle Eastern countries, while forging ties with
more than 1,000 chambers of commerce around the world."

"Live and Learn." This sentence has special meaning to Steve. In
an interview, Mr. Tsai, nearly 90 years old at the time, said that he
hoped that, on retiring, he could return to his hometown and spend
his days reading and learning in his ancestral home.

Lincoln University President Chang Tao-hsing (far right), awards Steve (far left) an
Honorary Doctor of Laws degree, and California Secretary of State March Kong Fong
Eu (second from left) an Honorary Doctor of Education degree, with Mrs. Chang in
attendance.

A Love Lasting 60 Years

Steve graduated from Dehua Normal School in the spring of 1942, along with six male classmates. Full of excitement at beginning their careers as teachers, the young men rented a small creek boat to take them back to Quanzhou.

As the boatman greeted them and they began to board, they heard a girl's voice, shouting from the distance: "Wait for me! Wait for me!" The seven boys turned to see a girl running towards them from a distance. As she came closer, they realized that it was a classmate a year below them, a girl surnamed He (hereafter Miss H), known for her many talents at Dehua Normal School. She ran up to the boat, and explained that she was headed back to Quanzhou for summer vacation, and asked to share the ride with them. The boys were excited to have a pretty girl along and shouted together, "Of course! Welcome!"

A Tight Squeeze

The girl was well known to all the boys. She was the star of the school drama troupe, and the lead singer of the choir. She was the favorite girl of almost every boy. When she asked if she could join them, the boys could not believe their luck.

In the present day, Quanzhou is more than 100 kilometers from

Dehua by road along the Quanzhou-Nanning Expressway, and by car the trip takes just under two hours. Back when Japan invaded China, there was a road, but the KMT Army had destroyed key parts of the road to block enemy movements, thus the journey had become an arduous trek of two or three days. In contrast, the boat would take them to Quanzhou along the Jinjiang River in about 40 hours.

The sun was sinking, and the boat carrying students slowly sailed into the night. Leaving Steve and Miss H at one end of the boat, the other boys gathered to whisper among themselves.

"What are you talking about," asked Miss H, coming up to them.

One of the boys answered shyly: "Nothing."

"Come on," she said. "Speak up."

"Well, there's an issue regarding your safety and wellbeing."

"My safety? What are you talking about?"

"Well, you see, this boat is really rather small, and it'll be a tight fit for the eight of us to sleep in the cabin. We're discussing the best sleeping arrangements for your comfort."

Miss H looked around at the boys. "You're taking this too seriously," she said. "Here's what we can do. Everyone take out your student ID cards and whichever one is youngest will sleep next to me." At this, she slyly turned and winked at Steve who was quite dumbstruck, having never received this kind of attention from a girl before.

"She was the dream sweetheart of all the boys in school," he remembered. "When she winked at me like that, it was like a joyful dream. I was really overwhelmed, and I struggled to maintain my composure in front of the others."

Miss H was an innocent girl, of medium build, with a fair, rosy complexion. She had a sweet smile and a lively demeanor. She spoke engagingly with a pleasant voice, neither fast nor slowly. She sang beautifully and expressed natural charm through her drama performances. Now, she looked through each of the boys' ID cards, and finally said, "Which one of you is Tsai? He's the youngest."

"The other six boys tried to hide their disappointment," he remembers. "Later, I learned that their original plan was to take shifts sleeping next to Miss H, but she had deduced their plans."

The bright moon shone high in the sky, sparkling off the river. From shore came the croaking of frogs. The boatman slowly paddled, matching the rhythm of the river as waves gently lapped against the bow. The students stayed up on deck chatting well past midnight, but slowly went below to the cabin to prepare for sleep, spreading their bedding in any available space on the cabin floor. The cabin soon filled with ostentatiously loud snoring as the six boys pretended to sleep, and Steve could feel six pairs of eyes fixed on him in the darkness.

For the first time in his life, here in this cramped cabin, the young Steve was sleeping next to a girl, and he felt like his heart would explode from the tension. On the one hand, he was scrupulously careful to avoid any physical contact with Miss H, lest she misunderstand his motives. On the other, he was sure the other six boys were working out how to tease him mercilessly for his predicament. Keeping his legs stiff as boards, with his hands tightly held to his sides, he closed his eyes and pretended to sleep for what seemed like hours. Soon, his whole body was aching, but he dared not move a muscle. "Suddenly, my throat started to itch," he remembered. "I simply had to cough - there was nothing I could do about it. When the cough came, my entire body shook and I lost my balance, lurching to the right towards Miss H. Immediately, six male voices called out in the dark, laughing: 'Steve! Are you all right?

What happened!"

Steve replied, "I'm fine. Don't worry. Go back to sleep."

Together, the "Gang of Six" called out "Stop after one touch. Stop when it is appropriate." Then they all laughed and went back to their snoring, leaving Steve with an implicit warning to watch his manners.

Time passed by agonizingly slowly. It was almost two o'clock, when the "Gang of Six" finally began to fall asleep one by one. But Steve was still unable to follow suit. His breathing was ragged and irregular. Maybe, he thought, she's as nervous as I am. Through a glimmer of moonlight coming through the roof slats, he could see that Miss H's eyes were closed, but he couldn't tell if she was actually sleeping.

Steve lay there for hours, with conflicting thoughts churning in his mind. It seemed as if Miss H liked him. But how should he respond to avoid being seen as foolish or ungentlemanly?

A Life-Changing Handshake

While his mind ached with these thoughts, his body was wracked with cramps from staying in one position for so long. Finally, he had to shift position and, in doing so, his right hand accidentally brushed against Miss H's left hand in the dark. Aghast, he was about to draw away, when she grasped his hand tightly.

Time seemed to stop, and the air itself seemed to freeze in place. For the first time, Steve, at age 17, had his hand held by a girl tightly. The gentle sounds of the river seemed to rage in his ears. While only a few minutes had passed by, the time seemed endless to him.

Somehow, in the dark, the other boys sensed something was amiss. The boy to Steve's left turned and put his hand on Steve, while another five bodies seemed to simultaneously shift to the right, in a seemingly silent warning. Steve felt forced to withdraw his hand from Miss H.

At this time, dawn was beginning to break, and they heard a rooster on shore crowing. The tensest night of young Steve's life was almost over, but a strong bond had formed between the happy couple. After pretending to waken, Steve and Miss H seemed to naturally hive off from the others, seeming like an inseparable pair of lovers, and studiously ignoring the looks they attracted from the others.

The next day, the boat arrived in Quanzhou. After thanking the boatman, the students disembarked.

The journey from Quanzhou to Tangdong would take an entire day of walking, so Miss H invited Steve to her home for lunch before he set off. Having barely slept a wink the night before, he followed her in a daze.

Miss H's mother was a teacher, and she also had a younger brother at home. Her mother greeted her daughter and her handsome young guest at the door with a smile.

During lunch, Miss H asked Steve many questions about himself and his family. It was the first time Steve had been on the receiving end of such an interview, and it made him a bit uneasy.

After the meal, in front of Steve, Miss H suddenly said to her mother that if Tsai did not object, she would like to accompany him back to Tangdong. She said she would spend the two-month summer vacation in Tangdong and do her summer homework there. "I heard his home is by the sea, with beautiful mountains and beautiful rivers," she said. "It sounds like a nice place."

Steve was surprised by her suggestion, but also delighted and enthusiastically welcomed her to come home with him. Her mother looked at the two of them, and finally agreed, adding, "Be careful."

"I will take good care of her," Steve assured Mrs. H.

The notion that Miss H wanted to spend the summer vacation at his house made Steve's mind race with joyful thoughts. Although they were only really beginning to get to know one another, he began to suspect that Miss H had strong feelings for him. He was careful not to betray his excitement, but his heart was leaping.

Back in Tangdong, Steve's mother was also very happy to welcome this slim, beautiful girl who her son had brought home.

The house had a guest room on the second floor, with a beautiful view of the sea. Miss H spent the summer in this room, with Steve in the next room, and Mrs. Tsai one room over.

Soon the Tsai family and the entire neighborhood was completely taken with this charming guest from Quanzhou.

The sudden appearance of this young woman in her home greatly pleased Mrs. Tsai. She understood that her son was upright and honest and would not take such things lightly. She was thoroughly impressed with their young visitor and peppered Steve with questions: What does her family do for a living? Who is in the family? What kind of friendship do you have with her?

A Moonlit Beach

Steve's home lay at the southernmost tip of Tangdong Village, a peninsula with the Pacific Ocean to the east, and a bay to the west connected by a long sandy beach. The white crests of the waves surged beneath a blue sky, while local fishermen tended their oyster and clam beds in the bay.

Steve told Miss H that the oysters in his hometown were the best in the world, and still maintained this view later in life, even after eating oysters all around the world, including Taiwan and the United States.

This beach, just a short walk from the Tsai family homestead, became a place where the young couple would spend many happy hours.

Each morning, they would wake up and open the windows to enjoy the summer sea breeze. After breakfast, the two young people would work on their homework, and then each read something of their choice for pleasure. At that time, their favorite books included Ba Jin's Torrents Trilogy, Shen Congwen's novels, Lu Xun's essays, Tian Han's plays, the poetry of Ai Qing and Xu Zhimo, as well as the novella "Ghost Love" by the Shanghai writer Xu Xu. They also loved reading Chinese classics such as "The Dream of Red Mansions". From time to time, the two laughed or shed tears in response to their readings and would maintain a constant commentary on the characters in their novels or would fall deep into discussion on the artistic conception of poetry.

Steve took copious notes, turning them into essays for publication in Quanzhou's "Dazhong Daily". He also wrote serialized chapters of "Diary of a Normal School Student" in the same newspaper.

The two young people passed an idyllic summer, luxuriating in a daily fairy tale. "This was a kind of joy I had never before experienced," he remembers. "We both loved singing. She would start singing at the drop of a hat. I was a fairly good singer, but I couldn't compare to her."

The Ruyuan Pavilion lay at one end of the beach, and it took about an hour to walk to the other end. After dinner every day, Steve and Miss H walked the beach hand in hand, strolling slowly and enjoying pleasant times. As night fell, the white sand of the beach would shimmer in the moonlight, in stark relief to the dark sea. They sang together while enjoying the beautiful scene, with the boundless sea as their audience.

"Our voices - one soprano, one tenor, perfectly complemented the sound of the waves. When we finally exhausted our voices, we lay down on the beach, looking up at the bright moon."

They sang popular songs of the day, including Zhou Xuan's "The Wandering Songstress" and so on. In school, they had learned many anti-Japanese songs, along with lyrical and passionate ballads, and they sang these to each other under Tangdong's night sky. Aside from their singing and the waves, the whole world seemed to hold still. Then, they would lie together and talk about books and poetry, and then talk about their future plans.

It was a hot summer, and when they returned to the village late at night, the villagers were still outside, fanning themselves and trying to catch the sea breeze. Seeing the couple strolling and singing, older people looked on with envy of their youth and passion, while some of the younger people would join in singing. Soon, they were joined by other young couples, and the seaside rang with the chime of young voices.

For a while, Steve worked as the headmaster of the elementary school but was later called away to assume a teaching post at the neighboring Shenhu National Key School, joined by his second brother and cousin. At this time, Miss H was still in her second year of studies, so she took a leave of absence and accompanied Steve to Shenhu as a music teacher.

Reason Triumphs and Beauty Leaves in Anger

After arriving in Shenhu, the two lived separately in their

respective teacher dormitories. Shenhu is also on the coast, and the comforting familiar sounds of the sea followed them to their new home. But, unlike in Tangdong, here they were apart from family and friends, and in isolation the intensity of their love affair grew, but remained thoroughly chaste, with even walking hand in hand being an experience to remember.

Although Steve was still very young, he did not allow himself to be overcome by passion. First, he realized that marriage at the time was out of the question: He was barely able to care for himself, let alone a family. Second, his family was still in a precarious situation following the death of his father, so he had to take care of his mother, younger siblings, and nephews. Third, Miss H had not finished her studies and Steve had not established his career. He thus rededicated himself to overcome his years spent away from the classroom by engaging in strenuous self-study.

Thus, despite their ardor, the timing wasn't right. He hoped that they could take things slowly and eventually achieve their dream. Forcing rationality to overcome his emotions, he took Miss H aside and said bluntly, "Our love is irresistible, but our circumstances are difficult. If we're to ensure that we're never separated in the future, we must temporarily separate now. You need to return to school and complete your studies, while I have to complete my own self-studies and we can plan for our future together."

Miss H listened silently, her eyes wide, filling with tears. Without a word, she turned and went back to her dormitory.

The next morning, Steve found a letter on his desk:

"Steve, I am leaving. Don't ask where I am going or what I will do." She had left without a farewell, leaving Steve stricken. He ran to the train station, but there was no sign of her.

Filled with regret over his impulsiveness, Steve chided himself for not being more caring for her feelings and self-esteem.

But it was too late, and it would be decades before they met again.

After this sudden farewell in Shenhu, one would hardly expect that this romance could be revived, or that Mrs. Tsai would play a key role in the series of unexpected events.

Where Are Her Fragrant Footprints?

At the end of 1978, the CCP opened the Third Plenary Session of the Eleventh Central Committee, deciding on a policy of domestic reform and opening up to the outside world. After being away from home for decades, Steve finally had the opportunity to return to his hometown.

In 1942, Miss H left the Shenhu School in tears. Steve looked for her everywhere in vain. In 1946, Steve met Tina in Xiamen, and the two were married in Taiwan in 1953. Before they married, Steve had told Tina about his first love story and, although the subject of his younger classmate did not come up again for many years, Tina had a sense that Miss H still took up a place in Steve's heart. In the 1980s, following China's opening up, Tina returned to Xiamen saying that she was looking for long-lost relatives, but Steve later learned that she was trying to track down his old lover for him, without success. His wife's generosity of spirit truly moved Steve.

In the autumn of 1987, the couple returned to China together, traveling to Beijing, Shanghai, Xiamen and Quanzhou. In Xiamen, he gathered together with his classmates from Dehua Normal School, to relive their youthful days on a cruise filled with good food and karaoke. Amidst the laughter, Steve's mind turned to Miss H, and he suddenly fell silent. Finally, he asked, "Why isn't Miss H, my best friend from that time, here? Can anyone tell me where she is?"

After an awkward silence, his classmates responded that no one knew of her whereabouts. "Please help me find her," said Steve. "If you can find her, I'll fly back to Fujian within 48 hours and we'll have a special reunion with all of us and our families, and Miss H."

A few months later, a letter arrived from one of his classmates. Recognizing the sender and the potential impact of the letter's contents, Tina opened it first, and then handed it to Steve with shaking hands. The letter was brief and to the point: Miss H had passed away.

Steve read the letter without any emotional reaction. When he finished, he calmly told his wife that the letter simply wasn't credible. If she had died, why were their no details? How had she died? Where was she buried? Full of doubts and questions, Steve immediately wrote back, asking his classmates to reconfirm.

A few months later, a second letter came, stating that the previous news had been incorrect, and that Miss H was still alive. Furthermore, a few days later, another letter arrived - a letter from Miss H, the first communication between the two in nearly half a century. The letter was written on February 16, 1989, and postmarked February 17. Forty-seven years had gone by since they had parted in 1942.

The 19-page long letter recounted fully every little detail of their relationship back then. Scenes from several decades earlier were related in page after page of stationery like a movie flashback. She wrote that she was sorry for leaving so impulsively that morning 47 years earlier, and that she recognized that his urging of reason over emotion had been correct.

Steve read the letter and sighed. He sat at his desk and began writing what would eventually become a 20-page letter, filled with details of his struggles and experiences, taking his family from Quanzhou to Taiwan and then to the United States. Steve also asked her to send him a photograph of herself from that year, or a copy of her graduation photo.

From her letter, Steve learned that Miss H had pursued a career in education. Her husband was a well-known overseas Chinese businessman, with whom she had several children, and was leading a happy life.

Steve sent the letter to Miss H's home address, but she was away in Quanzhou at the time, assisting her daughter following the birth of her grandchild. Miss H's husband received and read the letter. It looked like her husband had long known the story of her first love, but he was a kind and open-minded man. After reading the letter, he rummaged around to find her graduation certificate with its photograph. He then himself rushed to Quanzhou to deliver the letter and photograph to his wife and encourage her to reply.

Reunion

Steve received the letter with the all-important photograph, and he immediately recognized the beautiful eyes and smile of his first love. This photograph thus became a treasure to him.

Tina took the initiative to arrange for her and Steve to go to Xiamen immediately. Miss H and her daughter rushed from Quanzhou to Xiamen and stayed at a friend's house. There in the living room, Steve and Tina came face to face with Miss H and her daughter. Steve was overwhelmed at his first glance of Miss H. She, however, graciously first welcomed Tina and thanked her for traveling all the way from the United States to meet her. After simple introductions, Tina and Miss H's daughter made a quiet retreat, leaving the two old lovers to lock in an embrace of sorrow and joy. Steve was immediately transported back decades, and he wept silently. Finally, they sat and recounted the decades of life that they had spent apart, and of the suffering they had endured thinking of each other. In the end, Steve took them back to that morning when he found her letter on his desk.

"Why did you leave so suddenly? Why did you leave me?"

"When you talked about a temporary separation, I was terribly disappointed and acted impulsively. It was youth and arrogance, nothing more."

"I can't blame you. I should have been more sensitive to your feelings. I knew we would have to be apart for a while, but I didn't expect that it would be forever."

"Fortune is fickle. However, it's a blessing that we were finally reunited in this life. We're taking fortune from misfortune." In the vernacular, we had predestined affinity, but it was not our destiny."

At the time, people in mainland China were still quite poor, and Steve had asked his wife to prepare an envelope full of cash for Miss H to help her and her family. However, when Tina brought out the money and gifts, Miss H only accepted the gifts, and resolutely declined the money. Steve tried again himself to try to get her to accept, but she said, "Our feelings for one another should not be contaminated by money."

For many years thereafter, each year before Steve's birthday, his wife and children, despite the distance, would secretly arrive early in the Xiamen Gulangyu house to make preparations for a so-called "surprise party." They would invite Miss H and her husband to attend as a surprise to Steve. The two families would be together and celebrate Steve's birthday happily and harmoniously. Outsiders could not imagine that this birthday party contained a love story that had lasted half a century.

Later in life, Steve donated the funds to develop Jindong Avenue in his hometown. On the day the road was to be first opened to traffic, he invited Miss H and other Dehua Normal School classmates to participate in the opening ceremony. In the evening, everyone attended a party in the Tsai family's ancestral home. Miss H sang "The Wandering Songstress," the song that the two had once sung together on the beach in Tangdong.

In this way, Steve and his first love have maintained frequent contact for more than ten years, making up for nearly half a century of separation. Miss H's husband is a gentle and kind man, and very devoted to his family's happiness, which came as a great relief to Steve.

One day in 2006 or 2007, the phone rang, bringing news that Miss H had been hospitalized. Steve immediately began making plans to make the trip to her bedside, but she assured him that it was nothing serious and there was no need to worry, and insisted he not make the effort. A few days later, however, a second phone call arrived, saying that she had peacefully passed away.

More than 60 years earlier, it was their misfortune that their first meeting was too early. The two had separated in a moment of pique, with only a curt letter to announce her sudden departure. And it was misfortune that their reunion was too late. After 60 years, she left peacefully. Through their reunion and frequent communication, they had both achieved a sense of closure. Thus, a sad and beautiful love story came to a close, but the memory of it will live forever.

Steve's mood after Miss H's parting was captured by the lyrics to his favorite love song, "*The First Girl I Loved*," lyrics by Dai Wangshu, music by Chen Gexin:

I walked to end of the world, I looked through the distant clouds and trees. How many past events are worth counting? Where are you?

I can't forget your sad eyes, I know your silent affection. You lead me into a dream, but I forgot you in another dream.

Ah ... my dreams and the person whom I have forgotten, ah ... the first person I sent my blessing to.

I tended to the rose all day long but let the orchid wither.

Steve has been singing "The First Girl I Loved" for more than 60 years.

{{ **Part 2: Beginning of Wisdom** }}
Chapter Three

Crossing a Shallow Strait

Unbearable to Recall - The Last Ship out of Xiamen

In 1949, the CCP's People's Liberation Army routed the Kuomintang forces, and millions of panicked KMT refugees evacuated the Mainland for Taiwan. Steve and his family were witnesses to this nightmare. The Japanese were finally defeated, but the Tsai family, which had just gotten back together, now numbering more than 20 people, old and young, was forced to take the last ship out of Xiamen, headed for Taiwan.

The Great Turmoil of 1949

Steve's girlfriend, Tina, had graduated from high school at the time. She had an uncle in Taiwan and went there for a visit after graduation. However, the PLA unexpectedly fell upon Xiamen, hammering the city with artillery fire, causing a mass evacuation. Tina kept calling from Taiwan, urging Steve to leave for Taiwan as soon as possible.

At this time, Steve had resigned from his position and was free to leave, whether for the Philippines, Taiwan or anywhere else. When pondering this, despite having no other friends or relatives in Taiwan, he decided to go there to be with Tina and take the whole family with him.

The PLA siege of the city had disrupted all outward transport. No air or ferry service was available. Fortunately, Tina's uncle pleaded with Fuzhou Governor Yen Ling-feng, who had already arrived in Taiwan, and Taipei County Commissioner Mei Ta-fu, who helped secure entry permits and transport both to the dock and to leave Xiamen by ship.

Late at night, a military detachment was sent to escort the Tsai family to Taikoo Wharf, and they boarded the last ship to Taiwan.

At that time, Taikoo Wharf was in chaos, with thousands of refugees seeking transport amid the roar of artillery fire. Desperate, they scampered up ropes hanging off the sides of the boats. On the overloaded ships, the decks were crawling with bodies, looking like waterborne anthills. Soon, the ship began to list at anchor. For fear of capsizing with any more weight, the captain gave the order to weigh anchor.

As the ship left the pier, refugees fell screaming into the sea, with their family members already on board helpless to save them.

Professor Lin Tong-fa, chair of the History Department at Fu Jen Catholic University in Taiwan wrote in his 2009 "The Great Retreat of 1949," that the main embarkation points for the great retreat were Shanghai, Guangzhou and Qingdao. The actual number of refugees is in dispute, but Lin estimates that over 1.2 million people fled China for Taiwan between 1945 and 1953. Of these, active military and civil servants accounted for about half.

Steve was an eyewitness to this chaotic history. Lin Tong-fa's work doesn't touch on the evacuation of Xiamen, and Steve's story adds an important perspective on the events.

Today, more than 60 years later, he recalls those shocking days and wonders, "was civil war really necessary? Was there no other way?"

Steve with former Xiamen Mayor Huang Tian-chue who would later serve as deputy chairman of the ROC Overseas Community Affairs Council.

A Book Opens Up a New Path

In August 1949, Steve, then 24 years old, came to Taiwan with his mother, his eldest brother, and his eldest sister. All he had to his name was 5 taels of gold (about 155 grams). The following year, his mother fell ill, and the gold was used up for her medical treatment and, soon thereafter, for her funeral, leaving Steve nearly penniless.

A New Free China

When they first arrived in Taiwan, Steve's family temporarily stayed at the home of his girlfriend Tina's uncle in Beitou. Steve lived simply and frugally, staying at home, diligently studying and preparing to take the college entrance examination. His only leisure was occasionally going to the movies with Tina. Expenses such as bus tickets, movie tickets, and snacks had to be carefully budgeted. Going to the movies was no small affair; it took careful planning. After the show, they would walk together to the train station where they would share a drink, and then walk home half-hungry.

Soon after, the family moved to a Japanese-style house owned by the eldest brother in Jiutiaotong, on Taipei's Zhongshan North Road. Following their mother's death, the eldest brother sold the house, and went with second brother back to Manila. Steve and his eldest nephew Ji Yang stayed in Taiwan and lived in a rented house.

Steve's first job after arriving in Taiwan was working for Taichung City Police Chief Hsieh Kui-cheng (formerly Chief of Police in Xiamen). He served as a Judicial Officer in the Taichung City Police Department. But after a few months, Tina persuaded him to resign and return to Taipei to become the editor-in-chief of the Taipei National Culture Press.

Steve saw that the newly relocated KMT government was trying to establish itself in a place that that was facing a strong military threat on the other side of the strait. Taiwan first had to survive before it could develop. To establish credibility and trust, the KMT needed to first improve popular morale. He recommended the writing of a book called "*A New Free China*" (Taipei National Culture Press) (Note 1). Published in 1951, this book reported on the plans and conditions of Free China's renovation and construction progress in Taiwan. The project enlisted the support of overseas Chinese and international public opinion. The publishing house's president was deeply impressed by the proposal and rented a small hotel room on Taipei's Chongqing North Road so that Steve could write in peace. He dove into the project, emerging occasionally to buy inexpensive meals at the nearby famous Yuanhuan market.

The new book came together quickly, providing a comprehensive overview of politics, justice, education, and society in Taiwan, and even mentioned that President Chiang Kai-Shek ordered the fatal shooting of the former Taiwan Provincial Chief Executive, Chen Yi, who was suspected of communist sympathies.

Steve wrote the text of the book, while images were collected by animator Huang Tsuo-xian. In 1951, Steve finally held his first book in his hands, 246 pages of coated paper. The weight of the book in his hand felt deeply satisfying.

Making Do in Difficult Circumstances - A National Athletics Initiative

In 1950, Steve (middle) assembles US military physical education consultant Dr. Chiang Liang-kui (far left), along with Central Air Command Colonel Chin An-yi (far right), Philippines overseas Chinese leader Hung Lee-pao (second right), and Chuang You-hsiung (second left) to plan a ROC-Philippines Basketball Tournament for the purpose of raising funds for the Tri-Service Stadium.

At the time, Taiwan was in a precarious situation. Chiang Ching-kuo, director of the General Political Department of the Ministry of National Defense, had initiated a nationwide campaign to modernize Taiwan, part of which included extending military physical training and sports to promote the development of civilian sports. But the effort was hampered by a lack of facilities. At the time, there was not a single basketball court in Taiwan that met international standards. The best quality court in Taipei was the at Military Police headquarters, but even this was an exposed court with no spectator seating.

Steve was friendly with the then president of the Military Sports Council, General Hu Wei-ke, and the two sought out Dr. Chiang Liangkui to discuss the possibility of securing a loan from the Bank of Taiwan to develop basketball facilities to host a large-scale international basketball tournament, inviting four basketball teams from the Philippines to compete against four local teams recruited from various armed forces units. Ticket proceeds and revenue from concession sales would be used to repay the loan.

Steve (front left) with his cousin, Philippine Sugar King Tsai Shishang (front right) attending the ROC-Philippines Basketball Tournament to raise funds for the construction of the Tri-Service Stadium. When the game ball was auctioned off, Tsai Shishang made the first and winning bids.

Following the Basketball Tournament, Steve was invited to visit the Philippines with the Ministry of National Defense Liangyou women's basketball team.

Four Philippine basketball teams assemble for the tournament to raise funds for the building of the Tri-Service Stadium, full of patriotic pride. Steve stands in the front row third from left, while Philippine Women's Association Chairwoman Chiu Chin-hsiang stands in the front row far right, and Chunsheng team honorary captain Tsai Shishang stands fifth from right. Teams from Taiwan are also pictured.

In the 1950s, ROC President Chiang Kai-shek and Madame Chiang invited the visiting Philippine Chunsheng basketball team to visit their Shihlin residence (Steve stands second from left).

In 1952, Steve speaks at the ceremony welcoming the Ministry of National Defense Liangyou women's basketball team to the Philippines. Team captain Hu Lee Mu-lan is at the far right, seated with teammates.

General Hu Wei-ke visits the Philippines. (From left: Philippines Overseas Chinese community leader Chuang You-hsiung, Philippine Sugar King Tsai Shishang, General Hu Wei-ke, Xinmin Daily News President Wu Chung-sheng, Steve and a photographer).

In the early 1950s, the Philippine national basketball team had dominated the sport in Asia, handing steep losses to teams from Nanjing and Shanghai. Steve's collaborators in this effort were aware of his relationship with the overseas Chinese community in the Philippines and valued his opinions. The plan quickly came together; and, with the active support of the military, a standard indoor basketball court was built off to one side of the Presidential Palace. Four basketball teams from the overseas Chinese community in the Philippines were invited to come. The captain of one of these teams was the cousin of Philippine sugar king Tsai Shixiang. On the first day of the tournament, the game ball was auctioned off for charity, and the buyer was none other than Tsai Shixiang. Local businesses were highly supportive of the effort and donated generously, quickly raising the funds needed to pay off the loan.

Overseas Chinese Teams Sets Off Patriotic Passion

The four Philippine teams visited three military bases throughout Taiwan and were warmly welcomed by provincial and local officials. Given his familiarity with the Philippines, Steve traveled with the team to assist in the arrangements and to extol the enthusiasm and patriotism of the overseas Chinese players, tying their visit to the new vision he had laid out in "*A New Free China.*" The press tour was a great success and helped bolster morale throughout Taiwan.

Mr. Chiang Ching-kuo visited the Philippine teams at the Beitou Hotel, presenting them with famous oranges from Yangmingshan as a gift.

On January 31, 1952, the Ministry of National Defense selected outstanding players from the various women's teams and organized the Liangyou Women's Basketball Team to visit the Philippines to play the Philippine Chinese Women's Basketball Team. Chief of Staff Chow Chihrou presented the national flag, and Chiang Ching-kuo's wife Chiang Fang-liang accepted it on his behalf. The delegation was led by Li Mu-lan, wife of Hu Wei-ke, Deputy Director of the General Political Department. Steve, in a consulting capacity, accompanied the team, responsible for liaising with the Filipino overseas community.

After the Liangyou Women's Basketball Team arrived in the Philippines, representatives from four Philippine-Chinese basketball teams invited Steve to dinner, and the local overseas Chinese clan associations also held banquets to welcome him, asking Steve to report on the recent situation in Taiwan. Steve's excellent knowledge of this topic led to his receiving a warm and enthusiastic welcome from the local overseas Chinese community.

Steve brought dozens of copies of his book "*A New Free China*" to present to attendees of the clan associations' reception dinners.

Unexpectedly, this book would open another door in his life.

Taiwan Correspondent for the Xinmin Daily News

At the dinner, Steve presented a copy of "*A New Free China*" to Xinmin Daily News photojournalist Mr. Su, who then forwarded it to Wu Chong-sheng, the newspaper's president. At the time, the Xinmin Daily News was the most influential overseas Chinese newspaper in the Philippines, and Mr. Wu was well-known in international press circles.

Upon receiving the book, Mr. Wu immediately contacted Su to contact Steve in Taiwan. Su told Mr. Wu that Steve was actually in Manila, and Mr. Wu asked Su Chun to immediately take him to see Steve. Upon receiving Su's phone call, Steve insisted he couldn't trouble Mr. Wu to come all the way out to see him, and they agreed to meet at a restaurant more convenient to them. On the spot, he offered to hire Steve as the editor-in-chief of Xinmin Daily News.

Steve was very grateful, but said that his fiancée was in Taiwan, making it difficult for him to stay and work in Manila. Mr. Wu persisted, encouraging him to bring Tina to Manila, but Steve was still reluctant.

Steve and Tina with well-known journalist Chang Jen-fei and his wife.

(left photo) In 1952, Xinmin Daily News president Wu Chung-sheng and his wife with Taipei correspondent Steve.

Mr. and Mrs. Tsai and colleagues from the Xinmin Daily News.

Still, he persisted. "I'll first appoint you a special correspondent in Taiwan with a monthly salary of US$500. Apply to the government for an office in Taiwan, and I'll provide office expenses of US$600 monthly. Whenever you're ready to accept the editor-in-chief post, just come to Manila." Swayed by Mr. Wu's passionate appeal, Steve accepted. That evening, Mr. Wu hosted a banquet at the Manila State Guest House, inviting the editor-in-chief Chang Chia-wei, the directors of the reporting and editorial departments, and Ms. Chen Pei-yuan, who would be Steve's primary contact at the newspaper. The atmosphere was warm and friendly as the new colleagues got acquainted.

After returning to Taiwan, Steve reported to the Ministry of the Interior and the Information Bureau and began preparing to establish a Taipei office for the newspaper. About a month later, he held a reception at Freedom House Hotel, celebrating Xinmin Daily News' new Taipei office, inviting major Chinese and foreign media representatives in Taipei. Other attendees included representatives from the Legislative Yuan, the Information Bureau, the Overseas Chinese Affairs Commission, and the KMT Overseas Working Committee. Shi Hsing-shui, chairman of the Manila Chinese Chamber of Commerce, also led a delegation to Taiwan to attend the opening. Chairman Shi said that the establishment of a special correspondent's office by Xinmin Daily News in Taipei would help develop the friendship between the Republic of China and the Philippines and would help facilitate the efforts of overseas Chinese to support Free China.

At the time, the Philippines was one of the world's leading voices supporting the continued presence of the Republic of China at the United Nations, and overseas Chinese in the Philippines strongly supported the ROC government. As special correspondent to a major Philippine daily newspaper, this helped Steve gain considerable social status in Taiwan. Steve recognized the importance of his new job and was determined to do the job well.

February 13, 2008, front page of the Manila Bulletin shows the paper's Chairman of the Board Dr. Emilio T. Yap (center) with the paper's Assistant Chairman (far left) and Manila Hotel president Mr. Lina (far right) with Steve and Tina, meeting to exchange viewpoints from the news and hotel industries.

Opening of the Xinmin Daily News Taipei office at Liberty House. Steve hosted a cocktail party for domestic and international news media and representatives of various industries. From front left: Overseas Chinese community leader Tsai Chin-Chiang, legislator Wu Chun-ching, Manila Overseas Chinese Chamber of Commerce president Shih Hsing-shui, Steve, Overseas Community Affairs Council deputy chairman Huang Tian-chueh, Tung Shih-fang of the Kuomintang Overseas Affairs Work Group. Back row: Government Information Office deputy director Mr. Chu, Chang Jen-fei of the Central News Agency, Yu Heng of the United Daily News, Ting Wei-tung of the Pan Asia Society).

Chapter Four

From Journalist to Entrepreneur

A High-Rise Building Built on a Single Salary

In 1951, Steve was hired as the special correspondent of the Philippines' Xinmin Daily News and its sister newspaper, the Manila Morning News. In addition to a monthly office overhead budget of US$600, he received a monthly salary of US$500. The salary was collected by Steve's second brother in the Philippines who would then bring the money to Taipei once a year.

At the time, six or seven thousand US dollars was considered a huge sum of money. The Korean War was still going on and a large number of US troops were stationed in Taiwan. Steve reasoned that the staff of the US Army Advisory Group in Taiwan would need a lot of housing, so he spent NT$140,000 to buy a piece of land and build a house in Tianmu, a scenic spot at the foot of Yangming Mountain in Taipei's northern suburbs.

The Korean War had ignited on June 25, 1950, and the following day, President Truman had ordered the US 7th Fleet into the Taiwan Strait.

The Korean War ended on July 27, 1953, but the US military advisory group remained in Taiwan. After the new house was completed, it was leased to an air force colonel in the US military advisory group for NT$6,000 per month on a three-year lease. The rent was paid in a lump sum of NT$216,000, immediately recouping the purchase price of the land and construction, with a 50% profit, which was then invested in buying a house on Taipei's Chongqing South Road.

When he first arrived in Taiwan, Steve had always lived in rented accommodations. Even after he got married, he rented houses on narrow, dark alleys in poor neighborhoods near the train tracks. With his new home on Chongqing South Road, he was happy to leave this nomadic life behind.

In 1979, the United States and the Republic of China broke off diplomatic relations. On March 1 of that year, the US military advisory group evacuated Taiwan and the tenants left. By this time, the value of the land in Tianmu had already skyrocketed, so Steve had the bungalow demolished and redeveloped the land into a high-rise building, significantly increasing the property value and rental income. This was also Steve's first land investment in Taiwan and, while it was very successful and lucrative, it paled in comparison with the large-scale projects to come.

From right: Steve, Philippine Sugar King Tsai Shishang. From left: Philippine paper industrialists Lin Hsi-ching and Yang Tsu-hwa, meeting to discuss overseas investment in Taiwan following the Republic of China's leaving the United Nations.

Tina visiting the Philippines, greeting Manila Overseas Chinese Chamber of Commerce president Shih Hsing-shui.

1968: Steve and Tina visit the Philippines, meeting with Philippine sugar industrialists Tsai Shishang and You Tsu-yi and their families for Christmas.

Steve meets with overseas Chinese community leaders to encourage investment in Taiwan. From left: Xinmin Daily News president Wu Chung-sheng, Mr. Yang, Secretary of the Manila Overseas Chinese Chamber of Commerce, Youth League director Mr. Li, industrialist Tsai Kui-lin, Manila Overseas Chinese Chamber of Commerce president Shih Hsing-shui, Steve, and reporters Huang Shih-yao and Wang Chin.

Steve was very conservative with his finances and investments. Owning his own home without a mortgage to maintain and having the rental income from the Tianmu property was an important turning point for his life and career in Taiwan, freeing him from worry about his job security. It also marked a new chapter in his life - moving from rootless restlessness to a more stable life. "Up until then, we'd had to be very careful with money," he said. "All expenditures were carefully considered. Minor prosperity comes from diligence and thrift, medium prosperity comes from hard work, and major prosperity comes from being in the right place at the right time."

This newfound stability gave him the financial freedom to become actively involved in domestic and foreign social welfare organizations and overseas Chinese enterprises. His involvement with these groups helped greatly expand his network and reputation.

Philippine-Chinese investment in Taiwan at that time made a great contribution to Taiwan's economic development.

Living Room Factories Create 150,000 jobs

Taiwan Becomes the Leading Exporter of Christmas Lights

In the 1960s, with Steve's encouragement, the chairman of the Manila Overseas Chinese Chamber of Commerce Mr. Shih Hsing-shui, organized overseas Chinese capital in the Philippines to establish the Overseas Chinese Life Insurance Company and the Overseas Chinese Property Insurance Company in Taiwan, with Steve serving as Managing Director, Deputy General Manager and eventually General Manager of both companies. Later on, through an introduction from Wu Chong-sheng, president of the Xinmin Daily News, Steve met Mr. Yang Tsu-hua, a paper tycoon in the Philippines. Mr. Yang came to admire Steve's personality and talent, finding him to be kind and serious. He felt that Steve's efforts to help overseas Chinese develop their careers in Taiwan had gone unrewarded and invited Steve to start a joint venture in Taiwan.

Together with Lin Hsi-ching, Mr. Yang had created the Philippines' largest paper mill, an expansive compound that had been nicknamed "Paper City." How would such a successful industrialist come to Taiwan to start a small company?

The Overseas Chinese Capital Funded Taishan Electric Industrial Company

One day in 1967, Mr. Yang called on Steve at the General Manager's office of the Overseas Chinese Life Insurance Corp. "Look at this magnificent office, you have here," he said. "You employ thousands of people working hard all day to create a large, fine company. But while you have the title, shareholders are a fickle lot, and they could replace you at a moment's notice, leaving you with nothing but the memories of efforts you made on behalf of others. You're a good man and would do anything for your friends. But you have to think of the future. You're a talented young man, and I want you to be my partner in a new business in Taiwan. A few days ago, I bought a small factory on Chongqing North Road, in Taipei, to make strings of Christmas lights."

Yang came to this small venture in Taiwan not only to make profits, but also to create employment opportunities. "Ornamental lights are one of the most labor-intensive industries and can provide tremendous opportunities for common people and military dependents in Hsinchu, Miaoli, and Zhongli." Steve felt the same way, and the two hit it off.

Yang insisted that the new company should be structured as an overseas Chinese investment business, bringing in increasing capital from overseas to buy land, build new factories, and install machinery and equipment to form one Taiwan's biggest producers of Christmas lights.

"I know your personality, and you have always been a patient person. This should be easy for you." These words of sincerity, trust, support, and encouragement touched Steve's heart. Recognizing the disparity in their financial resources in this partnership, Yang went on to say that he would put up his half of the financing first, while Steve could break his contribution in two halves: the first up front, and the balance when the factory was complete.

In this new company, Yang would be the chairman of the board and Steve would serve as general manager. Steve immediately began to make arrangements for the overseas investment, finding sites to build the new factories, sourcing production equipment, and developing export markets. The company would be named the "Taishan Electric Industrial Company."

It took a year of hard work to make all the necessary arrangements, and Taishan Electric Industrial Co., Ltd. was established as Taiwan's only overseas Chinese-owned Christmas light string factory. The company bought about 3,300 square meters of land on Taipei's Yongji Road to set up a factory, with more than 200 full time workers and more than 1,000 piece workers.

This marked the beginning of a new chapter in Steve's life, and it marked the start of a new charitable venture to which he would dedicate himself for decades to come.

At this time, Taiwan's Christmas light industry was still in its infancy, consisting of a few dozen small-scale manufacturers, mostly relying on orders from Japanese companies, and their output was negligible. But this was also a turning point for the development of Taiwan's Christmas light industry.

The industry had originated in Italy, and later moved to Japan. However, the 1960s saw sharp increases to wages in Japan, and these rising manufacturing costs made the industry unsustainable there, and the industry gradually moved to Taiwan.

Establishing a Guild to Promote Industrial Unity

Steve saw the strong need for the industry to continue to improve product quality, improve its export image, and strive to become the global center for production. This could only be possible through creating a united front.

At that time, most of the Christmas light manufacturers were based in Hsinchu, Miaoli, Zhongli, and Taoyuan. After a year of legwork and patient lobbying and deliberation, on May 4, 1968, the first industry-wide meeting was held, with 37 members. After three preparatory meetings, the Taiwan Decoration Bulb & Light-Set Exporters Association was formally established on July 12 of that year.

At that time, Steve was the managing director of two overseas Chinese insurance companies. Later, he served as the director of a third overseas Chinese-funded insurance company, the Youlian Insurance Company, and the general manager of the overseas Chinese-funded Taishan Electric Industrial Company. At the same time, Steve was working to develop a high-class large scale international tourist hotel, with hopes to make it the tallest building in the ROC.

He was also working for two Philippine newspapers in Taiwan. To minimize the necessary travel time to support the new Association, he dedicated a portion of his office on Xinyang Street in Taipei for the work of the Association and stated that he would do his best to advance the preparatory work of the Association, but he would be unable to serve as the chairman.

In 1968, Steve established the Taiwan Decoration Bulb & Light-Set Exporters Association.

The cover of a special publication celebrating the 35th anniversary of the establishment of the Taiwan Decoration Bulb & Light-Set Exporters Association.

However, internal conflicts between rival Association members resulted in a deadlock that could only be resolved by Steve serving as chairman. To ensure the Association's stability and success, he reluctantly took on the role for several years, and then left the position, finally returning to the job later on and serving as chairman for a total of 30 years. In this capacity, he also represented the Association on the board of the Republic of China Chamber of Commerce, where he served as Executive Director for 40 years.

Within a few years the Association had helped manufacturers upgrade their production equipment and greatly increase output while improving quality standards. From an initial group of 30 member firms, the Association's ranks quickly swelled to over 260, with over 600 representatives regularly taking part in Association proceedings.

This pure export industry was very labor-intensive, creating cottage industries with common people and military dependents doing piecework at home in a network of "living room factories," bringing in much-needed supplemental income and making a significant positive change in peoples' lives.

Export Price Verification Seal

In his tenure with the Association, Steve's proudest achievement was helping to obtain Taiwan's first "Export Price Verification Seal" specially authorized by the government for the Association. With this, the Taiwan Decoration Bulb & Light-Set Exporters Association was authorized to act on behalf of the government in verifying export prices for Christmas lights. Pricing created internal conflicts between manufacturers, who wanted to maximize prices, and distributors who wanted lower costs and higher margins. The resulting competition created chaos within the market as manufacturers and distributors sought to undercut each other and their competitors. Under the guidance of the Association, both sides agreed to a reserve price floor based on costs and market conditions. Each export consignment required a letter of credit that reported the actual selling price. Once the association had verified and approved the price, the bank would settle the payment. The International Trade Bureau of the Ministry of Economic Affairs would review the "Export Price Verification Seal." The director at the time was Mr. Vincent Siew, who later also served as Vice President of the ROC. However, Mr. Siew initially opposed the issuance of export authorization to the Association, telling Steve that the interests of the Association's members, including manufacturers and traders, did not necessarily align, and the Association's acting in lieu of the government for the export license might result in unintended consequences.

In 1969, Steve and his wife visited the Consulate General of the Republic of China in Malaysia, where their friend Consul General Chang Chung-ren introduced them to Vincent Siew, who was a consular officer. After spending time together sightseeing in Malaysia, Steve found himself deeply impressed by this enthusiastic young diplomat. Hsiao was later transferred from the Ministry of Foreign Affairs to the Ministry of Economic Affairs, where he made great contributions to national development. At this time, Steve served as the director of the Export Industry Association.

Mr. Siew and Steve had a very good collegial relationship, but Siew refused to grant authorization for the "Export Price Verification Seal" unless Steve could get all 600 Association members to agree to apply for permission for the Association to act in lieu of the government in this way.

Representing the Association, Steve stepped in to try to help all members reach an agreement that would meet the needs of all parties, while ensuring high-quality production and good profits. Steering all 600 Association members to reach such an agreement was a difficult task. Mr. Siew was probably expecting Steve to withdraw his proposal. Steve spent two years cajoling various member representatives, often with multiple back-to-back meetings that took him all over central Taiwan, at a time when Taiwan had no highways. Each trip to Xinzhu or Miaoli took an entire day of driving, often returning to Taipei late at night along dusty roads. Finally, his hard work and perseverance paid off, and it seemed that he had a final agreement in hand to take to the government.

At the last minute, however, he discovered that two Association members were backing out of the agreement and had written to the International Trade Bureau to express their opposition. This put all of Steve's hard work at risk. He rushed to Xinzhu, driving through the night and arriving early the next morning where he got the two holdouts to recommit to the pact. He took them to the post office to retrieve their letter before it was forwarded to Taipei.

Thus, the Association secured its preferential export authorization, and the experience highlighted the need for government/industrial cooperation. The Association quickly moved to leverage the unity of purpose of its members, establishing a headquarters in Taipei staffed by efficient work teams to coordinate the work of domestic producers and foreign distributors.

The Benefits of Livingroom Factories – Major Benefits for Military Dependent Communities

Steve once led a delegation of 20 Association members to organize exhibitions and sales fairs in over 20 locations in Europe and the United States to establish market relations. At the time, it was the most ambitious such effort Taiwan's Christmas light industry had ever staged, and was very well received, driving increased exports and bringing foreign exchange into Taiwan.

In the 1960s, the growth of the Christmas light industry helped create over 150,000 jobs for military dependent communities and the common people nearby in Hsinchu, Miaoli, and Zhongli, providing crucial income to non-mainstream labor forces including students and housewives who would use their free time after school or chores to string lights in their living rooms. Much of this income was spent on home improvements and these changes in village and town life gradually became apparent as originally destitute military dependents refurbished and expanded their houses and bought color television sets, with a thicket of TV antennas springing up on rooftops. This income was also instrumental in helping an increasing number of industrious students to seek further educational opportunities abroad in Europe and North America, and the income these living room factories brought in offered many families the means to emigrate abroad.

The King of Henan: Wang Ren-sheng

The story of Steve's involvement with the decorative light industry would not be complete without mentioning the "King of Christmas Lights," Mr. Wang Ren-sheng, who later became known as the "King of Henan."

Wang Ren-sheng was originally an elementary school teacher, but later went into business with the support of Steve and his wife through the Taishan Electric Industrial Company.

Many successful people owe a great deal of their success to a good mentor. Later in life, Wang Ren-sheng paid respect to those who had helped him in life by published testimonials in newspapers and magazines. In 2003, Wang celebrated the Association's 35th anniversary in an article, writing: "The greatest benefactor who contributed to my professional success was Mr. Steve Tsai. Mr. Tsai is a well-known entrepreneur in Taiwan. He was the general manager of Taishan Electric Co., and his children were my students. He was very impressed by my hard work, and we spoke frequently.

When I told him of my intention to change careers, he said he was willing to help. In 1970, I left teaching and came to work at Taishan Electric Christmas light factory. As the factory director and business manager, I have been inseparable from Christmas lights. Even though I was brand new to this industry and to business in general, Mr. Tsai saw my potential and gave me a lot of responsibility. The factory manager was in charge of production and the business manager was in charge of sales . At first, I was somewhat intimidated by the challenge. I studied hard and gradually made up for my lack of experience."

The June 21, 2006 issue of Business Weekly featured an interview with Wang Ren-sheng, including the following passage: "In Taipei, he met Steve, an honorable man and the parent of students at Guting Elementary School, where Wang taught. Steve asked him to leave teaching and pursue a career in business. This encounter changed the course of his life, bringing him to the Taishan Electric Company, where Steve was chairman of the board. After Wang had been at Taishan for several years, Steve appointed him factory director, making him responsible for raw material procurement, production and exports. Over the next few years, he fully mastered the entire operating process of the Christmas light factory. On the factory floor, he gained an education that possibly is unavailable at Harvard Business School, laying a firm professional foundation for his career in industry and commerce. Steve has said he took pride in appointing Wang to the post and setting the stage for his success, saying that Wang is intelligent and diligent, but that the key to his success is his devotion to the factory and the support of his family."

Over the next decade, wage inflation in Taiwan gradually pushed Christmas light production to other countries in southeast Asia and then to mainland China. However, the Association maintained its Taipei office to handle financial affairs, foreign orders, and foreign exchange settlement, providing important support for manufacturers who viewed the Taipei Association as a kind of business family.

While some viewed Christmas lights as a sunset industry, Steve disagreed. He saw that Christmas light use had expanded beyond public and private Christmas celebrations, and saw room to expand and saw the potential for production to move back to Taiwan as wages in China rise and as production is increasingly automated.

Steve served in the Christmas Lights Association for 38 years, during which Taiwan surpassed Japan as the world's leading producer, and while production eventually moved on to China, the industry as a whole is still largely controlled by Taiwanese businessmen.

Trustworthiness and Fairness Are More Precious Than Gold

Seek courage, and avoid carelessness, ignorance and injustice.

Stepping into Property Development

Steve's involvement in the Christmas light manufacturing industry also unexpectedly led him into real estate development. One of his first tasks in establishing the Taishan Electric joint venture was to find a suitable site for the factory. His experience as a journalist led him to first dig through Taipei City Government records, including the Taipei Urban Development Plan. While the Plan was public information, few people ever paid it any attention. Through his research, Steve learned that Taipei's Yongji Road was slated to be widened from seven to 25 meters. The surrounding land was frequently flooded and had become an informal garbage dump. But based on what he found in the Urban Development Plan, Steve realized that this landfill could become quite valuable. Acquisition, however, would be a challenge. Ownership of the plot was divided among more than 20 different owners, some of whom proved difficult to track down. Most potential buyers would be put off by the complications and difficulties, but Steve diligently tracked down each of the stakeholders, sending inquiries as far as Central and South America. It took him seven years of tireless research, correspondence and negotiation, but he eventually secured title to the entire parcel at an average price of NT$700 per ping (each ping is approximately four square meters).

When Yang Tsu-hua's Philippine partner, Lin Hsi-Ching, learned of the real estate development opportunity, he asked to be allowed to invest in the land as well. The two partners came to an amicable agreement in which they would each hold one-third of the land, leaving one-third for Mr. Lin.

In 1971, the Republic of China withdrew from the United Nations, marking the country's greatest diplomatic setback since the retreat to Taiwan. This left the population in a state of heightened anxiety, and many sought to leave Taiwan, seeking safety and stability abroad, despite President Chiang Kai-shek's exhortations for calm and resoluteness.

Yang Tsu-hua and Lin Hsi-ching rushed to Taipei from Manila immediately. Worried about the possibility of an imminent CCP invasion of Taiwan, they urged Steve to sell the land so they might protect their capital. Steve, however, cautioned against hasty measures. "The withdrawal of the Republic of China from the United Nations does not mean that the Communist Party will attack Taiwan," he told his partners. "Based on factors such as Taiwan's international strategic position, the CCP will not rush into attacking Taiwan. Meanwhile, the urban development plan points to a strongly bullish market outlook. We should hold our position."

Unpersuaded, Yang and Lin insisted on selling the land. But, as the land was jointly owned by the three parties, a successful sale or development required all three partners to agree. In addition, a parcel of land subject to such an internal dispute would have trouble attracting bidders. Not only did Steve feel this was a mistake, but to sell now would have wasted all the time and effort he had spent on acquiring the land. Still, however, he valued the friendship of his partners over all other considerations, so he reluctantly agreed, but declined to look for a buyer himself. Through a mutual friend, Yang and Lin found a buyer willing to purchase the land at NT$50,000 per ping, realizing the partners a 70-fold profit. Yang and Lin were overjoyed, but Steve was still wary. He told his partners that he still had absolute confidence in Taiwan and to sell now would be to miss out on much greater profits in the future. He suggested that, rather than sell now, they could partner with a local construction firm to develop the land, but the partners were adamant about their decision to sell.

Then, Steve received a call from Yang in the Philippines. Yang felt conflicted about the decision to sell, especially considering the great effort Steve had put into acquiring the land. Yang and Lin were determined to sell and found the offer of NT$50,000 per ping too good to pass up. However, they had agreed to sell their shares to Steve, allowing him to purchase the shares with a down payment and to pay off the balance as the land was developed.

Elated by this turn of events, Steve sold his house on Taipei's Heping West Road, and used the proceeds to make the down payment to Yang and Lin. He then partnered with construction firms to gradually build ten commercial buildings and hundreds of residential apartments on the site, with the construction companies taking a 45% stake in the development. Steve would then sell off some of his allotted apartment units to pay off the balance to Yang and Lin.

A Garbage Dump Becomes a Golden Treasure

After Steve bought the land, another great opportunity came knocking. At that time, he was building Taiwan's tallest hotel in front of Taipei Main Station. The project called for three sub-basements, involving the removal of a great deal of dirt, and the cost of hauling this earth out of the city for dumping was prohibitively expensive. Instead, he had the dirt dumped at the Yongji Road site.

During this time, the value of the land had appreciated considerably, and construction firms lined up to partner with him on the development. However, during the planning stage for a ten-plus story high-rise, the first global energy crisis prompted the government to seek to save energy by limiting new construction to five floors, which for the Yongji Road site would mean the loss of 300 households. Still bullish on future growth, Steve adopted a strategy of phased development so as to ride out the crisis. Indeed, as Taiwan emerged from the shadow of these diplomatic and economic crises, real estate prices continued to rise, and the project's three-phase development allowed them to continue to take advantage of increasing property prices.

Steve was approached by a prominent Japanese entrepreneur who had the idea to build an automobile factory on part of the land, asking Steve to either sell the land to him outright or to enter into a joint venture. The negotiations took Steve and his wife to Japan and Hawaii, and the prospects seemed bright but, on September 29, 1972, Tokyo announced that it would be severing diplomatic ties with the Republic of China and establishing relations with Beijing. The announcement was met with angry protests in Taiwan, with Japanese goods and cars being burned in the streets. The Japanese investors took fright and withdrew the offer.

At the time, Steve saw three ways forward for this land. In order of his preferences, these were to enter into a joint venture for industrial development, build apartments for rent or sale, or sell the land.

Comradeship, Confidence and Courage

Though the automobile factory fell through, Steve pressed

forward with the development of the Yongji Road land, eventually securing a significant victory.

He earned this achievement, first through showing courage. To move successfully from journalism to business requires sense and boldness, and this showed in his seeing this plot as the diamond in the rough that it was. He said, "There are two kinds of characteristics that will prevent one from achieving greatness: cowardice and recklessness." He earned this achievement second through showing comradeship, showing willingness to sell the land, a step which was against his own financial interest. His partners showed lack of resolve for wanting to sell the land, but still showed righteousness in agreeing to sell their shares to Steve, even though he lacked the funds at the time. He earned this achievement third by showing boldness. To address the shortfall, Steve sold his beloved home on Heping West Road, and the family moved into a small, shabby rented apartment on Shida Road. He earned this achievement fourth by staying true to his moral compass. "Always be honest, sincere, and serious. Never resort to underhanded tricks," he said. Because of his strong reputation for righteousness, Lin and Yang were willing to sell him the land before he had raised the necessary funds, otherwise the plot would have fallen out of their hands entirely. Finally, Steve earned this achievement fifth by showed great confidence, refusing to submit to the prevailing pessimism about Taiwan's future following its withdrawal from the United Nations. On the contrary, he saw it as an opportunity.

When Taiwan withdrew from the United Nations, many Taiwanese were overcome by pessimism, and sold off their assets to emigrate. But a few years later, those who stayed enjoyed rapid economic growth. Many who had left eventually returned, but on arrival they found that the assets they had sold just a few years before were now priced out of their reach. Based on his clear observation of the situation, Steve remained bullish on Taiwan's prospects, refusing to bow to the conventional wisdom, and thus securing his greatest professional achievement.

This story, in which a garbage dump becomes a golden treasure, proved the saying "Trustworthiness and fairness are more precious than gold".

Steve often exhorted himself with the words "Seek courage, and avoid carelessness, ignorance and injustice." These words, which showed their magic in the story of the land investment, led Steve from one success to the next.

Chapter Five

Solving Two Crimes with Wisdom

A Murder in Xiamen

Before going to Taiwan, Steve solved a sensational murder case at the age of 23. This occurred in October 1948 in Xiamen, where Steve headed a criminal investigation squad.

At that time, there were a pair of brothers Huang Zemin and his fifth brother Huang Qinian from Dehua County. After the "July 7 Incident" in 1937, many refugees arrived in Xiamen, presenting Huang Zemin with a business opportunity. His family had long produced a medicinal plaster called "Wanying Ointment," sold in Xiamen pharmacies under the name of "Yi Tie Ling" Huang Qinian first produced and sold "Yi Tie Ling" with his elder brother, and then developed another ointment with his wife Huo Meiling, which was renamed "Yi Fu Ling" for marketing purposes.

In 1945, the United States dropped two atomic bombs on Nagasaki and Hiroshima, leading to Japan's surrender. Huang Qinian thought to capitalize on popular fascination with this amazing new technology, creating an "Atomic Ointment" that claimed to cure all kinds of boils and abscesses. Each of the two brothers had their own pharmacies, with the elder brother's located on Yongchun Road in Gulangyu, while the younger brother's was at No. 94 Zhongshan Road, Xiamen. Both brothers became rich from their businesses, but their greed contributed to frequent spats between them.

In October of that year, Huang Zemin and Huang Qinian returned from Xiamen to their hometown in a remote part of Fujian Province, but only the older brother returned, with the younger brother dying suddenly on the way back. Rumors quickly spread that Huang Zemin had killed his younger brother.

Despite rampant speculation, there was no evidence. The news reached Steve, but he felt there was something strange about it. The younger brother had died just over a day away from Xiamen, but the elder brother failed to notify the younger brother's wife to go to the funeral, instead hurriedly burying his younger brother. Steve said, "The Huang family is well established in Xiamen, and the death took place not far from Xiamen where he had many relatives and friends. As a matter of common sense, the body should have been transported back to Xiamen for a grand funeral, rather than subject to a hasty on-the-spot burial. At the very least, he should have waited for the widow to arrive. Also, what kind of illness did he have, and which doctor was he taken to see?"

Steve immediately sent people to investigate, and his agents were very effective. He quickly learned that the Huang brothers did have conflicts over their business interests. He began interviewing Huang Zemin at eight o'clock in the morning, and the informal conversation went well into the evening. Steve engaged with Huang Zemin as if they were old friends reuniting after a long absence. Based on the content of the conversation on the first day, Steve felt that the evidence was increasingly unfavorable for Huang. It seemed very likely that Huang's desire for wealth and the opportunity to benefit from a monopoly on the family's trade secret medicines provided a strong motive for murder.

Steve served as the leader of the investigation team but was absolutely opposed to the inhumane and illegal use of torture to extract a confession during the trial. Instead, he adopted a lighter approach that followed three principles. First, to maintain politeness and respect for the suspect before guilt was established; second, to arouse the suspect's sense of conscience; and third, to clearly explain the implications of a confession, emphasizing the potential leniency the defendant may find in court, particularly in a capital case, where conviction can bring death.

Captain Tsai, responsible for solving the Xiamen fratricide case.

Steve reasoned that, if a crime had been committed, the suspect would have a guilty conscience and would lie to protect himself. But lies beget more lies, and each layer of falsehood would create inconsistencies that would trip up the suspect in the telling. By careful examination and consideration, the interrogator could catch the suspect in a lie, thus breaking his defense and extracting the truth. Steve and Huang Zemin talked for two days and two nights. On the first day, Huang steadfastly maintained his innocence.

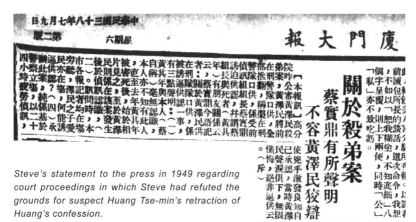

Steve's statement to the press in 1949 regarding court proceedings in which Steve had refuted the grounds for suspect Huang Tse-min's retraction of Huang's confession.

However, as the second night passed and the dawn began to break, there was a sudden downpour that shook the room. In a moment of inspiration, Steve suddenly rose to his feet and, amidst the flashing thunder and lightning, shouted: "Huang Zemin, your brother is here!" As the lightning glared off his haggard face, Huang Zemin suddenly burst into tears and confessed to killing his brother. Steve immediately brought in the stenographer Lan, who had been standing outside the door, to record the confession in detail. Also, just outside the door was Huang Aimin, Huang Zemin's son, the head of the criminal investigation team and reporters from various newspapers, all listening to the confession in real time.

Steve questioned Huang Zemin about the crime in front of everyone. He then sent someone to open the brother's coffin for an autopsy. The examiner discovered that Huang Qinian had been poisoned. Steve later discovered that the local coroner who had provided the original death certificate had been bribed by Huang Zemin. Because "Yi Tie Ling" and "Yi Fu Ling" both enjoyed a good reputation in China and Southeast Asia, the case was a media sensation.

This was one of several strange cases that Steve and his team cracked, and the news of these bizarre and twisted stories traveled widely, often through the work of Huang Feng, a reporter from Xiamen Jiangsheng Daily. Only 23 years old at the time, Steve became a celebrity in Xiamen, and even sixty years after the fact, Steve's wife and even his cousin would sometimes refer to him as "Inspector Tsai," much to his amusement.

A Bizarre Murder in Taipei Goes Unsolved for 50 years

Later, Steve would encounter another murder case, this time in Taiwan. The victim, Yao Chia-chien, an overseas Chinese, was a hotel manager in Taipei. The case ultimately resulted in four death sentences handed down to luminaries including university professors and senior police officers. Two others received life sentences. Disputes over the case lasted 49 years, making it the longest-lasting murder case in the judicial history of the Republic of China.

Steve was already working as a journalist at the time, but he retained his investigator's sense for systematically evaluating evidence and following clues, traits which were reflected in his reporting for the Philippines Xinmin Daily News and helped him attract quite a following among the overseas Chinese community and governments in Southeast Asia.

Yao Chia-chien was general manager of the Wuhan Hotel on Taipei's Hankou Street and an overseas Chinese from the Philippines. On July 18, 1959, Yao was found hanging from a door frame in a guest room in the hotel. Yao was a notable overseas Chinese, and his death attracted considerable attention. Steve was one of many who rushed to the scene, where the death was ultimately ruled a suicide by the coroner.

Yao's son, Yao Zhiguo, worked in the Philippines for a friend of Steve, the paper magnate Yang Tsu-hua. Returning to Taiwan upon news of his father's death, the son sought out Steve on Yang's recommendation. Steve accompanied him to the morgue to identify his father's remains. At the viewing, Steve noted that Yao's body had three small red pinpricks on both thighs. Questioning the coroner about the spots, Steve could not get a satisfactory answer.

Suspecting foul play, Steve went looking for a motive for murder. After interviewing Yao Chia-chien's relatives and friends, he discovered that Yao had been involved in an active dispute between Wuhan Hotel shareholder Huang Xuewen and others over equity and management rights. In fact, court proceedings for a civil suit over the dispute was scheduled to resume a few days hence.

A few days before his death, Yao Chia-chien had told those around him that he was struggling against powerful and malignant forces, and that he now had sufficient evidence to win his case when the court proceedings resumed. Furthermore, Yao announced that if he failed to win in court, he would go Zhongshan North Road, flag down President Chiang Kai-Shek's motorcade and make a traditional appeal by "bringing an accusation to the attention of the emperor."

His suspicions and curiosity aroused, Steve began to feel a sense of responsibility to see justice done. He interviewed hotel staff members to get a clearer sense of Yao's work and mood in the days leading up to his death but was met with a wall of silence. However, he discovered that the maid who had been serving Yao at the hotel was subsequently let go.

"The Emperor Qianlong Goes to the South of the Yangtze River"

The next day, Steve managed to find the maid. Yao was already in his seventies at the time, and thus this maid had been assigned to assist him exclusively. She told Steve that every night she would prepare a foot bath for Yao, and she remembered nothing out of the ordinary on the night of his death. Pressed for details, the maid remembered that Yao had been reading a book during his foot bath.

"Can you remember the name of the book," Steve asked. "Think carefully."

She thought for a while, and finally answered, "The Emperor Qianlong Goes to the South of the Yangtze River."

This answer confirmed his suspicions.

He took a deep breath and announced, "I'm sure of it now - this was no suicide. According to the coroner, the time of death was approximately two o'clock in the morning. And yet only two or three hours before his supposed suicide, he was reading one of the most beautiful and inspirational classics of Chinese literature? It simply doesn't stand to reason."

Steve asked himself, assuming Yao was murdered, who would have had the boldness and temerity to commit such a crime in a place as public as a hotel? Re-examining and analyzing the situation prior to Yao Chia-chien's death, Steve identified several people who could have been involved, including former senior police officer Huang Xuewen, National Taiwan University chemistry professor Chen Huazhou, and five members of the hotel staff.

The two forensic examiners to have examined Yao were among the first generation of forensic medicine specialists in Taiwan. One was Dr. Ye Zhaoqu, a forensic specialist from the Criminal Bureau of the Police Department of the Ministry of the Interior and a professor at National Taiwan University, and the other was Mr. Hsiao Daoying, a forensic doctor from the Bureau of Investigation of the Ministry of Justice.

The Wuhan Hotel case was reported in newspapers across Taiwan, and Steve's daily reports caught the attention of the overseas Chinese in the Philippines and beyond. In August 1959, a group of overseas Chinese signed a petition to the Taiwan authorities, strongly urging justice for Yao Chia-chien.

Also in August, a group of dozens of well-known Taiwanese from Fujian, including Hou Shunyin, Chen Kongxiong, Chen Mengmou, Zhuang Liming, and Chen Zongren organized the "Yao Chia-chien Homicide Support Association" to investigate allegations of official negligence among the police, prosecutors, and intelligence units.

The chairman of this Association was the Fujian-born Admiral Zhang Zhen (1884 to 1963) who had served as the adjutant to Sun Yat-sen, while Steve also served on the committee. Steve's daily reports on the case created an embarrassment for the government and the police; and, over the ensuing two years, he received over a dozen threatening letters and warning calls.

Under pressure from Steve and Yao Zhiguo, the authorities also actively conducted investigations. Finally, the forensic specialist Hsiao Daoying of the Bureau of Investigation was asked to re-examine the cause of Yao Chia-chien's death. His conclusion was that Yao was poisoned and then hung from the doorway to fake a suicide.

On December 13, the Bureau of Investigation stated that Yao had been murdered. On January 25, 1960, the Bureau officially announced that this was a homicide, and that Huang Xuewen and Chen Huazhou, and others had been summoned for questioning. On February 9, indictments were handed down for a total of seven suspects.

Chen Huazhou, the NTU chemistry professor, was accused of supplying the poison. Others under indictment included Wuhan Hotel accountant Lin Zuzan and staff member You Quanqiu, tenant Wang Aiyun,coworker Wu Liang, and Huang Xuewen's wife Yang Xunchun. All were eventually found guilty, with Huang Xuewen and four others implicated in the murder sentenced to death. Wu Liang and Chen Huazhou were sentenced to life imprisonment, and Yang Xunchun was sentenced to 16 years. The verdict explained that Huang and others had sought to use the hotel operations to repay their debts, but that sometime after Yao began serving as general manager, he discovered the scheme, and the plotters decided to kill him before they could be exposed.

After the verdict, Yao Chia-chien's son Yao Zhiguo made a statement, indicating his belief that Ye Zhaoqu's forensic conclusions were the result of bribery, and stated he hoped that the government would continue to pursue the investigation. Ye Zhaoqu was later dismissed from the Criminal Bureau and replaced by Dr. Yang Risong.

During the investigation, the Legislative Yuan held several hearings on the case and invited American criminal experts to participate in the autopsy. In total, Yao Chia-chien's body was subjected to nearly 20 post-mortems, possibly a record in Taiwan's history. Appeals from the various suspects resulted in nine hearings at the Supreme Court.

The Yao case resulted in lawsuits that went on for 47 years after his death. Huang Xuewen's death sentence was upheld eight times. In 1974, he was granted medical parole, but fled abroad and spent decades fighting extradition.

After repeated appeals, on November 23, 1976, with the exception of Huang Xuewen, the Supreme Court sentenced Yang Xunchun and the other five defendants to three to fifteen years in prison. By this time Professor Chen Huazhou had already died in prison.

In December 2005, the charges against Huang Xuewen were dropped due to the expiration of the statute of limitations. In August 2007, after 34 years of living in the United States as a fugitive, he returned to Taiwan seeking to clear his name. For Steve, this brought this strange case to a long-delayed close, though looking back, he noted that the case had additional victims, including the young children of Huang Xuewen and Yang Xunchun, whose lives were upended through no fault of their own.

{{ **Part 3: Beginning of Justice** }}
Chapter Six

An Inch of Land, an Inch of Blood

Remembering the Anti-Japanese War

At the time of writing his memoir, Mr. Tsai was almost 90 years old, but he still grew emotional and his eyes gleamed when he recalled the struggle against Japan.

The Fourteen Years of the Anti-Japanese War

In 1937, Steve was only just graduating from elementary school, but he was already beginning to participate in anti-Japanese activities. "For eight years, from the time I was twelve until I was twenty years old, anti-Japanese patriotic activities were an important theme in my life. In Xiamen, young men were actively opposing the Japanese. As a student, I went to the streets of the city to raise funds to support the front line."

"I acted in many anti-Japanese dramas and sang many anti-Japanese songs. They are all very passionate songs, such as 'On the Songhua River,' 'On Taihang Mountain, 'Flags Are Floating,' and 'Ode to the Yellow River. ‘"

"Among my favorite memories is singing the songs of the War of Resistance: 'The gun is on our shoulders, and the blood is on our

Towards the end of the War of Anti-Japanese Resistance, Steve worked in journalism, military intelligence, and, working for the Three Principles of the People Youth League, in propaganda.

chests. We want to defend China, and we all go to the battlefield... determined to carry forward the glory of the Chinese nation.'"

"That kind of anti-Japanese song was sung with great passion. If the effort to resist the Japanese had not been so tragic, perhaps our sentiments for our nationality would not be so deep. We see from this that adversity can shape our personality, creating a kind of patriotism and determination. This didn't come out of thin air - we were all aware of the terrible cruelty of the Japanese invaders. Our concern for the fate of our country and people inspired our patriotism. From elementary school to middle school, we were all engaged in patriotic anti-Japanese activities, and this included efforts such as eradicating illiteracy and promoting adult education. All of this was part of the active education work for the War of Resistance."

"In 1938, I joined the Three Principles of the People Youth League. In the words of Chiang Kai-Shek, "One hundred thousand youths become one hundred thousand troops; An Inch of Land, an Inch of Blood." I engaged in advocacy work and led a team at the Quanzhou Youth Army Guest House."

At the time, Chiang Kai-shek's strategy against the Japanese was to slowly give up territory in an effort to buy time, calling on "all citizens throughout China to rise up and defend the land and resist the invader." Steve has always held deep respect for Chairman Chiang. "Through eight years of war and resistance, the chairman led us to defeat Japan, cementing China's place among the great powers including United States, Britain and the Soviet Union. He also reunited Taiwan with China and abolished all unequal treaties."

During the Anti-Japanese War, Steve was engaged in military intelligence and propaganda work at the "Xingquan Command." After the victory, he handled the repatriation of Japanese overseas Chinese in Xiamen and served on a committee to deal with collaborators and property restitution in Kinmen-Xiamen District.

To this day, he clearly remembers the celebration Emperor Hirohito's announcement of Japan's unconditional surrender on August 15th, 1945. The announcement coincided with a local folk festival in which every household in Quanzhou City set up banquets for guests. At the South Street banquet, Steve heard the broadcast of the surrender announcement, and the streets exploded into a frenzy of celebration. People hugged and kissed in the street, singing and dancing. The city echoed with an outpouring of emotion, with feasting and celebratory drinking.

In September 2013, Wang Kang, an independent modern China history scholar from Chengdu, came to San Francisco to speak. Steve listened to the speech with great interest, and afterwards approached Wang Kang to ask questions and take photos with him.

In 2005, Steve speaks with Wang Kang (at left) after Wang presented a lecture. Second from right is World Journal president Hsiah Hsun-yi

Some hold that the United States' dropping atomic weapons on Nagasaki and Hiroshima in 1945 was a critical factor in China's victory in the war of resistance, but Steve has a different point of view. First, China had spent eight arduous years engaged in a guerilla war of attrition against the Japanese invader. In the first four years, China had used scorched earth tactics and strategic retreat to buy time that left Japanese supply lines weak and strained, smashing Japan's hopes to take China in three months. Second, by the time the United States entered the war, China had already been fighting Japan for four years, and Japan was already suffering from resource scarcity and heavy casualties. In the Chinese theater, Japan had committed millions of troops to a quagmire and faced inevitable defeat.

The bombing of Hiroshima and Nagasaki certainly helped speed up Japan's unconditional surrender, thus bringing forward China's victory in the War of Resistance and reducing Allied losses. The War of Resistance left a very deep impression on Steve.

Showing Bravery to Support a Just Cause, and a Blessing in Disguise

— Teacher Tsai and the widely rumored villager rebellion —

In 1944, 19-year-old Steve was arrested by the county government's security corps, but it turned out to be a blessing in disguise, opening up a new page in his life.

Disaster From Heaven

At that time Steve had volunteered to teach at the Jindong School in his hometown. But one day, he and more than one hundred men from the village were suddenly arrested by county officials and soldiers.

This was during the War of Resistance against Japan and the government was in constant need of new soldiers. Young men were recruited from the countryside, but sometimes the recruiting officers were abusive and coercive, causing local outrage and resistance. One such officer was confronted and beaten by few villagers in Tangdong. The following day, the local Quanzhou newspaper reported the incident as an anti-government rebellion that had resulted in villagers torturing military officers. As word of the incident spread, reports became more exaggerated and inflammatory, suggesting that Tangdong Village was in open revolt against the government.

A few days later, the villagers were astonished to find the streets full of uniformed armed soldiers, arbitrarily arresting male pedestrians, a total of 118 men in all. The eldest of the detainees was Tsai Chih-chang, a member of the Chinese United League in his eighties and in poor health. Mr. Tsai had travelled to the Philippines to promote Sun Yat-sen's revolution. He later returned to his hometown as a respected elder. It was ridiculous to suggest that such a man was capable of violent insurrection, and he was arrested simply because he was a local man. The youngest among those arrested was Steve Tsai, a 19-year-old teacher.

The captives were bound and escorted to Quanzhou City under armed guard. This ten-hour journey on foot was particularly difficult for the elder Mr. Tsai. After arriving in Quanzhou, they were detained in the Quanzhou Inductee Guest House.

The government intended to charge them with rebellion, accusing them of violently assaulting the military recruiters in a planned and organized operation, and accusing Tangdong Village of being in rebellion. On behalf of the arrested villagers, Steve argued that the charges were absurd, and that the government had arrested innocent people indiscriminately without checking the facts. He noted the poor quality of government law enforcement and insisted that the

Steve at Halong Bay,
Vietnam.

confrontation was only the result of spontaneous indignation on the part of a handful of villagers who did not understand the law. It was hardly an organized action, let alone a full-scale rebellion. There was no basis to make the false accusation that Tangdong Village was in rebellion.

By now, the incident had made national news, and Steve submitted reports to newspapers outlining the villagers' grievances and sent letters to fellow villagers all over the country. Word of the controversy reached an official from Tangdong, Tsai Ping-kun, director of the Quanzhou Xinghua Intelligence Office.

After Tsai Ping-kun gained a general understanding of the case, he told the county magistrate that this was a random arrest, and the priority should be to determine which villagers had actually been involved in beating the recruiter. That person should be arrested, rather than an indiscriminate mass arrest. "You've arrested revolutionary veterans?" he asked the magistrate. "You also arrested the teacher? Unless you get this under control, you will be responsible for the outcome. All of the arrestees must be released."

Chastened, the county magistrate admitted that his action was indeed too hasty and had harmed the innocent. As a first step, he proposed releasing the eldest and youngest detainees: Tsai Chih-chang and Steve.

Tsai Ping-kun personally accompanied the county magistrate to the Inductee Guest House, which was serving as a temporary detention center, to visit the detainees. When they arrived, they announced that Tsai Chih-chang and Steve would first be released.

To everyone's surprise, Steve resolutely refused to leave. "The county magistrate wants to let me go, but I won't come out," he said. "These 116 people who are still in detention rely on me as their spokesperson, and I intend to stay until they are all released."

Most of Steve's fellow captives were farmers or fishermen with only rudimentary education. Steve, in contrast, was young and had received a good education in Quanzhou and other places, had been a teacher, and had seen the world beyond Tangdong. As such, despite his young age, he had emerged as a leader among the group. He felt confident that the injustice of the government's indiscriminate arrest and persecution of these innocent men would be recognized and corrected, so they decided to protest their conditions and appeal to public opinion.

Tsai Ping-kun was quite impressed with Steve's boldness and generosity. "Young man," he said, "Your righteousness and courage are admirable, and I applaud your determination to stay with your friends in their hour of need. However, let's let this old man return home first. Then you can continue to negotiate with the county magistrate."

Steve's refusal to be one of only two to be released attracted widespread attention and sympathy and prompted the magistrate to rescind the indictments with all 118 villagers being fully acquitted. Unfortunately, one of their number, a man named Tsai Tianzan, died of dysentery before their release. Steve personally saw to the funeral arrangements. Later, a full investigation found that the men who had beat the military recruiters were some local hoodlums who had fled Tangdong following the incident and were never among those arrested.

Leaving the Classroom for the Front Lines

After regaining his freedom, Steve was invited by Tsai Ping-kun to visit his home. Steve also took this opportunity to thank him for his help. Tsai Ping-kun said, "You are so young, so ambitious, so outstanding. You are overqualified for being a rural teacher."

Tsai Ping-kun went on to say, "I ask you to help me today. Don't go back to your hometown, stay with me. I need someone like you to help me with my work."

Steve said, "I have always been a rural teacher. For me to abandon that and stay in Quanzhou to help you is too much of a departure for me . I don't know anything except teaching. What do you want me to stay for?" Tsai Ping-kun said, "I will take you to see the situation first-hand tomorrow."

The next day Steve arrived at the Xingquan Command office building on East Street in Quanzhou City. This building was taller than the county government building and was heavily guarded. Outside the main door stood two huge stone lions and two armed guards. All the way in, there were guards at every door, saluting Tsai Ping-kun who was dressed in plain clothes. Steve had never had the opportunity to observe such a high-ranking official at close quarters, and he was deeply impressed by the man's bearing. In fact, for the moment he forgot that he was actually one generation higher than Ping-kun in the Tsai family tree. As Ping-kun's distant "uncle," Steve had always called Ping-kun by his name, even though he was a high-ranking official.

Tsai Ping-kun's office was spacious and stylish. He said: "We are engaged in military intelligence work, and must keep our identities secret outside. Currently, the two major cities of Fujian, Fuzhou and Xiamen, have fallen to the Japanese, and the command headquarters in the Quanzhou to Xinghua areas are responsible for the first-line military operations in the war of resistance. The current commander is General Chen Zhong. I will take you to see him another day."

Steve said, "I don't know anything about intelligence work. I don't know anything. What can I do?" Ping-kun said, "I'm not asking you to be an intelligence officer. Instead, I need you to review and edit incoming intelligence. When raw intelligence comes in, you filter it, add your opinion, and then give it to me. I'll pass it up to the commander."

The intelligence collected at that time was mainly about the condition and movement of the Japanese forces in the occupied areas. Military movements were of particular concern for the combat commanders. There was also intelligence on collusion between traitors and the Japanese army, and intelligence on the activities of the collaborator troops on the islands in Quanzhou Bay. For the most heinous traitors, the command headquarters often sent out assassination squads at night to bring back the traitors' heads to be hung on the Quanzhou clock tower as a public reminder of the fate of the disloyal.

And thus, the rural schoolteacher became an intelligence officer on the front line of the Anti-Japanese War. The Intelligence Room served as a clearinghouse for incoming information from various sources. Steve and his team would seek to evaluate the importance and credibility of the information and collect various strands together to form a coherent picture, often sending out investigating teams to collect supplementary information. Every day, Steve was handling large amounts of first-hand intelligence. Through he wasn't physically on the front lines, his work and actions played a key role in the War of Resistance.

As an intelligence agent, Steve developed a cover as a reporter for the Evening Times, where he had previously served as a correspondent and editor. Later, he was promoted to chief correspondent, submitting daily articles based on domestic and foreign news, everything from local trivia to items of international consequence, accompanied by his brief commentary.

In this way, Steve, not even 20 years old at the time, found himself fighting against the Japanese, ferreting out critical intelligence from news reports and using a pen as a weapon.

In the autumn of 1944, Chairman Chiang issued a call for "One inch of land, one inch of blood, one hundred thousand youths become one hundred thousand troops," calling on young elites across the country to volunteer to join the army. In response to this great call, more than 100,000 college students, assembling like a gathering storm in response to this call, enlisted in the army in just one month. At this time, Steve was assigned to concurrently serve as part of the propaganda development team at the Quanzhou-Youth Army Reception Center. Though Steve had always been keen to participate in anti-Japanese activities at school, it still came as a surprise to find himself on the frontlines of the war effort.

After Japan's defeat, demand for intelligence agents dried up, but the aftermath of the war created the need for different kinds of work. Because of Steve's experience in intelligence work, he was sent to serve on two committees in Xiamen: the "Kinmen-Xiamen District Traitor Case Handling Committee" and the "Kinmen-Xiamen District Ill-Gotten Property Handling Committee." At the same time, he also served as the head of the investigation team in the Xiamen Police Station. Steve's work in Xiamen had two key focuses. The first was investigations of outstanding allegations of collusion and collaboration. During the War, there had been many instances in Xiamen and Kinmen of locals colluding with Japan, causing some locals to be framed, and some even to be killed. Such traitors were to be arrested as criminal suspects, and then handed off to the Military Court of the Military Committee of the Nanjing Nationalist Government.

The second task was the repatriation of Japanese nationals in the Guangfu District. Mustered in public before being put on a ship, the Japanese were pelted with stones from the angry crowd, despite the government's best attempts to ensure their safety.

Through the war, China's place in the world had changed, emerging from a century of turmoil and weakness to rank in the top four of the world's superpowers. This gave Steve a strong sense of honor for holding public office. He was determined to fulfill his duties responsibly, fairly and beyond reproach.

When Japan invaded China, traitors in the occupied area took advantage of the situation to prey on the common people. After the war, all those suspected of traitorous crimes were arrested, and Steve tried more than 100 such cases in Xiamen, many of whom were rich and powerful. Treason was a capital crime, and the defendants resorted to extreme measures to reduce or avoid their charges, including bribery with money, property and even young women.

Steve recognized his heavy responsibility and the need to be constantly alert and aware, respectful, self-reliant, and honest to prevent close relatives and friends from being used by others or for being implicated in corruption in attempts to sway him.

Once a friend introduced him to a great beauty who turned out to be the daughter of a man accused of treason under Steve's jurisdiction. As soon as he discovered this ruse, he immediately cut off all contact with the friend who had introduced them, saying, "You tried to influence me through the use of a beautiful woman. It's shameful that you would think so little of me or these important duties the nation has entrusted to me. I can no longer call you a friend."

To the woman, he said, "You and I cannot see each other again. Your father's case will be handled in accordance with the law, and whatever happened between us has no bearing on the case."

At the time, those convicted of treason who managed to escape the death penalty were still subject to lengthy prison sentences. However, some of the accused were from Taiwan, a territory controlled by Japan during the war. As such, they did not have Chinese nationality and thus could not be convicted of treason.

They were thus returned to Taiwan. Later, after he arrived in Taiwan himself, Steve met some of these men, and they remembered him well based on the fairness with which he had handled their cases. "If I had acted or spoken improperly against these men during my time as an investigator in Xiamen, my life in Taiwan would not have been so easy," he later said.

Steve still served as the editor of the Evening Times which had been moved from Quanzhou to Xiamen and was promoted to editor-in-chief.

At this time, the civil war between the Kuomintang and the Communist Party was raging in northern China. Following the Shenyang Incident, China had experienced 14 years of arduous resistance against Japan, but victory over Japan brought no respite from hardship as the domestic conflict immediately erupted into a full-scale civil war.

For Steve, who was in southern China, life was quietly undergoing tremendous changes. It was at this time that he met Tina, who he would later marry, making it possible for Steve and his family to leave Fujian for Taiwan.

Chapter Seven

Playing a Part in Taiwan's Economic Miracle

Unlocking Taiwan's Insurance Industry

The state of a country's insurance industry is an important indicator of the state of the country's overall development.

According to statistics from 2013, Taiwan had 30 life insurance companies and more than 20 property insurance companies, including subsidiaries of multinational insurers. But from 1945 to the early 1960s, Taiwan's insurance industry was small and under-developed. Steve played a critical role in the industry's entire development process, from initially persuading the government to enact legislative reforms ending the government monopoly on the insurance industry, to developing the industry to the point where insurance companies are found in all domains.

The Chinese financial crisis of 1948-1949 was one of the main reasons that Mainland China to fell to the Communists. Soon after the ROC government moved from the Mainland to Taiwan, the experience of this financial crisis led President Chiang Kai-shek to saddle Taiwan's financial industry with onerous restrictions.

In 1945, Taiwan was liberated from Japan, and the Central Government took over all the insurance companies in Taiwan. They then reorganized these into the Central Trust Life Insurance Bureau managed directly by the Central Government, and the Taiwan Life Insurance Company and the Taiwan Property Insurance Company managed by the Provincial Government. Once these structures were in place, the establishment of new insurance companies was prohibited up through 1960, when Shih Hsing-shui and other overseas Chinese entrepreneurs from the Philippines petitioned President Chiang to liberalize the relevant regulations and allow for the development of new insurance companies.

Steve said, "From Taiwan's retrocession to the early 1960s, Taiwan's economy still lagged far behind other countries, and was just beginning to gather some steam." Insurance is an important component of a country's social system, but at the time it was the weakest link. Businesses large and small, as well as individuals, all have insurance requirements, but with so few insurance companies operating, claims put the entire system under stress. The monopoly exercised by these companies essentially eliminated competition and was not in the interests of consumers or society in general.

The Overseas Chinese Insurance Corporation was established on April 27, 1961, the first insurance company to open since the reform of the insurance laws. This development marked the beginning of the Taiwan insurance industry's emergence from a dark tunnel and its gradual development into a fully functional insurance market.

These developments were in large part the result of the work of three men: Philippine overseas Chinese leader Shih Hsing-shui, insurance entrepreneur Yang Ying-lin, and Taiwan correspondent for the Xinmin Daily News Steve Tsai. Steve played a particularly important role in encouraging Shih and Yang to invest in the Taiwan market, and then lobbying for the necessary legal reforms. Steve emphasized that the market should open not only to this trio of investors, but also to local Taiwan entrepreneurs.

The Philippine overseas Chinese community was particularly well

1960: Steve visits the Philippines and meets with overseas Chinese community leaders to discuss the establishment of an insurance company in Taipei. (2nd from left, Xinmin Daily News president Wu Chung-sheng; 3rd from left, Manila Overseas Chinese Chamber of Commerce president Shih Hsing-shui; 2nd from right Youth League president Leu Huan-tsai; far right, photographer Wang Chin).

positioned to help Taiwan liberalize its insurance markets. First, the Philippines was a leading ally of the Republic of China in its anti-Communist stance and had long supported the ROC in the United Nations. Philippine-ROC relations were strong both at official and personal levels. Second, the Philippines had played an important role in assisting the retreat of the ROC military from the mainland, as units made their way from Zhoushan and Hainan to Taiwan. Third, the Philippines was the primary source of foreign investment in Taiwan, with investments including the 5-star Hilton, President, Asia World, Central and Taiwan Hotels, along with the Overseas Chinese Bank, Cathay Bank, and many other important financial institutions. Fourth, KMT Chairman Chiang Kai-shek had visited the Philippines in July 1949, meeting with Philippine President Elpidio Rivera Quirino, and had been warmly welcomed by the Philippine overseas Chinese community. Huge crowds lined the streets to wave at Chiang's limousine. Many had brought quilts and mats and had slept out the night before to ensure a good spot.

In his study "Philippine Foreign Policy," scholar Huai Ching-ru noted that during Taiwan's Anti-Communist period, the overseas Chinese in the Philippines "may have been the most loyal and patriotic among all Chinese in Southeast Asian countries."

When Calculating Cost-benefit, Think of the Big Picture

In the late 1950s, Steve would report on each visit to Taiwan by Shih Hsing-shui, President of the Manila Chinese Chamber of Commerce. Chang Chun, Secretary General of the Presidential Office, followed these reports closely and invited Shih to meet with the President.

Each time they met, President Chiang urged Shih to encourage overseas Chinese to return to Taiwan to invest, starting with the Manila Chamber of Commerce. Shih himself was not particularly wealthy, but he had warm feelings for his compatriots, was sympathetic to the downtrodden, and was not afraid to challenge authority. He enjoyed a high reputation in the overseas Chinese community. Two days a week, he would receive overseas Chinese petitioners at home, and seek to help them with their problems.

After each meeting with President Chiang, Shih would communicate the content of the meeting to Steve, who would then release the news to Chang Jen-fei, Deputy Interview Director of the Central News Agency.

Many times, Shih would call Steve and ask, "The President wants me to return to invest in Taiwan. What do you think I should do?"

Steve replied, "You have a good reputation in the global overseas Chinese community, and you love Free China. The overseas Chinese support you, and the President values you. If you don't act, who will?"

"Although investment decisions have to follow business logic," he continued, "you still have to consider how such an investment will benefit the people and the country. You need to think about what Taiwan needs. Therefore, I recommend you invest in the development of financial institutions, specifically banking and insurance. However, both markets are off limits to new entrants. The OCBC Philippines Bank investment is a special case and received special approval from the President. At present, Taiwan's insurance industry is monopolized by a few government-managed companies, which are insufficient to meet the needs of economic development in Taiwan. It is especially urgent to reform the insurance market, so I recommend you establish an Overseas Chinese Insurance Corporation. You have the ear of the President. Use it to this end."

Steve recommended: "When calculating cost-benefit, think of the big picture. If I'm overstepping, please forgive me, but if the government opens the market to us but does not allow others to enter, then we should insist that others are allowed to enter as well. Because our goal is to promote Taiwan's development, rather than snatch an opportunity away from Taiwan local entrepreneurs. If you do it this way, it will put you on the right side of history."

One morning in 1960, Shih called Steve to say that President Chiang had summoned him at 11:00 a.m. that day to hear his proposal to liberalize Taiwan's insurance industry. He asked Steve to come over and help him prepare.

Steve rushed to Shih's hotel, stopping along the way to buy a writing brush and paper. With Shih, he made the case for opening Taiwan's insurance markets to new entrants, and wrote up a two-page synopsis, using large brush strokes to make it easier for the President to read. As Shih was mostly in Manila, they added that Steve would serve as the Taiwan representative for this effort. A few hours later, the two men met again, and Shih happily reported that the President was receptive to the proposal and had delegated the matter to Vice President Chen Cheng.

A new chapter in the history of Taiwan's insurance industry was about to be written.

A few days later, Chen Cheng's office called and asked Shih and Steve to have dinner with Chen at his official residence on Mt. Yangming to discuss the lifting of the ban on new insurance companies. The two made their case while Chen ate slowly, occasionally stopping them with questions. Finally, he said, "The president has high regard for you and takes your advice very seriously. The president has entrusted this matter to me and explained that the first new insurance companies must be capitalized by overseas Chinese. The president hopes that this venture will succeed, because failure will have a negative impact on Taiwan's ability to attract further overseas Chinese capital. Therefore, the government will first approve the establishment of the Overseas Chinese Insurance Corporation. Depending on how this first venture fares, we will consider fully liberalizing Taiwan's insurance market." Steve responded, saying: "We believe that the establishment of new insurance companies in Taiwan will benefit the country's economic development, and thus we advocate comprehensive reform. Adding one or two insurance companies will not change things."

Chen Cheng was taken aback and replied, "I appreciate your position and your passion, but the president has considered the consequences of such a broad and sudden reform. It will lead to a frenzy of competition. Given your relative unfamiliarity with conditions in Taiwan, being overseas Chinese, your venture would have trouble competing against local consortia. I understand that you're motivated by a desire to help the nation, but the government above all is loath to see a venture financed by overseas Chinese capital fail."

Steve said, "We're very grateful for the kindness and consideration you and the president have shown us, and we appreciate the regard the government has for the overseas Chinese community. I understand your concerns that overseas Chinese ventures may have trouble competing here, but please consider this: these businessmen have long experience in establishing and operating insurance companies in different countries under fiercely competitive conditions. They have carefully honed skills in policy design, business management and capital utilization. While both international and local parties have different strengths and weaknesses, these characteristics are complementary and will allow for healthy competition."

As Steve spoke, Shih nodded his head in agreement.

Originally, it was Chen Cheng who sought to persuade Shih to accept the partial reform, but now the tables had turned, and Shih and Steve were persuading Chen Cheng to agree to comprehensive reform. While the conversation grew spirited at times, the tone was friendly and cooperative. The government recognized the patriotic spirit of the overseas Chinese community and saw the need to harness this love of country to drive Taiwan's development.

Chen Cheng politely concluded: "I will report your suggestion to the President."

Soon afterwards came the official announcement: the government would fully liberalize the Taiwan insurance industry, and Chen Cheng handed the matter over to Finance Minister Yen Chia-kan for implementation.

Tsai Wan-chun, the founder of Cathay Trust Group, heard that his clansman Steve was approaching the government to apply for the establishment of an insurance company. Tsai Wan-chun had expected that the market would only open to overseas Chinese, and asked Steve if he could be a co-investor. Steve told him immediately, "Brother Wan-chun, the insurance industry is about to be fully opened up. You can apply yourself without investing in our insurance company."

Overseas Chinese Insurance Corporation

As soon as the government opened the door, the first Overseas Chinese Insurance Corporation established a preparatory office in Steve's home on Chongqing South Road, Taipei. Shih Hsing-shui served as the office's director, with Steve as deputy director, volunteering his time and home to the cause. To comply with ROC Corporate Law, he spent NT$500 to print a prospectus and share subscription documents and to hold an organizational meeting.

On April 27, 1961, the Overseas Chinese Insurance Corporation was formally established on Taipei's Hankou Street. Shih Hsing-shui presided over the opening ceremony, and Minister of Finance Yen Chia-kan came to cut the ribbon.

Exactly two years later, on April 27, 1963, the second anniversary of the establishment of the Overseas Chinese Insurance Corporation was celebrated in Zhongshan Hall, and the official establishment of the Overseas Chinese Life Insurance Company was announced. Vice President Chen Cheng personally came to cut the ribbon.

While Americans like to start businesses in garages (e.g., HP, Apple, and more), Taiwan's original Overseas Chinese Insurance Corporations were started in Steve's living room, spending only NT$500 to obtain the needed financial licenses.

The main shareholders of the two companies were all businessmen and friends of Shih in the Philippines. Among the fifteen directors, twelve were from the Philippines and three were from Taiwan. Shih Hsing-shui was elected chairman. Among the directors from the Philippines was Yang Ying-lin(Note 1), a global insurance magnate. The three directors from Taiwan were Chiu Han-ping(Note 2), Steve Tsai, and Shih Hua.

The original plan had been to appoint Steve as general manager of the two Overseas Chinese Insurance Corporations. At that time, the general managers of financial institutions in Taiwan were mostly people from the mainland. Steve, only 36 years old at the time, felt that he was too young, and humbly recommended that Dr. Chiu Han-ping, former Minister of Finance of Fujian Province, President of Fujian Bank, legislator, and president of Soochow University, serve as the general manager of the two companies instead.

The board of directors thus reappointed Steve as the managing director and deputy general manager of the two companies. Chairman Shih offered Steve bonus shares as recognition for his

1963: Overseas Chinese Insurance Corporation General Manager Steve Tsai chairs an operational meeting.

(left photo) *January 20, 1962: While hosting the 3rd Miss China Pageant, word came that Yijiangshan Island had fallen. The event was immediately transformed into an event to raise funds for military supplies. College freshman Miss Fang Yu (at right) had just been awarded the title of Miss China, and in the latter part of the activities, served as master of ceremonies for the fundraising, with Steve (at left) representing the Overseas Chinese Insurance Corporation, going on stage after having made the highest bid for an item. In 1965, Fang Yu married future ROC Vice President Lien Chan.*

practical contributions in the planning and implementation. Steve respectfully thanked him for his consideration, but demurred, saying that his staff salary was compensation enough. Yang Fang-shan, Chen Yi-mao, and Tsai Hua-ren, all prominent figures in Taiwan's insurance industry, were also hired as deputy general managers in charge of business and finance. The management teams of the two companies were thus a who's-who of Taiwan's insurance industry.

An insurance company relies on a public perception of strength and requires impressive offices. Steve and Chiu Han-ping set their eyes on a building on Taipei's Kuanchien Street, a hub of Taiwan's financial institutions that was known at the time as Taipei's Wall Street. At the time, the Kuanchien Building was one of the tallest buildings in Taipei. The owner, Lin Chin-hsiang, was initially reluctant to sell. Steve knew that Taipei Mayor Huang Chi-rui was a friend of Lin's. The mayor kicked things off by acting as a go-between to allow Steve and Lin to get to know each other. It took Steve about a year to establish a friendship with Lin, and Steve finally bought the building for a little more than NT$70 million. To ensure good cash flow, Steve induced the Bank of America, at the time the largest foreign financial institution in Taiwan, to sign a long-term lease for the first floor of the building, income that would help recoup the purchase cost, leaving the rest of the building available for the new overseas Chinese insurers. The relationship with Bank of America not only brought needed income, but also cemented public perceptions of the robustness and resilience of the new firms.

Chairman Shih presided over the inauguration ceremony of the second insurance company, Overseas Chinese Life Insurance, in April 1963. He then returned to the Philippines, but suddenly died soon afterwards, sending shockwaves through Taiwan and the Philippines. Steve and Chiu Han-ping went to the Philippines to attend the funeral.

Shih Hsing-shui was a world-class overseas Chinese leader, and his death was a terrible blow for the country and society, and his loss was particularly hard on the two Taiwanese insurance companies started under his watch and guidance.

After the funeral, the two companies held a joint director's meeting in the Philippines and decided to restructure the organization. Under the original plan, Mr. Shih would serve as chairman of both companies, while Chiu would be general manager of both. Steve was the deputy general manager of both companies. Yang Ying-lin took over as chairman of the property insurance company, with Chen Yi-mao as general manager. Hung Kai-nian, who succeeded Shi Hsing-shui as chairman of the Manila Chinese Chamber of Commerce, took over as chairman of the life insurance operations, with Chiu Han-ping as general manager. Steve and Yang Fang-shan were full-time deputy general managers of the life insurance company.

Originally, shareholder investments were divided equally between the two companies. A joint directors' meeting issued a new resolution to give each shareholder the right to choose to consolidate their investment in one entity or the other. The two companies thus reorganized in a friendly and peaceful atmosphere. Later, Hung Kai-nian, chairman of Overseas Chinese Life Insurance, retired and gave his shares to Tsai Wen-hua, chairman of Philippine Pacific Bank. Tsai Wen-hua was elected as Chairman of Overseas Chinese Life Insurance, and Chiu Han-ping was reappointed as Vice Chairman, with Steve promoted to General Manager.

In later years, the Overseas Chinese Insurance Corporation became the Malayan Overseas Chinese Insurance Corporation, because Yang Ying-lin was the president of Malayan Group of Insurance Companies, and it was decided that the Taipei corporation would become an affiliate of this group.

In 1983, the China Insurance Group and Zurich Insurance Group signed a cooperation agreement to jointly establish the China-Zurich Insurance Group, thus folding the Overseas Chinese Insurance Corporations into an international insurance group.

In 1974, under Chiu Han-ping's leadership, the China Trust Company (now Chinatrust Commercial Bank) invested in Overseas Chinese Life Insurance, with Chinatrust chairman Koo Chen-fu concurrently serving as chairman of the insurance firm, and Jeffrey Koo Sr. serving as general manager. In March 1981, the company was renamed China Life Insurance, and the company was successfully listed on February 8, 1995.

▓ Note 1: Yang Ying-lin was born 1923. His family was from Nan'an, Fujian, and he gained fame in the Philippines as an entrepreneur and owner of more than forty companies, including two insurance companies: China Insurance Group and Great Pacific Life Insurance Company. Yang was also a heavyweight in Philippine politics, serving as ambassador to Beijing and Tokyo, respectively, under Presidents Aquino and Ramos. He later served President Estrada as a consultant to the Asia-Pacific Economic Cooperation Conference, and under President Arroyo he was appointed Special Representative of the Philippines to China, Japan and South Korea.

▓ Note 2: Chiu Han-ping (1903-1990) was born in Myanmar but returned to China to receive his Bachelor of Commerce from China's first university, Zhongguo Gongxue, and a Bachelor of Law from Soochow University. Later, he went to the United States to obtain a doctorate in law from the University of Washington. He subsequently returned to China to teach at Jinan University, Soochow University, and Jiaotong University, and Zhongguo Gongxue, while also working part time as a lawyer. He later served as a member of the Fujian Provincial Government, General Manager of the Provincial Bank, and Director of Provincial Finance, and was also elected to the ROC legislature.

Chiu Han-ping's son, Chiu Hungdah is a professor and authority on international law at the University of Maryland, former president of the American Law Society, and a professor of former President Ma Ying-jeou.

The OCBC Incident (I)

One night in February 1984, Steve was already asleep at his home in the United States when the phone beside his bed rang. Steve answered only to hear the anxious voice of Mr. Tsai Hsiao-ku, Chairman of the Overseas Chinese Bank of Taipei.

"Steve, I'm sorry to have awoken you," Tsai said. "But we have a big problem at OCBC (Overseas Chinese Banking Corporation) and we need your help. Please fly back to Taipei early tomorrow morning."

"What happened?," Steve asked.

Tsai told him that a consortium had been secretly buying up OCBC stock and now controlled more than half of the company's outstanding shares. "It's hard to say what's going on," he said. "The buyer is coming to execute the share transfer soon. The internal situation is also complicated. I can't talk about it over the phone. Please, come back at once."

Tsai Hsiao-ku handed the phone to Steve's second brother, Youhui, who was serving as a director and deputy general manager of the Overseas Chinese Bank and was one of Tsai Hsiao-ku's most trusted directors. Youhui told Steve, "We need you to come back and handle this. Be on the first flight in the morning."

Steve was reluctant to leave his family in the United States, but his loyalties to Chairman Tsai won out. After making his flight arrangements, he called ahead to make sure he would be met at the airport with a copy of the bank's charter. Chairman Tsai and Youhui met him at the airport, and he spent the drive back to Taipei reading the document.

The hostile takeover was being staged by a consortium led by the Cathay Trust Group under the direction of its chairman Tsai Chen-nan, a friend and relative of Tsai Hsiao-ku. A few days earlier, Tsai Chen-nan had turned up at the Overseas Chinese Bank and personally alerted Tsai Hsiao-ku of his intentions. "You will continue to serve as chairman, but I will send a team to the board of directors to help you handle important tasks."

"Steve, as you know, I am not willing to be anyone's puppet," said Tsai Hsiao-ku. "Chen-nan is giving me face because of my age but leaving me with an empty title. More importantly, the OCBC Bank was established with the special permission of the President, and the government entrusted me to manage the bank. Tsai Chen-nan is not an overseas Chinese. The fact that our bank is being taken over by someone who is not an overseas Chinese makes things difficult to justify."

Steve, who had been carefully studying the bank's charter as the car cruised through Linkou, suddenly looked up with an excited smile. "Don't worry," he said. "We can fix this."

Tsai Hsiao-ku was surprised and asked for an explanation, but Steve simply assured him, "We'll discuss it at the office tomorrow."

The final years of KMT rule in mainland China had been marked by rampant inflation. After the retreat to Taiwan, President Chiang was fearful of repeating the same mistakes there, and thus micro-managed the financial industry. At that time, Taiwan had few banks. Aside from a small handful of private banks, the sector was dominated by national banks, mainly the Central Bank and the Taiwan Provincial Bank, charged with issuing official currency. Shareholders of these institutions were thus richly rewarded.

President Chiang called on overseas Chinese to actively support the Republic of China, and several groups of overseas Chinese entrepreneurs recommended that the government allow overseas Chinese to return to Taiwan to establish investment banks to facilitate Taiwan's development. It was in this context that President Chiang had explicitly approved the establishment of the OCBC Bank and later the Cathay Bank, mainly with overseas Chinese capital.

In 1959, a preparatory office for the Overseas Chinese Bank was established. At that time, the Overseas Community Affairs Council developed a plan for raising the necessary capital from overseas Chinese in Asia, Europe and the Americas, with a requirement for proportional capital contributions from the various continents. However, this initial fundraising did not bring in the required funds. Steve published an article in the newspaper criticizing the plan, calling the new organization little more than a charity with little prospect of turning a profit. The council's funding plan had created conditions in which shareholders competed for power, but shirked responsibility. Moreover, the distribution of equity was too broad, and the company lacked a core group of influential shareholders to steer the company. Steve recommended discarding the requirement for geographically proportional capital contributions.

These problems led to years of delay in the establishment of the Overseas Chinese Bank. The establishment of such a bank, in addition to its economic impact, would have an even more important political impact. The ROC government was anxious. The delays were providing a propaganda victory for the CCP, which pointed at the lack of enthusiasm amongst the overseas Chinese community to support the KMT regime in Taiwan as an indication of the regime's lack of popular legitimacy.

Under the leadership of premier Chen Cheng, the Overseas Chinese Affairs Council was reorganized, appointing Chen Ching-wen, a Fujianese by heritage who was then chairman of the China Merchants Group, to replace Cheng Yan-fen, who had been in office for seven years, as the chairman of the Overseas Chinese Council. Chen Ching-wen flew to the Philippines in the first week of taking office. At the reception banquet, the majority of the attendees were overseas Chinese originally from Fujian. The hosts told Chen that, with a Fujianese leading the council, the subscription for the Overseas Chinese Bank would be successful. Their words proved to be true, and the necessary funding was raised that day.

Chen Ching-wen, the new chairman of the Overseas Chinese Affairs Council, was born in Singapore and studied in England. White-haired and personable, with a black pipe that never left his hand, he gave the impression of a true English gentleman.

Before he went to the Philippines, he met Steve for coffee to talk about the subscription for the overseas Chinese bank. Chen Ching-wen's acceptance of subscription by overseas Chinese in the Philippines to the Overseas Chinese Bank was tantamount to agreeing to abandoning the original share distribution plan, breaking the stalemate. This solution had begun when Steve wrote an article calling for abandoning the proportional distribution plan. The successful capital raise provided cover for Chen's cabinet to decisively instruct Chairman Chen Ching-wen to abandon the original plan and work with overseas Chinese in the Philippines to finally establish the OCBC Bank.

On March 1, 1961, the OCBC Bank officially opened with an initial capitalization of NT$100 million, and a shareholder base largely concentrated among overseas Chinese from the Philippines. Later, the capitalization increased by more than NT$10 billion, with the government stipulating that overseas Chinese capital should account for at least 80% in the initial stages (later 60%). This technicality was what had caught Steve's attention on the drive from the airport: Tsai Chen-nan was not an overseas Chinese and his ownership of over 50% of the shares of the OCBC Bank violated the regulations of the bank's charter.

But this technical regulation was not a guarantee of a successful defense. Business in Asia is driven by interpersonal relationships, which are sometimes stronger than black-letter law. The Cathay Trust Group had very good connections. Despite this, Steve slept well that night.

At 8 am the next morning, Steve arrived at the OCBC Bank headquarters on Xiangyang Road. After half an hour of discussion with Tsai Hsiao-ku and Tsai Youhui, Steve called the office of Yu Kuo-hwa, President of the Central Bank.

Overseas Chinese investment in Taiwan's financial industry involves four departments: the Ministry of Finance, the Central Bank, the Ministry of Economy Affairs, and the Overseas Chinese Affairs Council. It would be laborious and time-consuming to work the dispute through all four departments. The key was to identify one institution with the authority to provide the desired result. Based on his familiarity with Taiwan's financial industry, Steve knew that the most effective option was to go directly to the Central Bank, which presided over financial policy making. Yu Kuo-hwa, president of the Central Bank, was the most trusted financial leader during the regimes of both Chiang Kai-shek and Chiang Ching-kuo. Steve knew that Yu Kuo-hwa was the key man to help resolve this issue. He called Yu's secretary and bluntly explained that there was a developing situation that had the potential to cause financial turmoil if it was not resolved before the news became public. "Please tell President Yu that we are on our way to see him, and it's of the highest urgency that he sees us at once."

Hearing Steve's anxious tone, the secretary asked him to stay on the line. Within three minutes, the secretary returned to say that President Yu was waiting for them.

Steve and Yu Kuo-hwa were familiar with each other but did not have a close friendship. When the three men arrived at the Central Bank building, they were directly ushered into Yu's office, where Yu asked them to sit. Still standing, Steve said anxiously, "Mr. President, I apologize for barging in like this, but we're here on a matter of utmost urgency."

He explained how over 51% of the outstanding shares of the Overseas Chinese Bank had been surreptitiously acquired in a hostile takeover, and that the 21 directorships of the Overseas Chinese Bank had been bought. Incredulous, Yu Kuo-hwa asked Tsai Hsiao-ku, "Someone acquired a majority stake in your own bank without your knowledge?" Tsai Hsiao-ku stood in silence. While they stood there, tea was brought in, and Steve sought to diffuse the tension.

"President Yu, Chairman Tsai isn't to blame in this matter," he said.

"Why not?" demanded Yu.

"Over 80% of the founding shareholders are overseas Chinese from the Philippines, which now is plagued by political corruption and economic problems, with the peso depreciating drastically against the dollar. Overseas Chinese businessmen in the Philippines are desperate to raise funds, so it's little surprise that they would take the opportunity to sell their director's votes for cash. In this way, they could raise more than NT$100 million, enough to buy a small bank in the Philippines, or to rescue their local operations."

Steve continued: "In recent years, the new Taiwan dollar has appreciated considerably against the peso, making such a deal even more attractive. These shareholders have a legitimate interest in preserving their operations in the Philippines, and Chairman Tsai would not have been able to anticipate nor prevent this move. The original shareholders were born in China and, despite fleeing to the Philippines, they were true patriots. However, many of these men are now gone, and their shares have passed on to their children whose ties to China are not as strong. To them, their shares in the bank are merely an asset, like any other, and they won't hesitate to sell if the need or opportunity arises."

When this question of the change in shareholders occurred, Tsai Pai-sheng, son of Tsai Kung-nan, the first chairman of the Overseas Chinese Bank, transferred his inherited equity to Li Chi-chang, chairman of the Overseas Chinese Trust Company. However, Li Chi-chang suddenly died, and Li's son transferred the shares to Tsai Chen-nan's Cathay Trust Group. These factors plus the fact that Cathay Trust Group had already raised their offer price, made it evident that Cathay Trust Group intended to seize control of the Overseas Chinese Bank.

As Steve spoke, Yu Kuo-hwa nodded, and finally asked, "Do you have any specific suggestions?"

Steve said, "Cathay Trust Group's purchase of Overseas Chinese Bank stock has alarmed many of the Bank's shareholders. If this affair becomes public, it may cause a run on the bank."

Yu Kuo-hwa once again asked what he could do to help. Steve felt Yu would address the situation impartially and in accordance with the law. Steve told Yu Kuo-hwa about the clause in the Bank's charter that required overseas Chinese to hold at least 60% of the shares. Yu Kuo-hwa listened, and then rose to his feet.

"But under what identity did Tsai Chen-nan buy his OCBC Bank shares?," he asked.

Steve replied, "He posed as an overseas Chinese." He explained that Tsai Chen-nan's wife, Chen Pao-chi, had originally been a director of the Overseas Chinese Bank, and had used her status as an overseas Chinese from Costa Rica to buy the shares.

"If that's the case," Yu Kuo-hwa said, "he used the identity of an overseas Chinese to purchase the shares. What can I do?"

"This is the problem," said Steve. "We don't really know if someone is an overseas Chinese. We have to check. Tsai Chen-nan is a household name in Taiwan, born and raised here, and is the head of a large consortium. His personal and family activities are in the news almost every day. Most people don't believe that he is an overseas Chinese."

Yu Kuo-hwa replied, "But, if you say his status as overseas Chinese is fake, you still have to provide evidence."

"As private citizens, we don't have the resources to access such information," said Steve. "But for the government, it would be as easy as a phone call or searching official documents."

Yu Kuo-hwa was silent.

Steve continued, "There is an unconfirmed rumor that Taiwan's Overseas Chinese Trust and Investment Company was previously bought by a local consortium. More than half of the shares are held by overseas Chinese in the Philippines, purchased at the behest of Wu Ho-su of the Shin Kong Group. Like Cathay Trust Group, it is also a local consortium."

"I also heard that, after you heard about this incident, you asked Jeffrey Koo Sr. to tell Wu Ho-su to return the stock to the shareholders of Overseas Chinese Trust within three days. According to the articles of association, shares of specially approved overseas financial institutions can only be held by overseas Chinese. Non-overseas Chinese are not allowed to touch them. According to the grapevine, Wu Ho-su returned these shares immediately without complaint."

At the time, Wu Ho-su's Shin Kong Group and Tsai Chen-nan's Cathay Trust Group were both powerful local consortia. The Overseas Chinese Trust and Investment Company, which Wu Ho-su sought to buy, was also a financial institution like the OCBC Bank, mainly capitalized by overseas Chinese in the Philippines and, following regulations, the majority of shares were controlled by overseas Chinese. Wu Ho-su said at the time: "President Yu has given me three days to return the shares I bought, but I am willing to make the transaction in three minutes."

This entire incident had unfolded several years previously but had gone almost unnoticed by the general public. Steve knew that Yu Kuo-hwa was involved in this event but sought to give Yu face by referring to it as "unverified rumors".

Yu did not deny Steve's account of the incident, and Steve then proposed that the current dilemma be handled in the same way as the previous incident as a show of government impartiality. The parallels between the two cases were striking: both centered on financial institutions founded and ostensibly controlled by overseas Chinese. Both were hostile acquisition targets of local companies. The only real difference lay in personal relationships, where the chairman of the Overseas Chinese Trust, Li Chi-chang, was the son-in-law of the famous Yu Hung-chun, three-time president of the

ROC Central Bank, while the chairman of the Overseas Chinese Bank had no such entanglements.

Steve noted that the Overseas Chinese Trust provided an instructive precedent to follow and following this would avoid the appearance of double standards or personal favoritism by the government, which would be difficult to explain to the overseas Chinese investment community.

Still, Yu Kuo-hwa insisted, "If you can't provide proof that Tsai Chen-nan is not actually an overseas Chinese from Costa Rica, how can I act?"

Steve noted, "We have diplomatic relations with Costa Rica. Through the Ministry of Foreign Affairs, you can ask the ROC embassy in Costa Rica to make inquiries into Tsai Chen-nan's business operations and status there. When did he register his company? Does he qualify as a resident? Does he pay taxes there? The answers to these questions will provide a complete picture of his actual national status."

At this time Steve asked Tsai Hsiao-ku to speak. He noted that Cathay Trust Group had spent several billion new Taiwan dollars to purchase his shares in the Overseas Chinese Bank. If this was actually overseas Chinese capital, there would be ample records of the inward remittance of such a huge sum. At this, Yu Kuo-hwa's facial expression softened somewhat. He excused himself and left the office.

Ten minutes later, he returned. "I called Minister Hsu at the Ministry of Finance and asked him to expect you at his office. Please explain the situation to him. I've already instructed the Minister on how to proceed."

Yu Kuo-hwa personally escorted the visitors to the elevator. As they waited for the elevator to arrive, Steve said, "President Yu, we have great confidence in you, and hope you can see your way to helping us." Yu Kuo-hwa nodded silently but exchanged a tight handshake with Steve.

As soon as the elevator door closed, Tsai Hsiao-ku blurted out, "Steve, wow! You really let him have it! We came here to ask him for help, but you really put him in a corner. How do you think things stand now?"

Steve said, "Don't worry, you'll win."

Tsai Hsiao-ku replied, "I don't see how!"

Steve said, "As we were leaving, he answered me with his handshake. The way he held my hand tightly was a message: 'Don't worry.'"

The three of them went straight to the Ministry of Finance. Hsu Yuan-tung, the Director of Finance, met them at the door and ushered them into the office of the Finance Minister, Hsu Lee-te. The Minister did not stand on ceremony but sat while the guests stood before his desk. "President Yu has explained this matter to me," he said. "Chairman Tsai, how can you claim to be the chairman of this company when you don't even know who owns your stock? You can't even keep track of who has the majority shareholding? You only first became aware when someone is about to make a transfer of ownership? How did you become so confused?"

In the face of this tirade, Hsiao-ku and Youhui were dumbfounded and remained silent. Steve addressed them, saying "Let's go." Hsu Yuan-tung said "Hold on, tell the Minister what's going on."

Steve replied, "What is there to say, Minister? We are here to discuss major financial matters with you, not personal matters. Given your attitude and tone, it seems there's nothing to discuss."

Hsu Yuan-tung tried to defuse the tension. "This is just a misunderstanding, and the Minister is just being blunt. There's no other meaning."

Minister Hsu remained silent, staring at the three men. Steve said, "Minister Hsu, I'm afraid I simply cannot accept the way you have denigrated my elderly colleague. If it were President Chiang standing here instead of you today, I can hardly believe he would have spoken in such a way. When the Republic of China was fighting for its life, retreating from Hainan, Zhoushan and the Yijiangshan Islands, only overseas Chinese from the Philippines stepped forward to offer assistance, including my colleague Tsai Hsiao-ku, and President Chiang was deeply grateful for his efforts. You are young and don't know this history, and your criticism is unwarranted. I didn't bring him here to be scolded by you. But given the way you are speaking to him, I feel that we should leave and perhaps discuss it some other time."

At this time Hsu Lee-te said, "There has been a mis-understanding. I apologize, let's all just calm down."

Once the tension had dissipated, he continued: "President Yu has provided detailed instructions, but I still need to ask you some questions. If the government convinces Tsai Chen-nan to return the shares he's bought, the government will not be involved in negotiating the price. You'll have to address this directly yourselves."

Steve said, "This should not be a problem. The purchase happened only recently, and everyone is aware of the price."

Minister Hsu asked, "What if Tsai Chen-nan insists on a different price, for example NT$1000 per share. Will you buy at that price?"

Steve smiled and replied, "He wouldn't dare, Minister. The purchase price is easily verified. If he plans to sell the shares back to us at inflated prices, he'll have to deal with the legal liability of having violated the articles of our corporate charter and his having held the shares illegally. We'll offer to buy the shares back at the original acquisition price, plus a preferable rate of interest. He'll make a decent return on the transaction, but it will be within reason. As head of the tax authority, you have access to the tax records on the transaction, thus the entire matter will be transparent to you."

With this, the guests took their leave and Director Hsu escorted them out.

Despite their best efforts, news of the affair still got out and dominated the financial press for the following month.

From Cheng Chou-min, founder of the Taiwan Asia Trust Company, Tsai Chen-nan later learned that Steve had played a key role in interfering with his plan. He contacted Steve directly and, after a couple weeks of negotiation over the phone, they reached a deal in which the Overseas Chinese Bank would coordinate a repurchase of Tsai Chen-nan's shares for NT$500 per share, but the shareholders who had sold their shares to Tsai in the first place were not interested in repurchasing those shares, so the Bank had to seek buyers elsewhere.

The repurchase entailed a huge amount of capital, and the Philippines' economy was in a recession at the time. Both the media and government urged Cathay Trust Group to sell the equity. A minority of the directors, including Cheng Chou-min and Tsai Neng, temporarily repurchased additional shares on behalf of the seven other directors, and then began to look for new buyers in the overseas Chinese community. These seven directors put up 50% of the repurchase price, and then used the stocks as collateral, with Cathay Trust Group putting up the balance as a loan.

Steve went to see Yu Kuo-hwa again, suggesting that the government should temporarily become a shareholder with the aim to later sell the shares to overseas Chinese. The purchase of this fraction of the shares was eventually made by the Executive Yuan Development Fund through the China Commercial Bank at a NT$10 per share discount provided by Chen-nan. The shareholders of Overseas Chinese Bank and Cathay Trust Group held a signing ceremony to repurchase the shares. The event caused a sensation among the financial press and the venue was packed with reporters. Chairman Tsai Hsiao-ku and Steve represented the buyers, and Tsai Chen-nan represented the seller, signing the contract at Tsai Chen-nan's office on Taipei's Dunhua South Road. At the time, it was the largest single equity transaction since Taiwan's retrocession.

Replying to a reporter's question, Tsai Chen-nan recounted the story in very frank terms. "I believe the Overseas Chinese Bank has a very promising future, so I purchased a majority of the shares. It was a tasty morsel, but now I'm being forced to spit it out. It turns out there was someone whispering in Tsai Hsiao-ku's ear - a fellow clansman and friend of my father. My father had told me before - anything related to the Overseas Chinese Bank, go see Steve. We've always had a good relationship, and his role in this affair came as a surprise to me."

Indeed, Steve and Tsai Wan-chun, the founder of Cathay Pacific Bank, had a close friendship dating from the co-founding the Taiwan Philippine Chua (Tsai) Clan Association. Tsai Wan-chun later introduced his son Tsai Chen-nan and Steve to each other, and the two had been friendly for many years.

When he had arrived in Taiwan to assist in this affair, Steve soon realized that his adversary was his good friend Tsai Chen-nan, leaving him in a difficult position of having to choose between friendship and social justice. Justice was the painful, but obvious, choice.

However, this did not completely resolve the matter. In March 1985, legislator Wu Chun-ching and others raised pointed challenges to Yu Kuo-hwa and Hsu Lee-te. First, Cathay Trust Group knew that it had violated the regulations by purchasing a majority stake in the bank. Therefore, in addition to returning the stock, there remained an outstanding issue of how the Cathay Trust Group should be punished. Second, the Executive Yuan had used development funds to purchase shares in the Overseas Chinese Bank without the consent of the Legislative Yuan. Third, the government believed that the Cathay Trust Group was not owned by overseas Chinese and therefore was not eligible to purchase a majority of the bank's equity. But the development funds were also not overseas Chinese capital, so how could these funds legitimately be used for this purpose?

At the time, Yu Kuo-hwa, who had since been promoted to Premier, responded that the government's highest priority was maintaining Taiwan's financial stability. According to the regulations, the majority ownership of the Overseas Chinese Bank must return to overseas Chinese, and the government had stepped in to temporarily acquire the shares due to a lack of available overseas Chinese capital, with the intention of unloading the shares into the proper hands as soon as possible.

However, despite this controversy in Legislative Yuan, the OCBC crisis had finally passed, with the bank's majority equity safely returned to overseas Chinese hands. The Bank, emerging from this crisis, underwent a full reorganization. Based on the government's shareholding, the Central Bank appointed Lin Lee-hsin, the general manager of the Agricultural Bank, to serve as the managing director and general manager of the Overseas Chinese Bank. His arrival at his new assignment inevitably resulted in some misunderstandings. He was under the impression that Steve was a member of the establishment faction within the bank, and that the influence of this faction needed to be addressed if the institution was to be effectively reformed.

"After a period of butting heads, we soon achieved a common understanding that we both had the same goals," Steve remembers. "This paved the way for a period of stable growth for the Overseas Chinese Bank under President Lin's fair and honest leadership."

Due to significant amounts of firm equity changing hands, the board of directors was reorganized, along with the bank's management.

Following these events, Steve increased his holdings, and his continued efforts contributed significantly to the firm's subsequent success. At the board meeting on June 30, 1984, a new slate of 21 directors was elected, including seven standing directors: Tsai Hsiao-ku, Lin Lee-hsin, Tsai Shao-hua, Steve Tsai, Tsai Neng, and Cheng Hsin-hsin. The appointment of each standing director was confirmed by the Ministry of Finance for a three-year term. In total, Steve served as standing director for 15 years.

An OCBC birthday party. From left, Managing Directors Steve and Tsai Neng, Taiwan Province Governor Chiu Chuang-huan, KMT General Secretary Ma Shu-li, Managing Directors Cheng Hsin-hsin, Tsai Shao-hua, and Cheng Wei-huang.

The first three OCBC Chairmen of the Board : (from top) Tsai Kung-nan (May 26, 1960 to December 2, 1975), Tsai Wen-hwa (December 3, 1975 to March 1, 1976), Tsai Hsiao-ku (March 1, 1976 to December 18, 1984).

OCBC Former General Manager and Managing Director Lin Lee-hsin.

1997: OCBC Managing Director, Steve (second from left); Chairman of the Board Tai Lee-ning (third from left), and Managing Directors and supervisors.

The OCBC Incident (II)

This seemed to mark the end of the crisis for the Overseas Chinese Bank, but it was quickly followed by a major event that, on the surface, seemed unrelated to the OCBC.

The Overseas Chinese Bank crisis occurred in February 1984. The following February saw the onset of a new crisis involving the Taipei Tenth Credit Cooperative (TTCC), which quickly developed into the largest financial crisis in Taiwan's history.

The chairman of the TTCC at the time was Tsai Chen-nan's brother Tsai Chen-chou, under whose management the TTCC engaged in illegal operations, the details of which are beyond the scope of this book. However, the fallout from this incident greatly damaged the credibility of the Cathay Trust Group, leaving it unable to re-sign existing investors as their standing agreements came up for renewal or to attract new ones.

On March 3, 1985, the Ministry of Finance and the Central Bank announced the reorganization of the Cathay Trust Group. The Bank of Communications was assigned to form a joint banking group with the Agricultural Bank and the Central Trust Bureau to create an escrow facility for the Cathay Trust Group. During the reorganization, it came out that Cathay Trust Group had extended an illegal loan of nearly NT$17 billion to Tsai Chen-chou's Cathay Plastics Group and its affiliated companies. The furor following these disclosures saw both Cathay Plastics and the Cathay Trust Group, the two main components of Tsai Chen-nan's family's holdings, quickly shuttered.

Finance Minister Lu Run-kang, his predecessor Hsu Lee-te (since transferred to the Ministry of Economic Affairs), Kuomintang Secretary-General Chiang Yan-shih, and Kuomintang Party Director Kuan Chung all resigned in the fallout.

Yu Ching-tang, the eighty-nine-year-old KMT veteran and former Minister of the Interior, emotionally and forcefully denounced the TTCC affair at a Standing Committee meeting of the Bank of Communications. He was so overcome that he suffered a stroke and died on the spot.

Prosecutors arrested and imprisoned Tsai Chen-chou on charges related to the scandal, and he later succumbed to illness on the eve of his sentencing.

The fallout from the scandal amply shows how narrowly the Overseas Chinese Bank avoided all of several undesirable outcomes: being directly caught up in the scandal, causing a run on the bank, or having the bank either being shut down or taken over by the government. The ensuing fallout would have irreparably damaged relations between the government and the overseas Chinese investment community, a fate prevented in large part due to Steve's subtle and quiet diplomacy and maneuvering.

Tsai Chen-nan's financial career came to an end with the government takeover of the Cathay Trust Group, and he shifted his interests elsewhere, indulging his penchant for gourmet cuisine by opening the Shengli Plaza Shopping Center in Dalian in 1992, with a menu featuring many of his signature creations. He followed this up with restaurants in Shanghai and Hangzhou and the Straits Club in Taipei.

Steve was invited to the opening of these restaurants and was subsequently a frequent visitor. Steve often praised Tsai Chen-nan as a young, ambitious and open-minded entrepreneur who does not bear grudges, treats others humbly, and is known for his tolerance. Every time the two met, they greeted each other warmly.

Steve would later recall this episode of saving the Overseas Chinese Bank and emphasize his respect for Tsai Chen-nan's grace in defeat.

Steve (far right) with former Ministers of Economic Affairs Hsu Lee-te (far left) and Lu Run-kang (second from right).

Taiwan's First Five-Star International Hotel Chain

In the 1960s, Taiwan's tourism industry was underdeveloped. In 1973, construction was completed on the Taipei Hilton Hotel, financed by overseas Chinese investors from the Philippines.

Taipei's Hilton Hotel was Taiwan's the first entry of a large-scale high-end hotel chain in Taiwan and, at the time, was the tallest building in Taiwan. As such, it plays a very special role in Taiwan's tourism, hotel, and architectural history.

However, the hotel's development was difficult, and the construction process was full of obstacles that Steve and his team methodically overcame. At the time, the hotel was known for setting three records: the tallest building in Taiwan, the largest number of guest rooms (at more than 500), and the highest budget for interior decoration (US$8000 per guest room, not including construction costs).

In the 1950s, tourism development was just one of countless problems facing Taiwan, but one with the potential to attract foreign currency and to raise Taiwan's international image. In the 1960s, the government announced incentives to attract investment for large-scale, high-class international-grade hotels. Large-scale meant 500 rooms or more, and high-class meant with decoration budgets exceeding US$8000 per guest room. Applicants would have to demonstrate ownership of the proposed development site. Based on long-term low interest loans from the "China-US Fund," hotel investment applicants were required to put up at least 50% of the capital in their own funds, with matching government loans.

Steve recruited the Philippine Overseas Chinese Yachia Sugar Industry Group Corporation to invest in Taiwan's Huayang Investment and Development Company, which originally planned to build an office building for lease in Taipei. Following the development of the government loan program, Steve suggested a change of plans to develop a high-end, large-scale international tourist hotel on the site. Steve served as executive director and deputy general manager of Huayang at the time. The general manager was Lin Wei-pai, a prominent overseas Chinese from the Philippines, known as Taiwan's "Godfather of Golf" for his role in developing the sport there. The chairman was Tsai Wen-hua, the Philippines' sugar king and chairman of the Pacific Bank, who also served as vice chairman of the Overseas Chinese Bank.

Based on his experience in journalism, Steve realized the development potential of international tourism in Taiwan, but the only international-grade hotel in Taipei at the time was the Grand Hotel, supplemented by a small handful of smaller hotels such as the United Hotel and Ambassador Hotel.

In 1973, Huayang completed the capitalization of the Taipei Hilton Hotel project, bringing the first international hotel chain to Taiwan. At 20 floors and standing 71 meters tall, the building was 11 meters taller than the Presidential Palace.

The first challenge was to find a suitable location. Lei Chun-tao, a friend of Steve's from the financial sector, recommended the site of the Shuanglian Christian Church, on Taipei's Zhongshan North

Road. Huayang director Tsai Shixiang came to Taiwan to preside over the negotiations and was about to sign a contract, when Lei Chun-tao came forward with some inside information: the Ministry of Finance Property Bureau was planning to auction off a prime site. Steve immediately set out with Tsai Shixiang to inspect the site and found it to be much more favorable than the Shuanglian land. They immediately suspended their current negotiations and began making preparations to bid on the new site, located on Zhongxiao West Road, directly across from the Taipei Railway Station.

This corner lot, measuring about 30,000 square feet, was currently occupied by the Ministry of Economic Affairs and the Bureau of Gold and Copper Mining. Steve felt this site presented a great opportunity and encouraged Huayang to bid. With the approval of the board of directors, Shixiang and Steve were sent to bid on behalf of the company. Determined to take the prize, they opened their bid at NT$30 million, considerably above the reserve price. This proved to be a winning strategy, and the shareholders were overjoyed by the acquisition.

However, securing the site was only the first of a long list of challenges on the road to building the Hilton Hotel. They estimated that the development would require more than US$20 million, a huge sum at the time.

Under the loan terms, Huayang needed to raise US$6 million of its own funds, and could borrow the remainder at 5% over 20 years. At the time, open market bank lending rates were all above 12%, with loans maturing from five to seven years, thus this 5% arrangement with a longer maturity not only would greatly reduce the borrowing costs, but also provide an important competitive advantage for future operations. The board instructed Steve to pull out all the stops to secure the loan.

But there were other issues to address. First, following

construction regulations for a building of such height would mean they could only build on 40% of the available lot, making it impossible to construct the desired 500 guest rooms. Second, regulations required the provision of at least 15 elevators for various functions. Third, as the building would be within three km of the runways at Songshan Airport, the height limitation was set at 60 meters, while the company's development plans called for a 71-meter, 20-floor tower.

Finally, the groundbreaking was soon followed by the ROC's withdrawal from the United Nations, which caused a crisis of investor confidence in Taiwan and the hotel project. This will be discussed further below.

Building regulations at the time had failed to keep pace with Taiwan's development, unnecessarily limiting development areas and requiring excessive elevator service. Following current regulations, the company would end up with a tall, skinny observation tower, rather than a hotel. Thus, the first step was to carefully examine all the building codes to find an acceptable solution.

Steve brought in a prominent hotel designer from Hong Kong to collaborate with the famous Taipei designer Haigo T. H. Shen to address the hotel's design issues, but without success. Subsequently, he took on the task directly, pouring over the relevant building regulations and documents, and finally found what he thought was an effective loophole regarding setback requirements from major roads. He quickly brought this to the attention of Haigo T. H. Shen, who broke the bad news that, while this loophole technically existed on paper and is well known to architects, it almost never meets with regulatory approval due to a lack of clear definitions of "major roads." Steve felt that the fault here was in the government's failure to provide clear definitions in its legislation. Developers paid high premiums to secure corner lots, especially on major thoroughfares, and this regulatory ambiguity thus prevented these investors from securing their anticipated returns, making the government liable for their losses. He turned to Wang Chang-ching, who was highly experienced in public works. Wang expressed his sympathy and his willingness to help, but he was not sure where to start.

Wang noted that securing a precise definition of "main arterial roads" must extend beyond a verbal definition but must be accompanied by concrete actions. They launched a full research project, hiring student workers to carefully calculate traffic flows during different times of the day, and then turning over this data for expert analysis to determine a definition of "main road." Legislative remedies were also required, but the project could not wait for that. Lee Ru-nan, deputy director of the Public Works Bureau, had a deep understanding of building regulations and was more pragmatic than Wang Chang-ching. Steve sought a meeting, but without success. Repeated attempts left Steve suspicious that Lee might be deliberately avoiding him. Finally, he arranged a meeting through a mutual friend, at which he explained the efforts he and his company had already undertaken to clarify the "main road" issue, noting that these were tasks that Lee's department should have completed long ago as a matter of course as part of their government responsibilities, and then pushed the issue with the Legislative Yuan to improve existing building regulations. Lee Ru-nan promised to deal with it, but Steve continued to push, sending messages to the director of the Public Works Department, and escalating the issue to the Department of Land Affairs at the Ministry of Interior, which was responsible for construction within Taiwan.

In addition to these formal channels, Steve actively worked informal channels, instructing his secretary to form a close relationship with the director of the Public Works Department by taking him out for dinner every night after work, with conversation centering on relevant regulations and possible workarounds. But the feedback was uniformly unfavorable, and the consensus was that the hotel would be impossible to build, leaving only the option of developing an office building. The office building project would be much smaller, and therefore it could be entirely self-financed.

At this desperate moment, there came a ray of hope. In 1967, the central government announced the promotion of Taipei City to a municipality directly under the Central Government. On July 1 of that year, Steve was invited to attend a celebratory reception for the promotion of Taipei City at the Grand Hotel. At the reception, Taipei Mayor Kao Yu-shu was drinking with the commander of the US Defense Forces in Taiwan but excused himself to speak to Steve.

"That's a prime location you've secured," said the mayor. "It's the perfect spot for a tourist hotel."

"That's true," replied Steve, "but we've come up against a wall of regulations that make the hotel project impossible."

After hearing Steve describe the difficulties he'd encountered, Kao told him: "Come see me tomorrow. There's a clause in the regulations that says that if a project is in the national interests, the mayor of a special municipality has the authority to approve specific construction projects, without ministerial approval."

Kao instructed Steve to prepare the required report and bring it to him the following morning. Steve could hardly believe his ears. He immediately returned to his office and wrote the report without telling anyone.

The following morning, he delivered the report in person to the mayor, who read through it quickly and said that he fully supported the construction of an international tourist hotel in Taipei as a priority in the national interest. "I say this is a main road. Therefore, it's a main road," he said. "It's part of the mayor's remit to cut through unnecessary red tape." At the same time, he reduced the number of required elevators from 15 to 5, signing off on the project.

"I'll take this to the Department of Public Works and follow up with them directly," he told Steve.

With the stroke of a pen, the mayor had helped resolve two intractable problems. But the overall height of the building remained a difficult issue in terms of flight safety for Songshan Airport. However, an exception had been carved out for structures close to the Presidential Palace. The hotel's proposed site, at No. 30, Section 1, Zhongxiao West Road, was considered close to the Presidential Palace, thus relieving it from the airport restriction.

In addition, the hotel project required approval from the Ministry of the Interior. Steve therefore called on Hsu Ching-chung, Minister of the Interior. Given Taiwan's location in an earthquake fault zone, the construction of tall buildings required extensive consultations.

Steve came prepared, noting that Tokyo is also prone to earthquakes, but already boasted towers reaching 52 floors. "This project only entails the construction of a building less than half that height," he noted. "In addition, this project is important for the national interest. Professional experts are in agreement on the feasibility and safety of the proposed building. This is not a time to be timid. Hold public hearings to hear from experts. As long as the experts sign off on the project, there is no reason to worry. This is a critical step for Taiwan's development, and a failure to move forward with this project with ensure that Taiwan will never develop a modern metropolitan skyline."

He noted that the extensive delays had already significantly increased the project's costs and presented a significant obstacle to the government's efforts to attract overseas Chinese capital. This project would be a bellwether for Taiwan's future development, he stressed, and failure to move ahead with the project could encourage foreign investors to retreat from Taiwan.

Minister Hsu was swayed by these arguments and assured Steve that the project would receive the required authorization. Steve pushed the Minister to immediately announce the approval to the journalists sitting in the Minister's waiting room. When Hsu hesitated, Steve noted, "This project has been on hold for two years due to red tape and regulations. We are ready to break ground, but now approval from your ministry is holding us up again. Given this hesitation, I'll have to go out to those reporters and announce that the project has been scrapped because we couldn't secure approval from the Ministry of the Interior."

Hsu attempted to placate Steve, assuring him that the project would be approved, but asked for two or three days for the necessary processing.

Upon leaving Hsu's office, Steve stopped to talk to the reporters. "Minister Hsu has agreed to approve the hotel project and will provide the required dispensation in three days," he told them, and the announcement was made in the following day's newspapers.

However, just as all these other obstacles were seemingly resolved, there came a problem with the loan, an issue which originally had seemed one of the easier challenges. The Council for United States Aid within the ROC Executive Yuan notified Huayang that the China-US Fund loan funds would be granted to another company, and Huayang's only chance of receiving funds was if the other project did not go forward. Steve found that the competing company did not actually own the site for their proposed development. Instead, it had simply signed an agreement with the actual landowner, which held that if the financing and official approval were secured, the company would partner with the landowner in the remainder of the planning and then the construction of their proposed hotel. Steve was incensed. "This is completely illegal," he said. "The incentives for this program clearly require that the applicant own the land outright with no debt. If the applicant doesn't own the land, how can it possibly apply for financing?" If financing were approved, any disagreement between the parties would have the potential to blow up the entire project. The prestige and reputation of the government would be on the line here."

Steve went to the official residence of Yen Chia-kan, Premier of the Executive Yuan, on Chongqing South Road. Yan concurrently served as the chairman of The Council for United States Aid within the ROC Executive Yuan. He listened to Steve's complaint but did not reply beyond saying that he would review the case.

The next day Steve went to report the matter to Finance Minister Kwoh-Ting Li. Lee received him politely, saying that the loan decision had been made at a meeting chaired by S.Y. Dao, Secretary-General of the Committee for Economic Cooperation of the ROC Ministry of Economic Affairs. He asked, "Mr. Tsai, do you think there's a problem here?"

"I have no doubt as to Secretary Dao's trustworthiness and honesty," said Steve. "But where did this go wrong?"

Lee promised to investigate.

Events began to unfold quickly. Steve remembered, "I was not mistaken. At that time, the leadership and members of the Council for United States Aid within the ROC Executive Yuan were very trustworthy. Within a month, the Council corrected the mistake and cancelled the original qualification for the competitor's loan preference and promoted Huayang to first place". Huayang shareholders rejoiced at the news. Thus, the complex construction technology problems had been solved, as had the basic financing problems. However, there was another surprise coming.

As the date approached for the hotel's groundbreaking ceremony, on October 25, 1971, the Republic of China withdrew from the United Nations. This raised concerns among the corporate directors, fearful that Taiwan may fall to the CCP, and that their investment would be nationalized. Steve was summoned to Manila for an emergency board meeting where he tried to assuage their fears. He noted Taiwan's international strategic importance and the deterrents arrayed to discourage CCP aggression. He also noted that the investors had already sunk considerable funds into the project that could not be recovered by cancelling the project.

After hearing Steve's statement, some directors suggested a change of plans, and to build a hospital on the site, rather than a hotel.

Steve responded by saying that this change would necessitate completely restarting the entire application process, and that the favorable loan scheme would not cover hospital construction. In addition, the construction and equipment requirements for hotels and hospitals were completely different.

In the end, Chairman Tsai Wen-hua resolved the dispute with a compromise. Originally, the hotel would be owned and operated under the name of the Huayang Group. Now, he suggested that the group license the hotel to the American Hilton Hotel Group, and that the Hilton Group would directly manage the property. The involvement of this international business group in the project would lend some protection against potential expropriation following a CCP invasion.

The proposal was unanimously approved, but the terms subsequently proposed by Hilton were too unfavorable to Huayang and amounted to granting the Hilton Group control over the property for 30 years.

Due to frustration with the final terms, Steve decided to

withdraw from the project, despite the countless hours he had sunk into it. In 1973, the Taipei Hilton Hotel was completed and opened its doors. Freed from the need to spend its own capital, the hotel was immediately and immensely profitable, and the appreciating value of the hotel and its land provided the Huayang shareholders with considerable returns of NT$4 to 5 billion. In 2002, the Huayang Board decided not to renew its agreement with the Hilton Hotel Group. By this time, most of the original shareholders had passed on, and their children and grandchildren decided to sell the property. In January 2003, the new owners changed the name of the property to the Caesar Park Taipei.

Steve noted that the Huayang lot was a unique development location, and the Hilton Group was the gold standard of the global hospitality industry. News of the sale of the plot struck him as a terrible lost opportunity for the shareholders and led to several sleepless nights for him.

Nearly 50 years ago, a prime lot of 800 pings (30,000 square feet) in Taipei was available for less than NT$30 million. In 2013, such a location would command nearly NT$9 million per ping.

"Holding the property would be a lasting legacy for the shareholders' children and grandchildren," Steve said. But the plot was sold without much consideration, a decision which still caused him to sigh regretfully.

Nowadays, Steve cannot bring himself to visit the site out of sadness. Still, the Hilton, today known as the Caesar Park Hotel, bears an indelible imprint of Steve's efforts.

Chapter Eight

A Crosswalk in the Real Estate Market

Planning Taiwan's Construction Management Industry

Among Steve's many titles, from 1988 to the writing of this book in 2014, he served as Chairman of the Chiaofu Construction Management Company, a title which hides a story of social service.

What is a "construction manager"? Steve metaphorically calls the construction management industry a "crosswalk," protecting the legitimate rights and interests of home buyers, the construction investment industry, and banks, providing objective and reliable professional services. (The Taiwan definition of "construction management" is quite different from the American definition.)

In Taiwan's "pre-sold housing" system, a developer will secure approval and permits for a residential project, and then pre-sell 50% to 60% of the units before construction begins. Thus, the purchaser makes a down payment on the property and begins to make installment payments long before the property is ready to move in.

Developers use the land as collateral to secure bank loans, and then make loan payments using funds from the installment payments they receive on the pre-sold units. Unscrupulous developers, however, may misdirect these pre-sale revenue streams to other purposes, such as funding other development projects, or as venture capital. If these investments turn bad, they could be unable to finish the initial development project, leaving the unit purchasers holding the bag. Several large-scale failures like these had led to considerable social unrest.

Even when projects were completed, they were still subject to significant disputes regarding the size of the final apartments, the materials used and substandard construction quality. As Taiwan's real estate market grew rapidly, these disputes threatened to overwhelm Taiwan's judicial and regulatory systems.

In the early 1980s, Steve, then managing director of OCBC Bank, had a birds-eye view to the chaos this lack of regulation was causing in the domestic real estate markets, and the spillover effects for buyers and the overall financial industry. In response, the Executive Yuan established an inter-ministerial task force including officials from the Ministry of Finance, the Ministry of Economic Affairs, Ministry of the Interior and Academia Sinica, sending researchers on fact-finding trips to the United States, Japan and Europe. They returned with a new concept for Taiwan: the construction manager. In 1985 and 1986, the Ministry of the Interior promulgated regulations that encouraged the real estate and finance industries to launch private construction management firms. The regulations required that at least 30% of the shares of such companies belong to banks, and that the three coordinating ministries review and approve such companies. As a standing director of the OCBC, Steve was appointed to concurrently serve as a director of the Chiaofu Construction Management Company in which the OCBC had a significant stake and was elected chairman of the board.

During his tenure, the construction management industry expanded to areas beyond Taipei, and thus the regional association, Taipei City Construction Managers Association, was upgraded to the Republic of China Construction Managers Commercial Association. He was re-elected and served as the chairman for two terms of six years, finally stepping down as he approached eighty years old, a tenure he remembers as a "cruel" challenge, but also a "glorious mission."

In 1992, three days after being elected as the chairman of the Taipei City Construction Managers Association, Steve he visited President Lee Teng-hui with two requests: First, to implement the new construction management system and relevant policies to stabilize Taiwan's real estate market. Second, to accelerate the plans to list OCBC on the Taiwan stock market.

In the case of Overseas Chinese Bank's shares, Steve was later appointed by the bank's board of directors to call on Minister of Finance Wang Chien-shien and Director of Finance Chen Mu-tsai. The two parties reached a consensus, and the bank was successfully listed. Regarding system implementation, Lee Teng-hui may have referred the matter of the construction manager industry to the relevant agencies, but unfortunately there had been no further progress.

In his first week as chairman of the board, Steve successively called on the heads of the relevant ministries and relevant business organizations, along with selected legislators, to promote the early passage of needed legislation for the construction management industry. He then held a press conference to publicly explain the impact and importance of this new industry in policing the construction industry, enforcing

Inscription by Li-Fu Chen for the Republic of China Construction Managers Commercial Association.

1994: Commercial Times reports Steve assumes control of the Republic of China Construction Managers Commercial Association.

industry professionalism, service quality and ethics.

He noted that professional construction managers would review all details of a construction project's financing and marketing, along with the financial health of the builders, and assess collateral and loan securities. Such oversight would also help construction firms reduce their borrowing costs, thus reducing overall construction costs, savings which could be passed on to the consumer, who would also benefit from increased confidence in the security of their real estate investments.

In his work, "Research on the Future Development of Construction Manager Companies," Professor Chuang Meng-han notes, "With professional and independent project oversight, the construction industry will be able to raise funds more easily and provide consumers with credible service quality guarantees. Thus, home buyers will feel secure in making their installment payments as the liquidation of the construction firm would become the responsibility of the construction management firm, which is then obligated to either complete the project or provide full refunds to purchasers."

The development of the construction management industry thus presents an important win-win for home buyers, builders, and banks. Despite this, the industry's development was not all smooth sailing, mainly due to the determination of builders seeking to protect their vested interests, leading them to oppose reforms through backroom political pressure.

In fact, the establishment of the construction management industry would significantly reduce the financial and social risks inherent in housing transactions, providing much needed security and transparency.

Steve also criticized the government for its failure to

energetically back the initiative.

Steve published an article in the thirteenth issue of the Construction Manager Quarterly entitled "Re-examining the Legal Context of the Construction Management Industry". The article stressed the need for a transformation of the construction industry, and clearly noted the long-term benefits of establishing the construction management industry, including the establishment of a third-party mechanism to ensure the safety of real estate transactions, thereby creating consumer trust and confidence.

A public hearing held by the Legislative Yuan deliberating the development of the construction management industry, with Steve and his colleagues invited to attend. Steve was the first to speak, reporting on the progress of the association and problems that needed to be resolved. He spoke loudly, emphasizing the importance and urgency of the legalization of the industry. The other witnesses echoed his sentiments, positioning the construction management industry as a critical reform initiative that would improve social security, and called for increased regulation.

Fifty-nine legislators from different parties, including Lai Shyh-Bao and J.T. Cho, jointly proposed a bill during the fourth session of the Legislative Yuan to formulate laws to regulate the construction management industry. However, stubborn resistance from the Construction Investment Association ensured that the bill fell short of majority support.

Steve said, "The cornerstone of democratic politics lies in the National Assembly, and the operation of the National Assembly is determined by the majority. However, we've seen the inability of the Legislative Yuan to overcome industry objection, despite overwhelming public support."

A Challenge and a Mission

Steve remembered, "To overcome these objections, the board of directors and I visited the ROC Construction Investment Association, as well as the directors and board members of the Taipei, Kaohsiung, and Taiwan Provincial Associations. To win support, I visited almost all the relevant legislators, some more than once, sometimes visiting their local representative offices, and sometimes going to the Legislative Yuan several times a day for days on end. I had to convince people to meet me, to listen to me, to agree with me, to attend the relevant legislative session, and to represent us correctly. It was thankless work and could be very frustrating."

Steve continued, "After nearly half a century of serving industrial and commercial organizations both at home and abroad, which took my time and attention away from my own business dealings and my family, I felt I owed it to these organizations to see this through."

The development of Taiwan's construction manager industry also attracted attention in mainland China.

When Wang Daohan, chairman of the Association for Relations Across the Taiwan Straits (ARATS), met Sun Yuan-fang, general manager of Taiyi Construction Management Co., in Shanghai, he noted the title "Construction Management Corp." on his business card with curiosity. Sun explained how Taiwan's construction management industry worked, and Wang was struck by the similarities between industry conditions in the mainland and Taiwan. After inquiring, he learned about Taiwan's construction management industry. He was particularly interested in how the industry safeguarded the interests of real estate consumers and investors. The following day he brought his assistant to meet Sun and, in the ensuing discussion, encouraged Taiwan-based construction management operators to extend their operations to the mainland.

After heading the Taipei and the National Construction Management Industry Associations for 12 years, Steve stepped down from his active roles but continued to serve as honorary chairman as the industry continued to push for legislative establishment and regulation. Despite his advanced age, he continued to support the efforts of his successors, including Chao Hsi-chiang and the current chairman Tsao Fen-ping. Tsao, in particular, brought excellent knowledge and experience to the effort. He had previously directed local urban planning in Canada with excellent results. Over the succeeding years, Steve and Cao remained in close contact, and Steve carefully followed the development of related legislation.

1986: Republic of China Construction Managers Commercial Association. Chairman Steve (right) leads a delegation of over 60 people for Taiwan's construction industry to visit the Shanghai-Hangzhou Development Zone (to the left is Association secretary Huang Yi-feng).

Steve (4th from left) leads a delegation from Taiwan's construction industry to mainland China.

Chapter Nine

Responsibility for the Nation

As the United States and Canada Cut Diplomatic Ties, the ROC Establishes Offices to Promote "Business Diplomacy."

I've been busy all my life and there just aren't enough hours in the day. But for 40 years I volunteered my time and energy to serve many industrial and commercial organizations. Although I have never received a penny in compensation, I have received something more precious: the love and respect of the people I represent. I will always do my best to live up to their expectations.

- Steve Tsai

Severance of Taiwan-US Ties

At 9 p.m. local time on December 15, 1978, President Jimmy Carter announced in Washington that the United States would establish diplomatic relations with Beijing on January 1 of the following year. Simultaneously, at 10 am Beijing time, Chinese Premier Hua Guofeng made the same announcement in Beijing.

Just seven hours before this announcement, at 3 a.m. on

December 16th, Taipei time, the US ambassador to the Republic of China, Leonard S. Unger, called on President Chiang Ching-kuo to inform him of the coming developments.

Steve clearly remembered President Chiang addressing the nation on television the night of December 16. The loss of US diplomatic recognition represented the Republic of China's greatest international setback since the government had withdrawn from the United Nations.

The president seemed overwhelmed and distracted. His hair was uncombed, and a button on his jacket had gone unbuttoned. A sense of deep humiliation spread through Taiwan, and people reacted with disappointment and outrage. Protesters took to the streets, shouting into the cold winter wind. A mob lay siege to the US embassy, with small groups scaling the walls and flying the ROC flag. Some cut their fingers to write patriotic slogans on the walls in their own blood.

This incident also opened a new chapter in Steve's life: promoting the ROC's national diplomacy through business, establishing Chamber of Commerce offices in two countries without diplomatic relations with the Republic of China, namely the United States and Canada.

The day after President Chiang's televised announcement, the Executive Yuan held a meeting in Zhongshan Hall to discuss the self-reliance of Taiwan's business sector. Executive Yuan President Sun Yun-Suan presided over the meeting, which was packed to the walls with anxious businessmen. Sun said that, since World War II, the Republic of China has been fighting side by side of its closest ally, the United States. Today, when Taiwan was facing its most difficult times, the United States has abandoned us. The country must be self-reliant and focus on economic development. We must mobilize the entire country in the name of self-reliance.

After the meeting, Sun instructed the Republic of China General Chamber of Commerce to send personnel to establish an office in Washington before the US completed its shift of diplomatic relations to Beijing, thus maintaining uninterrupted, if unofficial, diplomatic relations with the US.

Steve speaks to a meeting of the Manila Overseas Chinese Chamber of Commerce.

The Chamber of Commerce then held an emergency meeting in response to the government's self-reliance campaign. It was unanimously resolved that Steve, the organization's executive director, would travel to the United States to establish the Washington office. Time was of the essence, as there were less than two weeks left before Washington would establish formal relations with Beijing. Adding to the urgency, Taiwan at the time had a foreign trade deficit with Japan, but a surplus with the United States, making Taiwan-US trade absolutely vital to Taiwan's continued economic development.

The following day, Steve took the first flight to Washington and went straight to the ROC embassy where he explained his mission to Ambassador James Shen and asked for his assistance. Steve had long known Ambassador Shen from the days when he served as the special correspondent to the Philippine Xinmin Daily News. At the time, Shen was the English Secretary to President Chiang, and later served for many years as Director of the Central News Agency. Unfortunately, it was a sad reunion, and Steve found his old friend utterly despondent. "We have to lower our flag and close the embassy," he said. "I'm packing up and going back to Taiwan. There's nothing I can do to help." Steve swallowed his disappointment and flew immediately to San Francisco, home of the largest and most influential Chinese community in the United States.

Steve also lived in San Francisco and was close friends with Chung Hu-pin, the local consul general of the Republic of China. Chung told Steve that Beijing had already anticipated his mission and had requested the US State Department to not acknowledge the ROC Chamber of Commerce as a diplomatic channel. "And if Ambassador Shen can't help you, what can I do?"

Steve recognized the bind the officials found themselves in but persisted. "Diplomats used to be in charge, but now this is a private matter," he said. "If you can't help in an official capacity, at least give me the benefit of your experience. How can we achieve these aims?" Chung suggested Steve approach the California state government to establish an NGO to promote Taiwan-US trade. However, one obvious obstacle would be that the resulting organization would not be able to use the name "Republic of China".

Steve reported the situation to Chen Chi-ching, Chairman of the Republic of China Chamber of Commerce, noting the difficulties he was having securing assistance from the embassies and consulates in Washington and San Francisco and the additional problem of using the ROC name. Would it be possible, he asked, to establish a representative office that didn't use the country's name?

Recognizing the gravity of the situation, Chen called an emergency board meeting to discuss the issue. The result was an emphatic no: the office must explicitly use the country's name in its title.

Steve was ordered to stay in San Francisco and continue to press the issue. Through an official from the Consulate General, Steve was introduced to an experienced American lawyer. He explained that he was tasked with establishing a pseudo-official representative office for the Republic of China in the United States, that the office need not be located in Washington, DC, but that it must use the name "Republic of China General Chamber of Commerce in the United States." The lawyer noted that, with the clock ticking towards the severing of official ties, submitting an application with these terms now would be taking advantage of a narrow window of time to do something that would not be legal later. The lawyer asked if Steve had any argument in favor of establishing the office with that name.

Steve said, "The General Chamber of Commerce (of the ROC) was not established in response to the imminent severing of diplomatic relations between Taiwan and the United States. In fact, this institution was established in Nanjing, the capital of the Republic of China, in 1946." He then produced official documentation and press reports to substantiate this claim. He also noted that the Communiqué on the Establishment of Diplomatic Relations between the United States and the People's Republic of China promised that "The American people will maintain cultural, commercial and other unofficial relations with the people of Taiwan."

He pointed out: "In the past, problems in Taiwan-US business relations could be resolved through diplomatic channels. Now that diplomatic relations are being revoked, the Chamber of Commerce seeks to establish an office in the United States to maintain business relations between Taiwan and the United States, as stated in the communiqué, providing support, services and communication channels. If American businessmen want to hold exhibitions in Taiwan, the office can connect them with agents to find the appropriate channels. Likewise, Taiwanese companies who want to come to the United States can contact US government agencies or industrial and commercial counterparts through the office. This organization is legitimately established, and there can be no reasonable objection."

The lawyer found the argument persuasive and set about submitting the required documents.

On January 1, 1979, the United States officially severed diplomatic relations with the Republic of China. However, through the efforts of Steve and his lawyers, the application for the establishment of the General Chamber of Commerce of the Republic of China in the United States was submitted and approved by the California state government without difficulty. Steve found office space for the organization in a Market Street office building that already housed several foreign consulates in San Francisco.

Steve not only contributed to the establishment of the new office but paid for several thousands of dollars of legal fees out of his own pocket. The first director of the US office was Wu Ching-tang, a career diplomat at the Ministry of Foreign Affairs, and graduate of the International Diplomacy Department at National Chengchi University. Fluent in English and Spanish, he had begun his career translating Spanish documents for President Chiang Kai-shek and Madame Chiang.

At the time the office of the ROC Chamber of Commerce in the United States was established, Wu Ching-tang, as ROC Ministry of Foreign Affairs director of the Office for Central and South American Affairs, was seconded to the Taiwan Provincial Government as the director of the Foreign Affairs Office. Based on his qualifications and experience, the Ministry of Foreign Affairs selected him to head up the new organization.

The inaugural meeting of the ROC National Chamber of Commerce in the United States was held on the top floor of the Bank of America Headquarters Building on California Street in San Francisco. Chen Chi-ching, Chairman of the Chamber of Commerce, led a delegation of the executive directors from Taipei, joining a who's-who of local, state and federal officials and influential businesspeople.

Despite the severing of official diplomatic relations, ties between the two sides remained warm and enthusiastic. Still, the lowering of the ROC flag, accompanied by the national anthem, brought tears to the eyes of crowds of overseas Chinese, still in shock over the US change in diplomatic recognition. As of March 1, 1979, the ROC Chamber of Commerce in the United States assumed the unofficial diplomatic role of liaising between the two countries.

Wu Ching-tang also engaged in public diplomacy, keeping up an active calendar of high-profile social and professional engagements to ensure regular and positive publicity for the ROC Chamber of Commerce in the US media. His work was characterized by pragmatism and urgency, keeping in close coordination with Steve and consulting with him over major decisions. During his tenure, he actively promoted bilateral economic and trade relations between Taiwan and the United States by providing critical information to American businesses, visiting chambers of commerce across the United States, and contacting Chinese businessmen in the United States to develop trade with Taiwan. Wu Ching-tang also established strong ties with the San Francisco Chamber of Commerce and the US Department of Commerce's Western Pacific Regional Office, and the two sides cooperated closely on the development of Taiwan-US economic and trade relations.

1979: Establishment of the US office of the Republic of China Chamber of Commerce. From left, Chamber of Commerce Chairman Chen Chi-ching, and executive directors Lin Hsi-chen, Steve Tsai, Chiang Meng-mo, and Hsieh Wen-chin welcome guests.

The US office also co-hosted a Taiwan-US economic and trade seminar with the Department of Commerce's Western Pacific Regional Office, with more than 200 economic and trade VIPs from both sides meeting and dining on the deck of a China Shipping Company cargo vessel anchored at San Francisco Terminal.

Three years after the establishment of the new office, Wu Ching-tang was called back to Taiwan to serve in the Ministry of the Interior, leaving the US office temporarily without a director. Steve stepped into this role, serving as acting director for more than a year. Under his leadership, the office continued to promote commercial ties between the two countries, and further strengthened ties with local, state and federal officials to promote Taiwan-US economic and trade exchanges. Steve's son Solomon and daughter Tenny could often be found in the office, helping out in an arrangement Steve referred to as "buy one, get two free." Steve had other commitments at this time, and when he could not continue serving as acting director, he recommended that Hung Tu, an experienced ROC diplomat, take over the position of director.

Following the severing of official ties, the ROC government established a "North American Affairs Coordination Committee" in the United States to handle exchanges between the two countries,

Hung Tu, second US office director of the Republic of China Chamber of Commerce.

Steve (right) represents the Republic of China Chamber of Commerce in signing a memorandum of understanding with a foreign counterpart.

but the ambiguous name of the organization led to confusion among American businesspeople and ordinary citizens, who intuitively sought out the ROC Chamber of Commerce in the United States to handle their questions and concerns about Taiwan. The office gradually came to embrace this role, providing information and services where possible, and providing referrals to relevant agencies or the Coordination Committee as needed.

At that time, the U.S. had a large trade deficit with Taiwan, and this was a potential source of friction between the two countries. Actively seeking to reduce this deficit, the ROC government required certain imports to be sourced only from US companies and sent delegations to the US to seek out opportunities for importing US goods, often coordinating with staff of the ROC Chamber of Commerce office.

In September 1986, the director of the ROC Chamber of Commerce in the United States was invited to deliver remarks on the state of Taiwan-US relations to a meeting of United States governors in Colorado Springs. Director Hung's speech would touch on current policies and practices designed to reduce the bilateral trade deficit. Before the speech, he floated an idea with Steve: the attendees of the conference were all important officials, and this seemed a good opportunity to invite them to personally visit Taiwan. Steve gave his support to the proposition, and Hung Tu successfully arranged a delegation of officials and prominent individuals from the thirteen western states to visit Taiwan in November of the same year. During the visit, the chairman of the ROC Chamber of Commerce Wang Tseng hosted a banquet to warmly welcome the visitors.

In the 1980s, the United States and Israel signed a bilateral free trade agreement, inspiring Taiwan to seek a similar arrangement with the US in the belief that this would not only strengthen bilateral economic and trade relations, but also effectively balance the Taiwan-US trade deficit. However, the US was concerned about

1973: ROC Premier Chiang Ching-kuo (right) meets the supervisors of the ROC Chamber of Commerce, with executive director Steve at left.

Official document authorizing Chamber of Commerce executive director Steve to establish a representative office in the United States prior to the severing of formal diplomatic ties.

1st director of the ROC Chamber of Commerce US Office Wu Ching-tang, meeting in San Francisco with Steve, serving as Director of the International Liaison Center of the Chamber of Commerce.

Steve (4th from left) leads a delegation representing the ROC Chamber of Commerce to the Coordination Council for North American Affairs office in the US (established March 1, 1979).

Steve and Tina, with their second daughter, Elizabeth, meeting with US Department of Commerce Pacific region director Newhart, representing 13 states in the western United States.

the lack of official relations and about Beijing's response, and the US ignored this proposal.

In 1988 and 1989, Hung Tu led delegations of groups in meeting with the US Trade Commission, and sponsored a series of seminars at Loyola University Law School in Los Angeles to press the case for a bilateral free trade agreement.

The U.S. Department of Commerce office in San Francisco had a wide jurisdiction over the Western Pacific Region, covering more than a dozen states including Hawaii. After Hung Tu took over as director, he and Steve continued to maintain good and close interaction with Department of Commerce personnel in San Francisco and, in April 1985, Hung Tu was invited by the US Department of Commerce's office in St. Louis to deliver a keynote speech at a China-US Trade Seminar, along with Vincent Siew, then director of the ROC Bureau of International Trade.

After the San Francisco office was fully established, Steve moved on to replicate the effort in Toronto. While the situation there was completely different than what had transpired in San Francisco, Steve focused on securing the most key outcome: that the name "Republic of China" would continue to be recognized and used without change.

After the establishment of these two offices, Steve continued to engage in international commercial diplomacy on behalf of the Republic of China with counterparts in various nations.

Steve also served as the chairman of the Taiwan Decoration Bulb & Light-Set Exporters Association. In this capacity, he led multiple delegations to Europe, the Americas, New Zealand, Australia, North Africa and Southeast Asia, along with Eastern Bloc countries including the Soviet Union, Hungary, Poland, Yugoslavia, the Czech Republic and Romania.

During one visit to the Taipei Chamber of Commerce in Rome, Steve arrived in the midst of a transport strike, shutting down the city's public transport system and taxi services. Determined to make his 9:00 am meeting, Steve woke before dawn and left his hotel at 6 am, walking in through the rain-soaked streets of Rome for more than two hours, arriving in plenty of time.

At the time Steve was nearly 55 years old. The English secretary and retired diplomat Peng Chung-yuan who accompanied the delegation noted Steve's commitment to the mission, especially considering that he wasn't being compensated for his time or efforts.

The ROC Chamber of Commerce also published a monthly English-language magazine for distribution to their Chamber of Commerce counterparts in other nations, to keep the world abreast of new advances and developments in Free China and to introduce new business opportunities. This was a critical aspect of the Chamber's mission of assisting foreign businessmen in finding buyers and sources in Taiwan, with the Chamber acting as a clearinghouse of information and contacts between Taiwan and the rest of the world.

Despite Steve not taking a salary, considerable funds were required to support the Chamber of Commerce's work. As Taiwan's economy expanded, the organization received increased membership dues from member companies, along with additional support from the ROC Foreign Trade Development Association, taken from a national foreign trade levy of 0.0625% on foreign exchange transactions. However, these funds were earmarked specifically for the development of trade and commercial ties; no funds were available to support the organization's business diplomacy work. This was a frequent topic of discussion between Steve and Sun Yun-Suan, the Minister of Economic Development and Foreign Trade.

A compromise was struck to expand funding to the Foreign Chamber of Commerce Liaison Center. At the same time, the management and supervision of the ROC Chamber of Commerce was liberalized to turn responsibility over to a new generation of leadership, with the 1973 Business Organization Law requiring by-elections of directors and supervisors, thus increasing representation among Taiwanese industrialists and businesspeople. That year, Steve was elected as the Chamber of Commerce's executive director, a role he would fulfill until stepping down in 2014. This 41-year

Taiwan Provincial Governor James Soong speaks at the University of California, Berkeley, and meets with overseas Chinese community leaders (from left, UC Berkeley Chancellor Chang-Lin Tien, James Soong, Steve, and Asia-region venture capitalist Hsu Ta-lin).

Steve and Tina meet President Ma Ying-jeou at a banquet hosted by the Bay Area overseas Chinese community.

tenure made him the most senior and experienced director in Chamber history. Throughout his service to the Chamber, he never received a penny in compensation, serving out of dedication to the organization's membership.

Steve asks the President about the Status of Taiwan as a Nation at Advisory Meeting

In response to Taiwan's persistent economic downturn, President Chen Shui-bian convened a meeting of the Economic Development Advisory Committee with 120 representatives from industry, academic think tanks, and the ruling and opposition parties, for extensive discussions and brainstorming.

Steve was selected by the Presidential Palace to serve as an industry representative to the committee, which was divided into five sub-committees, each tasked with a particular facet of the overall problem: employment, investment, cross-Strait relations, industrial competitiveness, and financial prospects. Steve was assigned to the Finance group, but also met with members of the other groups.

The Committee met from July 23rd to August 18th. In the financial group meeting, Steve and CITIC Financial Holdings Chairman Jeffrey Koo Sr., Fubon Group President Tsai Wan-tsai , Dongsen Housing Chairman Wang Yingjie, Hongtai Construction Chairman Lin Yu-lin and others made the case for halving the land value-added tax. This proposal was adopted on August 17, along with a one-year suspension of the securities transaction tax. At the time, the group estimated that these two tax cuts would reduce government revenue by nearly NT$200 billion, a shortfall to be made up by the central government. What was the rationale for this tax cut? Steve noted the sluggishness of the real estate market at the time, and that the suspension of these taxes would spur the real estate market and help promote Taiwan's overall economic growth.

When discussing the proposal, the advisory members of the Economic Development Council, including Central Bank President Perng Fai-nan, Finance Minister Yan Ching-chang, and Deputy Minister Chen Chung also spoke on the critical nature of the situation and did not oppose the measure.

At the meeting, Steve noted: "The proposed tax cuts will stimulate the economy and increase the tax base. If we don't enact these cuts, businesses will fail or leave, reducing the overall tax base. The current recession is not entirely caused by economic factors, and I hope that the government can propose short-term emergency measures to prevent further economic deterioration and to restore corporate confidence."

At a later plenary meeting, Steve said: "Temporary tax cuts are expected to increase investment, increase consumption and taxation, stimulate the economy, and restore people's confidence."

The proposal to halve the land value tax was later promulgated by the Legislative Yuan and signed into law by President Chen on January 30.

News reports at the time said that, with the new law, "anyone who transfers land ownership within two years will be eligible for a 50% reduction in transfer taxes. The purpose of the amendment is to promote economic development, but the extent to which it will do so is currently unknown, though the measure is a clear benefit to those transferring land title."

However, the passage of the law quickly brought results. In March, just two months after the passage of the new law, Rui Hsieh-ming, associate professor at the National Open University published two articles noting that the tax reduction had boosted real estate transactions by over 50 percent over the previous year, and this had been accompanied by a gradual recovery in the stock market, along with commissions and sales for manufacturers and industrial parks. Other hopeful signs included the development of new industrial and science parks and the purchase of an office building by Cathay Life Insurance Corp. for a record NT$1.18 billion.

In August of that year, the Economic Development Committee met again for a two day follow up meeting, chaired by President Chen and attended by the heads of various ministries. Steve spoke at the plenary meeting. He had not prepared a speech but spoke from the heart on matters he had long considered.

"President Chen, today I want to ask you about our national identity," he said. "You ran for president in accordance with the provisions of the Constitution of the Republic of China, and upon your election, you were sworn in according to that Constitution. However, your rhetoric suggests you feel that the Republic of China no longer exists. As the leader of the country, you owe your office to the Constitution of the Republic of China, but now you deny the very existence of this country. This leaves us with a crisis of identity. Where are we going as a nation?"

Years later, recalling this event, he said, "President Chen was sitting in the first row, directly in front of me while I was speaking. After I left the podium, Chen stepped forward to shake my hand." Chen Che-nan, the Deputy Secretary-General of the Presidential

Office, accompanied Steve to his seat and said, "The questions raised in your speech are very important, and the President will answer them. In the future, whether it is a matter of national affairs or personal matters, just come to us directly."

Upon arriving in office, President Chen had urged a re-thinking of previous President Lee Teng-hui's policy of patience in regard to cross-Strait relations. At the urging of local industry, Chen had instead adopted an approach characterized by "active openness and effective management."

When Steve spoke at the cross-Strait group, he pointed out that the "three direct links" should be implemented as soon as possible to further develop cross-Strait relations. This approach had broad support among Taiwan's industrial elite, along with a return to the "1992 Consensus."

Steve addressed the cross-Strait advisory group, mentioning Vice President Annette Lu's opinion that the transfer of funds from Taiwan to China by Taiwanese enterprises was unsustainable, threatening to deplete Taiwan's foreign reserves. Steve felt that Lu was incorrect and called for the government to rationalize relations with China and eliminate chaotic conditions.

These recommendations were gradually adopted and implemented. Many years later, recalling the meeting, Steve marveled at the sweep of change he had witnessed in Taiwan since first arriving there at the age of 24. "It was a process of blood and tears," he said of his active role in Taiwan's emerging prosperity. His deep love of Taiwan brought him great anxiety in the face of Taiwan's deepening economic crisis. "When I spoke to President Chen at the conference, it caused me consternation, but I was completely sincere in my concerns."

Economic Development Advisory Committee member Steve poses with President Chen Shui-bian.

President Chen Shui-bian's formal appointment of Steve to the Economic Development Advisory Committee.

總 統 用 牋

實鼎先生大鑒：為解決當前經濟問題，落實經濟優先政策，

特舉行經濟發展諮詢委員會議，期能匯集各界智慧，研提具

體對策，為國家經濟長遠發展奠定宏規。特函敦請

出任諮詢委員，出席會議，共策嘉謨，無任企幸。耑此，順頌

時綏

陳 水 扁 敬啟

九十年七月十八日

Openly Talking about Cross-Strait Relations at the Great Hall of the People in Beijing

In 1990 Steve was included in a cross-Strait business delegation to Beijing. Coming not long after the June 4 Tiananmen Square crisis, this was a sensitive time. The delegation stayed at the Diaoyutai State Guesthouse, and a banquet was held at Great Hall of the People, and many important leaders were there. Steve spoke to the group about cross-Strait relations. At the time of writing this book, Steve said that his assessment of cross-Strait relations presented to the group in Beijing had proven to have been correct.

The 60 attendees at the banquet included members of the National People's Congress and CPPCC Standing Committee. In his welcoming speech, Yang Side, director of the Office of Taiwan Affairs of the CCP Central Committee noted that China continued to welcome a steady stream of visiting delegations from Taiwan, but that the hospitality was decidedly one-way, with visits from the mainland to Taiwan subject to onerous restrictions, along with additional obstacles placed on journalists from Mainland China working in Taiwan. He also cited China's generosity in offering

Taiwan two pandas but criticized Taiwan's foot-dragging on the offer. While the tone of the speech was relaxed, the subtext was quite hostile, and the Taiwan delegation felt that a strong response was in order, and that it should be presented by Steve.

Taking the podium, he first stressed that this meeting was, in essence, a big family gathering. Speaking calmly and with sincerity, he said, "Today, we are gathered here as overseas Chinese, Taiwanese Chinese, and mainland Chinese - all brothers and sisters in a big family. For us overseas Chinese, coming here has the feeling that a married daughter feels upon returning to her parents' home. None of our delegation are elected leaders or civil servants. I myself am an overseas Chinese and a businessman. We are very concerned about our compatriots in the motherland, so we came to learn. I am very grateful to our hosts for this warm welcome, and I feel that it is rare for so many members of our family to come together and share a meal. This is a time to speak frankly on issues of common concern. If we give offense, it was not intended, and we hope that our comments will be received in the spirit of sincerity and toleration."

He paused for a moment, as applause filled the hall.

"Just now, our host has brought up some aspects of the relationship between Taiwan and the mainland. If you will allow me, I will respond with my personal thoughts."

He noted that exchanges require the clarification of cross-Strait relations, saying that the relationship between the two sides of the Taiwan Strait is not a father-son relationship where the central government controls localities, but rather a sibling relationship. "Our host just said that the relationship between the mainland and Taiwan is unequal and non-reciprocal. I think international relations are about equality and reciprocity. In this context, the meaning of equality and reciprocity is that I offer a concession, and you, out of reciprocity, offer up an equal concession. But brotherhood is about love, not equality. It focuses not on reciprocity, but on mutual assistance. I am able to help you, and I will. You are able to help me, and you will. Brotherhood and international relations are different."

"Taiwan is like a brother who left home and worked hard to build his own fortune and reputation in a free system. This brother has great ambitions. Although he has gone through hardships, he will eventually achieve success. Therefore, one must not underestimate this brother. He has had a successful career and is rich as a result. Today, Taiwan does not come as a supplicant, but out of homesickness. He has been away from his family for too long and has come back to see how he and his family can help each other."

"Cross-Strait non-governmental relations are like a pair of lovers," he continued. "In the early days, they would sneak around secretly, just as people from Taiwan would secretly return to China to visit family, given that Taiwan had not relaxed regulations on family visits. Later, changes in public sentiment prompted the government of the Republic of China to change these regulations, and these gradual changes have improved the relations between people on both sides of the Taiwan Strait."

Steve went on to point out that the mainland had proposed direct talks between the Kuomintang and the Communist Party over cross-Strait issues, but this was a complicated issue in Taiwan as both of these entities had their roots in mainland China, creating suspicion among the people of Taiwan that these talks might not have their best interests at heart. In this regard, in his 1990 inaugural address, Lee Teng-hui recommended the talks proceed not between political parties, but on a government-to-government basis. This is a thorny issue because the mainland side insists that there is only one China, and therefore only one government. Given this impasse, it is too early to begin political negotiations, and our current efforts should be devoted to cultural and economic exchange. These exchanges will help create a relaxed atmosphere, with both governments taking a hands-off approach, allowing for the flowering of trust and affection between the two sides. He went on to discuss the favorable trade and investment terms that mainland China had proposed to encourage Taiwanese investment in the mainland. These policies had been issued by the State Council, not the National People's Congress, and keeping the policy implementation at a lower administration level allowed China latitude to amend the policy at any time, leaving Beijing considerable flexibility.

As for the status of mainland journalists in Taiwan and the panda issue, Steve noted that "Taiwan is a society ruled by law, and everyone, including the president, is subject to formal legal procedures." He raised the example of how Lee Teng-hui had recently convened a national conference, inviting representatives from all walks of life at home and abroad to attend, including Taiwan independence leader Peng Mingmin. Peng had been living in the United States for many years, under threat of arrest and prosecution if he returned to Taiwan. Given President Lee's invitation, reporters asked the Chief Prosecutor of the Taiwan High Court for clarification on the issue. The prosecutor stated clearly that the arrest warrant for Peng remained in effect and that the President did not have the authority to unilaterally dismiss the charges against him. Similarly, Steve noted, while President Lee may welcome reporters who are CCP members to Taiwan to conduct interviews, ROC law holds that the Communist Party is still a rebel group, and CCP members may not legally enter Taiwan. This is a case, he said, of facts on the ground moving too fast for the ROC legal framework to keep pace, and the only legal way for such reporters to visit Taiwan is to first give up their Party membership.

Remembering the scene many years later, Steve recalled, "Taiwan High Court Prosecutor General Chen Han was a good friend of mine. I asked him back then about the similarities of these two cases. How would he have handled the arrival of Peng Mingmin in Taiwan? He replied that he would have been arrested and interrogated upon arrival, and possibly detained for prosecution. I asked him, 'Even though he's a VIP, arriving at the express invitation of the President?' He replied simply by saying that Taiwan's judicial system is independent. It was a similar issue with the pandas. Taiwan's laws still included provisions that prohibited the import of most items from China, which was under a government seen as illegitimate."

In the context of these developments, Steve noted that, "To welcome Taiwanese businessmen to mainland China, two major obstacles need to be removed: first, the rights and interests of Taiwanese businessmen must be protected by law; second, the constant threat of military force must be removed. Cross-Strait ties can't be solved with an abacus or a sword. The real source of tension in cross-Strait relations is China's refusal to preclude the use of force against Taiwan."

At this time, Deputy Director Wang of the Taiwan Affairs Office of the CCP Central Committee stood up and said that the mainland has three prerequisites for using force against Taiwan: foreign invasion, a declaration of Taiwan independence, or internal unrest.

Steve replied, "Deputy Director Wang, I understand that these are the three prerequisites for your use of military force, but most people in the world don't know much about these three conditions. They only know that you will not give up the threat of military force against Taiwan. The general trend of cross-Strait relations should seek peace and mutual prosperity. Why resort to threats of violence? You could change the prevailing tone by inverting your proposition: 'China wants peaceful reunification, and reunification will be achieved by peaceful means unless one of these three conditions occurs, following which we may consider using force as a last resort.' Moreover, the third item of these premises is very vague. What does 'internal unrest' actually mean? Taiwan is emerging as a pluralistic and democratic society, where people may express emphatic opinions on anything, and often take to the streets in protests which lead to clashes with police. Is this 'internal unrest' that would justify force by mainland China? Proceedings in Taiwan's Legislative Yuan often erupt into fist fights. Is this 'internal unrest'?"

He went on to question the guarantees provided in the trade and investment concessions made to Taiwanese businessmen, encouraging his hosts to put these measures on a more permanent and legally robust footing. He raised the example of the Shanghai Pudong Development Zone, the largest industrial development zone in the mainland, noting that investors are only guaranteed usage rights, but not ownership rights, and that even then, the price of land is more than double that of comparable locations in Taiwan. He criticized the opacity of pricing policies. Upon hearing this, Gu Mu, who served as the deputy prime minister in charge of economic affairs, immediately asked his secretary to call Shanghai to inquire about Steve's allegations. By the time Steve had finished speaking, Gu Mu had already received a reply from Shanghai, and told Steve, "This is indeed the case, and it really needs improvement."

Steve also analyzed the evolution of Taiwan's cross-Strait policy. "For more than 40 years, Taiwan had been preparing to counterattack and retake the mainland. Today, Taiwan's military posture is entirely defensive in nature, and focuses on reunification through peaceful means based on the Three People's Principles. Whereas the former president Chiang Ching-kuo had insisted on a hardline approach of "no contact, no negotiation, and no compromise" with the mainland, his successor President Lee Tung-hui had recently declared that the Republic of China is willing to negotiate with the CCP as the government of an economically and politically free China. This represents an historic turning point, that amply demonstrates Taiwan's sincerity. With that, he closed his remarks to thunderous applause.

Gu Mu took to the podium to say, "Recent years have seen a

great expansion in cross-Strait exchanges, along with delegations of visiting legislators, each of which comes speaking in very pleasant but circumspect language. This evening, Mr. Tsai has spoken very plainly and meaningfully on a very sensitive topic." Gu expressed his appreciation for Steve's straightforwardness and urged everyone at the meeting to keep his words in mind as they moved forward.

2008: Chen Yunlin, chairman of the Association for Relations Across the Taiwan Straits meets Steve at Taipei's Grand Hotel on the occasion of the first such high-level delegation to visit Taiwan from mainland China.

{{ Part 4: Beginning of Trustworthiness }}
Chapter Ten

Recalling Highlights of a Career in Journalism

Small Stories about Important People

Steve left the mainland for Taiwan at the age of 24. He not only witnessed and participated in the era of Taiwan's economic miracle from its beginning during the difficult postwar years, but also, as the special correspondent in Taiwan for the Philippine Overseas Chinese Newspaper for more than 20 years, interviewed many influential people, both Chinese and foreigners, documenting Taiwan's remarkable transition and development in a long journalistic career. While the actions of these influential people have long since been published in news articles or dispatches, some interesting tidbits related to these people have left many unforgettable memories for Steve during his journalistic career.

Two Heroes of World War II Meet in Taipei

On June 18, 1960, US President Dwight Eisenhower became the first American president to visit Taiwan. He was greeted at the airport by ROC President Chiang Kai-shek, commander of the Allied Chinese Theater in World War II. Photos from the day show a young man standing between the two presidents, identified in the photo captions as "Steve Tsai." None was more surprised by this

June 18, 1960: US President Dwight Eisenhower is welcomed at Taipei's Songshan Airport by President Chiang Kai-shek. Visible between the two historical figures is journalist Steve, standing next to White House spokesman James C. Hagerty.

1953: Steve (far right) with Philippine overseas Chinese community leaders Wang Chin (far left) and Tsai Ping-hsuen, on the occasion of President Chiang's birthday.

President Chiang meets with General Douglas MacArthur at Taipei's Songshan Airport. The Korean War broke out on June 25, 1950. Two days later, US President Truman ordered the US 7th Fleet into the Taiwan Strait, with MacArthur visiting Taiwan on July 31. President Chiang met the general at the airport. After resting at the Yangming Guest House, the two leaders co-hosted a joint military strategy session. His mission accomplished, General MacArthur left the following day for occupied Japan. In 1960, General Dwight Eisenhower, then US president, arrived in Taiwan. These three legendary figures of World War II met in Taipei at key moments, exerting a great impact on future events.

than Steve himself, catching sight of his face on the front pages of the next day's newspapers.

Is This Garment Cool?

Each October, on President Chiang Kai-shek's birthday, overseas Chinese delegations would come to Taiwan from all over the world to wish him well, including overseas Chinese in the Philippines. Usually, the celebration would also include Madame Chiang, and Chiang Ching-kuo over dinner or tea. Steve had covered such events involving President Chiang many times in the Presidential Palace or in Taipei's Zhongshan Hall.

On one such occasion, the President's mood, usually very formal and serious, was rather cheerful and relaxed. The members of the Philippine delegation were wearing a traditional Philippine garment of linen, better suited to the humid tropical climate of the Philippines than western suits, and that were considered appropriate for formal occasions. During the course of the meeting, the President suddenly reached out and touched the fabric of his visitor's clothing asking curiously, "Is this garment cool?" but given his Ningbo accent, the visitors misunderstood him as suggesting that the garment had "only cost two yuan" and replied that actually it was rather expensive and cost several hundred yuan. Surprisingly for someone usually so stern and formal, President Chiang found the misunderstanding to be amusing, and they all laughed together.

Mahjong and Bridge

At another such birthday, many reporters were gathered at the scene. Normally, the President would have a speech prepared in advance, but on this day he spoke extemporaneously. Steve recalled him saying that Chinese people are smarter than foreigners but are unable to work together to a common purpose. As an example, he recalled a foreign friend telling him: "Chinese people are good at mahjong, but not good at bridge." His point was that mahjong rewards offense and defense, improving one's own chances of winning by denying opportunities to one's opponents, whereas bridge requires tacit understanding and mutual trust.

Chiang Ching-kuo Delivers Fruit to Beitou

In the early 1950s, four overseas basketball teams from the Philippines came to Taiwan to compete with Taiwanese teams and raise funds for the Tri-Service Stadium. All of the teams stayed together at a hotel in Beitou. One night, Steve and his cousin Tsai Shixiang, who had come as the teams' chaperone and leader, received a call from the security guard at the hotel's main gate, informing them that a VIP had come to visit. The two immediately went downstairs only to find an unexpected visitor: Chiang Ching-kuo, Director of the General Political Department of the Ministry of National Defense, had made a special trip to bring the players oranges from Mt. Yangming and to welcome the players.

Tsai Shixiang felt obliged to acknowledge the gift in kind. He quickly patched through a call to the Philippines, asking his friends to immediately send baskets of famous Philippine mangoes. Once the mangoes arrived, the two Tsai cousins personally delivered them to Chiang's official residence in Taipei, thus initiating a sort of "fruit diplomacy" between the Republic of China and the Philippines.

Chiang Wei-kuo's Secret Bridal Chamber

Steve had visited General Chiang Wei-kuo many times, mainly to talk about military training. At that time, Chiang served as Commander of the Armored Corps, and later also served as the President of the Tri-Service University and Director of the Joint Combat Training Department. Steve recalled that Chiang had received training in many of the world's most elite military schools in Europe and the United States, as his father was preparing him for a key role in the ROC military.

Chiang Wei-kuo married Shi Ching-yi in 1944, but she died during childbirth in 1953. In 1957, Chiang secretly married Chiu Ru-hsue in Japan. While the Taiwan press had been tipped off to the event, there were no interviews as no one knew where he was.

General Chiang Wei-kuo

At that time, Hu Wei-ke, deputy director of the General Political Department of the Ministry of National Defense, was also a good friend of Chiang's. After Chiang and Chiu returned to Taiwan, Steve and Hu visited them in downtown Taipei, at a house where they were "on their honeymoon." "Wei-kuo is more relaxed and personable," recalled Steve. "He likes to tell off-color jokes, in stark contrast to Chiang Ching-kuo, who is always very serious." Even as reporters from around Taiwan were seeking out the newlyweds for a scoop, Steve was visiting them in his capacity as a friend and kept the account to himself.

Hu Shih, Hu Shih?

On April 8, 1958, the 68-year-old Hu Shih flew from the United States to Taipei Songshan Airport. His son Hu Tsu-wang and grandson Hu Fu came to meet him at the airport, along with a crowd of more than 500 ROC dignitaries, showing rare deference for a scholar.

As a reporter, Steve interviewed Hu Shih at the residence of National Taiwan University President Chien Shih-liang on Fuzhou Street, Taipei. He asked Hu Shih about his views on freedom and democracy, his plans for his life in Taiwan and the prospects for the future development of academics in Taiwan.

Hu Shih told Steve that he had not come back to retire and would continue to serve the nation and people as long as he is needed and able. He emphasized the need for real freedom and democracy, and the importance of academic freedom.

Steve's interview of Hu Shih was published in the weekly magazine of the Philippines Xinmin Daily News. The article title was "Hu Shih, Hu Shih?" The Chinese characters for the first "Hu Shih" and the second "Hu Shih" were identical. The first "Hu Shih" refers to the person "Hu Shih." The second "Hu Shih" carries the meaning "Where are you going?"

The following day, Hu Shih was sworn in as the Dean of the Academia Sinica, with President Chiang Kai-shek delivering congratulatory remarks, and with political figures such as Chen Cheng and Chang Chun attending, and Steve on hand to record the events.

Li-Fu Chen Sees Greatness in Little Things

One year, Li-Fu Chen's son returned to Taiwan from the United States and rented Steve's house in Tianmu. Steve did not meet the young man at the time, handling the three-year lease through a lawyer. However, he only stayed one year before leaving Taiwan. Li-Fu Chen wrote to Steve to apologize for the inconvenience caused, saying he would continue to pay the rent in accordance with the lease. Given Chen's high status and professional importance, Steve was impressed that he had taken the time to personally attend to the matter. He replied to thank him for his concern, but to please not trouble himself, as Steve could simply find another tenant.

Chen replied that he was touched by Steve's generosity, but he insisted that he was bound by honor to adhere to the contract. Chen, who was well-known for his calligraphy, also provided Steve with his own calligraphic works several times, including more than one hand-written scroll that was used as the master for two large wooden plaques that were respectively mounted

Li-Fu Chen

at Steve's ancestral home and at a public office

important to Steve.

O.K. Yui Respects Everyone

Steve once interviewed O.K. Yui, Premier of the Executive Yuan. Steve asked, "You are the Premier, and you have a strong public reputation for kindness and wisdom and have enjoyed great personal and professional success. How have you achieved these things?"

Yui protested modestly but said that he felt the highest human principle is to treat everyone you meet with respect. Even beggars have their self-esteem and are entitled to respect. Even a judge presiding over a criminal trial owes due deference to the defendant. Respect everyone, and you will be respected by everyone, and have friends everywhere.

Prior to the KMT's retreat to Taiwan, Yui had served as Minister of Finance and President of the Central Bank. Later, in Taiwan, he served as chairman of the Bank of Communications, the Farmers Bank of China, the Bank of Taiwan, and chairman of the Taiwan Provincial Government and concurrently as the commander of the Taiwan Provincial Security Command. From 1954 to 1958, he served as the Premier of the Executive Yuan, and then again as the President of the Central Bank.

Yan Hsi-shan Talks About Right and Wrong

Steve said, "I am very grateful for my time as a journalist; it helped me learn a lot. If I could do it all over again, I would again choose to be a journalist. This was an excellent career that exposed me to all kinds of people with very different life experiences. To be a good journalist, you must realize that your work could have a strong impact on society, so you must also have a strong sense of fairness and ethics. The journalist must collect the required relevant information, interview all the people involved, and analyze

General Yan Hsi-shan

Calligraphy presented by General Yan Hsi-shan to Steve.

the information to clearly depict the facts without fear or favor. However, a journalist is not a judge."

Steve once interviewed Yan Hsi-shan, the first Premier of the Executive Yuan and Minister of Defense after the Republic of China government moved to Taiwan.

Yan had commanded KMT forces against the CCP at the Battle of Taiyuan in Shanxi, one of the most famous military engagements of the Chinese Civil War. Later, in Taiwan, the government ordered a monument erected to commemorate the event.

Yan was erudite and talented, the author of two influential books arguing against Communism.

During their interview, Yan took the initiative to ask Steve about his work as a journalist and how he approached his responsibility to reporting the news. Steve replied in line with what you can see in the paragraph above. Yan was very pleased with Steve's responses and wrote a calligraphic scroll for him as follows: "Amongst men, matters of right and wrong should be clear to all, but paradoxes abound. There is a duty in journalism to put in extra effort when facing these paradoxes, and to pay careful attention to achieving long-lasting peace and harmony." Steve always cherished this scroll, and it not only hung on the wall of his home in Taipei for many years, but he committed it to memory and often quoted it to his journalistic colleagues.

Lee Teng-hui Attempts to Change Opinions over Tea

After being elected as the chairman of the Construction Managers Association of the Republic of China, Steve visited President Lee Teng-hui to discuss regulations affecting the construction industry.

On September 14, 1999, Lee had proposed at the National Executive Conference that Taiwanese enterprises should exercise restraint and patience when investing in mainland China. Upon learning that these comments were not well received among Taiwan's construction industry, Lee invited Steve and other industrial leaders to the Presidential Palace for tea, hoping to bridge their differences.

"Lee was very thoughtful and attentive to his guests, personally pouring us tea and serving us snacks. The conversation was very polite and deferential, with Lee asking for our input on national policy. The meeting had been arranged through mutual friends; and, based on the cordial exchange, President Lee was left with the impression that he had successfully brought us around to his point of view. However, while we had treated the head of state with due courtesy and respect, we were quite firm in our position."

Steve's assessment of Lee included praise and criticism.

"He was very successful as the Governor of Taiwan Province and had made considerable improvements on his predecessors in terms

of government effectiveness and intragovernmental communication. But he used his position as KMT Chairman to undermine the KMT, thus earning the contempt of many people."

2001: Steve meets President Lee Teng-hui.

The Three Shens

As a journalist, Steve was in frequent contact with the government's official spokesmen. Three of the earliest happened to be surnamed Shen: Shen Chang-huan, James Shen, and Shen Chi. Beyond their surname, the three also shared similar career trajectories. All had previously served as personal secretary and government spokesperson for President Chiang Kai-shek and were then transferred to important positions in the Ministry of Foreign Affairs. Shen Chang-huan had been the Minister of Foreign Affairs, while James Shen was Ambassador to the United States, and Shen Chi was the representative to Germany. When Shen Chang-huan served as spokesman, the Central News Agency had not yet been established, so he performed his duties from the government spokesperson's office. A man of great personal force and little patience for delicacy, as Minister of Foreign Affairs he was famous for his dramatic facial expressions and expressive body language, sometimes biting his lower lip to show resolve and speaking with great force.

In contrast, Shen spoke cautiously and calmly and was quite urbane. Steve lived in San Francisco at the time and had frequent contacts with the playwright Shen Yue, Ambassador Shen's daughter, and her husband Hsu Ta-lin, known as the father of the Asian venture capital industry.

Of the three, Shen Chi was the most gentle and elegant, with a highly personable manner similar to a university professor.

Steve said, "The three had all previously served as the English secretary for President Chiang, so they were not only highly fluent in Chinese and English but were also very loyal."

"At that time, the situation across the Taiwan Strait had changed a lot, and the relationship between Taiwan and the United States was uncertain. The 'Three Shens' were the president's closest staffers and were key players in nearly half a century of cross-Strait affairs and Taiwan's international diplomacy." These three men knew the inside details of many important events, but always kept what they knew to themselves.

In 1958, a terrible artillery battle exploded over Kinmen. Hundreds of journalists from around the world gathered in Taipei and requested permission to go to the front lines, including Steve. Shen Chi, director of press affairs at the time, called a press conference, after which he privately told Steve that visiting Kinmen would be very dangerous, and urged him to consider his own safety and retract his application. Many years later, both Tsai and Shen were living in the San Francisco Bay Area, and continued their friendship, with Steve inviting Shen Chi and his wife to attend the 20th anniversary of the opening of his hotel. Looking back, he expressed his heartfelt gratitude for Shen's sincere concern for his safety so many years before.

Hu Wei-ke Publishes the 25-Volume History

Hu Wei-ke was a vigorous general who later became a fighter for defending Chinese culture, and this story also became involved with Taipei politics.

Born to a Chinese father and a British mother, Hu was handsome and fluent in both Chinese and English. In his youth, he was practically a member of the Chiang family, and treated Chiang Ching-kuo and Wei-kuo as brothers. In the Mainland, he served as Dean of the R.O.C. Air Force Academy in Jianqiao, Hangzhou.

On January 21, 1948, the day after announcing his resignation in Nanjing, President Chiang Kai-shek went to Hangzhou and spent the night at the Air Force Academy where General Hu Wei-ke was in charge.

When Steve met Hu, he was serving as deputy director of the General Political Department of the Ministry of National Defense and was also deputy to Chiang Ching-kuo, in which capacity he heavily promoted the development of sports in military training.

Hu's wife, Lee Mu-lan was an Indonesian overseas Chinese who indulged her love of orchids in her garden on Taipei's Yunhe Street. Mrs. Hu had led the Ministry of National Defense's Liangyou women's basketball team to visit the Philippines. The story goes

December 6, 1950: Chiang Ching-kuo and Hu Wei-ke attend the graduation ceremony for the 5th Political Cadre Class.

1966: Vice Minister of National Defense and former Air Force Academy President Hu Wei-ke worked to republish a 25-volume history of China to preserve Chinese history and culture, appointing Steve to the editorial committee, responsible for overseas distribution.

that Hu Wei-ke and Chiang Ching-kuo had a disagreement and Hu decided to resign from being Chiang's deputy.

One day, Steve and General Hu and his wife were drinking tea and chatting in the Hu's orchid garden when Chiang Ching-kuo and his wife came to visit. Chiang urged Hu to stay at his current position, but Hu insisted on resigning, and was later appointed as the director of the Ministry of Defense Planning Bureau.

At that time, mainland China was in the throes of the Great Cultural Revolution, which devastated traditional Chinese culture there.

Hu Wei-ke was deeply saddened by these events and resolved to do what he could to protect and promote Chinese culture.

Hu Wei-ke submitted a proposal to republish the 25-Volume History of China. With approval from President Chiang, funds were raised to have the collection photocopied and published by the Taipei Publication Office for distribution at home and abroad. Hu served as chief editor and coordinator, with Steve recruited to be an advisor at the publication office in charge of overseas marketing.

There Goes Chiang Kai-shek, and also My Bible

On July 10, 1949, President Chiang Kai-shek visited the Philippines in his capacity as leader of the Kuomintang, marking his first overseas trip, for a conference held at the summer resort of Baguio. Chiang was a Christian and was in the habit of reading the bible and praying every morning and evening. While in Baguio, his bible went missing, and Ambassador Chen Chih-ping immediately arranged to borrow a bible from the famous Philippine newspaperman and the president of Xinmin Daily News, Wu Chong-sheng, who was also a leader of the local Christian community.

When the conference ended on July 12, Chiang and his entourage flew out for Taiwan. Watching the plane take off from the balcony of his Baguio home, Wu Chong-sheng commented to his wife, "There goes Chiang Kai-shek, and also my bible."

At just that moment, the doorbell rang, and a well-dressed diplomat who claimed to represent the Republic of China in the Philippines respectfully handed Wu a letter of thanks from the President along with the missing bible.

Wu only visited Taiwan for the first time in 1961 for a meeting of prominent newspapermen. Speaking at a briefing organized by the Central News Agency, he recalled the story of his "flying bible" and suggested that the tale vividly showed the character of President Chiang and his attention to detail.

The Three Directors of the Judicial
Yuan Whom I Know

*Steve had interactions with Lin Yang-kang, Lai Ying-chao, and Lai
Hao-min. What these three men have in common is that they were all
once the head of the ROC Judicial Yuan.*

Ah-Gang Bo's Legendary Capacity for Drink

Taiwanese political leader Lin Yang-kang was affectionately called
Ah-Gang Bo. He had served as the mayor of Taipei, the chairman of
the Taiwan Provincial Government, the Minister of the Interior, the
Vice President of the Executive Yuan, and Chief Justice of the High
Court (April 17, 1987 to September 1, 1994). One evening during his
tenure at the Taiwan Provincial Government, Lin invited Steve to
his official residence in Taichung's Chunghsing New Village with
the director of the American Institute in Taiwan also in attendance.
Steve took the train to Taichung's Yuanlin Station, where Lin sent
a car to meet him. That evening, the wine flowed freely, and Steve
surprised his host with his ability to keep up with the drinking.

Years later, Steve was serving as Managing Director of the
National Builder's Society and was scheduled to deliver the keynote
at their Society's annual meeting. Before he went on stage, Lin Yang-
kang took him aside and reminded him of that evening at his home

long ago. Lin noted how surprised he had been at Steve's capacity for drinking. "How did you do it," he asked. "What's your secret?"

Steve replied "Knowing your reputation, before I accepted your invitation, I consulted with an expert on how to hold my liquor better. He told me that, when I first arrived at the station, I should eat one or two bawan (dough made of sweet potato starch filled with a savory stuffing). This would leave an oily lining in my stomach, helping me stay sober longer." Lin was so delighted with the story that he later recounted it to the entire meeting before delivering his own speech, bringing howls of laughter from the assembled guests.

Steve remembered Lin as being very cultivated and approachable, and possessing a remarkable memory, allowing him to remember the names of everyone he met. He was rightly famous for his love of good wine but, after taking up his political career, he quietly cut back on his drinking, though going to great lengths to disguise his temperance, including using a special thick-walled glass to give the appearance that his glass held more wine than it actually did. In this way, he could regularly drain his glass in honor of his guests without becoming drunk.

Eventually, the winds of political change caught up with Lin, and he was forced out of public life by Lee Teng-hui. But this did not dim his love of life, and Steve found him in good spirits when he visited.

Recalling his visits with Lin Yang-kang, Steve said emotionally, "If Lin Yang-kang had become president instead of Lee Teng-hui, history would have turned out very differently. The KMT wouldn't be in the mess it is now, the younger generation would have stayed within the party and you wouldn't have had Lee Teng-hui sparking infighting within the party. Lin Yang-kang's kind-heartedness and excellent character would have informed his presidency, and thus Taiwan, and you might not have the blue-green antagonism that plagues Taiwan today."

Lai Ying-chao Loves to Sing "Orchid Grass"

Following the 1979 break in diplomatic relations between Taiwan and the United States, the ROC Chamber of Commerce sent a delegation to Europe to promote trade and economic diplomacy. Lai Ying-chao, with a JD from Harvard University, wound up working in the Ministry of Finance and joined the delegation as a consultant for three weeks. The whole delegation worked intensively every day, building deep friendships.

"He was a very accomplished young man with a deep legal understanding, a high-ranking official but one who carried himself with deep kindness and humility."

After the delegation returned to Taipei, everyone was very busy. Lai Ying-chao was taken on as Deputy Provincial Governor under James Soong, and later became Director of the Judicial Yuan. These increased responsibilities left little time for the old friends to meet.

Steve had served as the executive director of the Republic of China Arbitration Association for nearly two decades, and Lai was occasionally invited to attend the Association's annual meeting as a guest speaker, with the dinner often followed by karaoke, at which Lai, a native of Yilan ("lan" means "orchid"), would sing "Orchid Grass".

Lai Hao-min Helped Me Win a Lawsuit

The barrister Lai Hao-min, who graduated from National Taiwan University and the University of Tokyo, was a founding partner of the Wanguo Law Firm, in which capacity he was Steve's legal counsel. In 1995, in a case regarding an OCBC loan to Liang Pai-hsun, the chairman and the managing director were sued for breach of trust. Steve asked Lai Hao-min to help him defend the case, which went on for several years.

The facts of the case were confusing and unfavorable for the defendant, and some defendants resorted to questionable tactics. Lai solemnly told Steve, "You must not ask anyone to engage in any improper activities, otherwise I cannot be your lawyer. I understand that you are innocent, and I believe the law will eventually find in your favor."

"I asked Lai Hao-min to be my lawyer. He told me to stick to the law and not to seek out unofficial assistance."

"Every time he spoke on my behalf in court, his arguments were clear and powerful, and were widely admired."

In the end, Liang Pai-hsun was found guilty and imprisoned, but OCBC Chairman Tsai Shao-hua and Managing Director Steve were both exonerated.

During Chen Shui-bian's presidency, Lai Hao-min was appointed to the Central Election Commission. He exercised his duties in accordance with his professional principles and personal integrity and developed a reputation among the public for fairness and probity. As a result, when Ma Ying-jeou became president, he was promoted to the chairmanship of the Central Election Commission.

"I had just come back to Taipei from the United States and called him to congratulate him on his appointment. I visited him at his office and, when I was leaving, I mentioned that I was glad that President Ma had recognized his abilities, but that he really should have appointed you as Chief Justice. It was just an idle comment, and it never occurred to me that the appointment would actually take place a year later."

"Mr. Lai combines a keen legal mind with enthusiasm and deep kindness. He knows no fear or favor in executing the law, not favoring one political party over another."

Post-War Sino-Philippine Diplomatic Relations

— An Evaluation of Three Ambassadors: Chen Chih-ping, Chou Shu-kai, Chen Chih-mai —

In the early post-World War II period, the Republic of China and the Philippines maintained close diplomatic relations, and the Philippines was home to hundreds of thousands of patriotic overseas Chinese who supported a free motherland. Steve was the Taiwanese correspondent of the Xinmin Daily News, the largest Chinese-language newspaper in the Philippines, and he naturally paid special attention to the relations between the two countries.

Following the end of the civil war, the government of the Republic of China moved to Taiwan and was in dire need of support from the international community. The United States was the ROC's most important global ally, while its most important ally in Southeast Asia was the Philippines, the wealthiest country in Asia at that time.

During this time, Steve wrote a special report in the Xinmin Daily News, commenting on the performance of successive ROC ambassadors to the Philippines after the war.

At the time, nearly every overseas Chinese family in the Philippines had extended family in southern Fujian, which made the Chinese community in the Philippines of interest to Steve.

Steve spoke highly of Ambassador Chen Chih-ping, believing that he had achieved "practical diplomacy" and reached out to President Chiang Kai-shek after he arrived in Taiwan, and was instrumental in arranging the Baguio Conference at which Chiang discussed anti-Communist strategy with Philippine President Quirino.

When Chen assumed his post in Manila, he brought a well-regarded chef with him to cater informal banquets at the ambassador's residence to entertain President Quirino and other government officials.

This helped establish a deep friendship that facilitated communication between the two countries, as Quirino would frequently visit Chen at the ambassador's residence without going through diplomatic procedures. Before long, Chen began sending his chef to the Presidential Palace to cook for the President.

However, Chen was not warmly welcomed by the overseas Chinese community, which was closer to a later ambassador, Chen Chih-mai. Chen Chih-mai had been transferred to Manila after

Steve (right) interviews ROC ambassador to the Philippines Tuan Mao-lan.

Steve (left) interviews the ROC ambassador to the Philippines Hang Lee-wu about the ROC's withdrawal from the United Nations.

serving in the United States for many years. "The two Chens were very different people. Chen Chih-ping's courtly diplomacy was highly effective for Eastern countries, while Chen Chih-mai's classical diplomacy was appropriate for Western countries."

Chen Chih-mai had served as a professor at Peking University, Tsinghua University and Southwest Associated University. He had also served as ambassador to Australia, New Zealand, Japan and the Holy See. He was deeply talented but had a rather rigid diplomatic style.

As mentioned earlier, the government of the Republic of China was in a very difficult situation, and the Philippines was an important ally of the Republic of China, putting great responsibility on the ambassador.

In Sino-Philippine relations, a key diplomatic point of contention was a 25-year-old case related to Philippine immigration quotas following the end of WWII, limiting inward annual immigration to 500 people per year from China in an attempt to prevent infiltration by Communist spies. In 1949, the Philippines announced that this quota would be cut back to 50 individuals, and later to zero.

Therefore, in the wake of the civil war, many Chinese seeking to reunite with their family members in the Philippines were restricted to visitor visas lasting three to six months and, when they overstayed these visas, they became illegal immigrants. Nearly 3000 such immigrants started new lives in the Philippines, marrying and starting families. They petitioned the government to grant them immigrant status but were refused.

On October 9, 1954, Chen Chih-ping stepped down as ambassador to the Philippines. On December 9, 1955, the new ambassador Chen Chih-mai came to Manila to assume the office. During the 14 months that that the ambassadorship was vacant, the issue of the 3000 illegal immigrants' status was revived, with

Steve and Tina visit Ambassador Macapagal of the Philippines. To the right is Chairman Chiu Han-ping of the Sino-Philippines Friendship Association.

Steve (front left) interviews Philippine President Garcia (front center) during his visit to Taiwan. Tina is at the rear right.

1992: Steve (left) interviews Philippine President Estrada (right).

a Philippine legislator proposing that if they failed to leave the country, they should be flown out on military planes and pushed out with parachutes over Hong Kong or China.

Chargé d'affaires Chou Shu-kai, acting Ambassador, believed humanitarian principles demanded that these visitors be immediately be granted legal status, allowing them to remain in the Philippines with their relatives. The Minister of Foreign Affairs in Taipei, Shen Chang-huan, noted the critical importance of ROC-Philippines relations and that the status of the illegals should be resolved as quickly as possible without damaging diplomatic ties. At that time, pro-Beijing UN member states began making annual proposals to "restore" China's UN seat of the Beijing government, while the Philippine government insisted that the seat should remain with the Republic of China. In Shen's view maintaining the support from the Philippines' UN delegation was of critical importance, and all other matters paled in comparison.

The situation became a diplomatic flashpoint as Philippine legislators sought to exploit the issue for election advantage, accusing the stranded migrants of stealing jobs from Filipinos.

Steve believed that, among previous ambassadors to the Philippines, Chou Shu-kai had the best understanding of the political situation in the Philippines and of the overseas Chinese community. He understood that the domestic politics of the issue in the Philippines was primarily aimed at short-term election advantages and focused on mobilizing a wide network of overseas Chinese leaders to work with the ROC government in lobbying Manila to legalize the immigrants in return for their paying some kind of fine.

Minister of Foreign Affairs Shen Chang-huan reported on the case to the Legislative Yuan in Taipei. In response, Steve published an article in the Xinmin Daily News, presenting a calm and detailed analysis of the issue. He promoted Chou's pragmatic approach, believing that Shen's approach prioritizing the United Nations seat, while understandable in theory, risked further alienating important allies.

Eventually, the illegal immigrants were granted permanent resident status prior to June 1975 when Manila switched diplomatic recognition to Beijing. Eventually, nearly 2000 of the 2745 migrants remained in the Philippines.

Chou Shu-kai later served as ROC ambassador to the United States, Ambassador to the United Nations, and Minister of Foreign Affairs, leading a delegation to attend the UN General Assembly in October 1971. It later fell to him to announce the Republic of China's withdrawal from the UN. Upon his return to Taipei, he was greeted at the airport by President Chiang Ching-kuo. The following year, when Chiang reorganized his cabinet, he appointed Chou to the Council of Political Affairs and, in 1978, he appointed him ambassador to the Holy See, a post he held for the next 13 years, during which Steve frequently visited him when business brought him to Europe.

During Chou's time on the Council of Political Affairs, Steve was very busy with his career and the two had few opportunities to meet. Then one, late one evening in 1991, Steve and his wife were having a late supper at a Yonghe Soy Milk restaurant on Ren'ai Road in Taipei. Suddenly, Chou Shu-kai walked in, and the old friends greeted each other warmly. "Chou seemed to be in good health. We talked for nearly an hour," Steve remembered. The conversation turned to the way in which the Republic of China had left the United Nations, with Steve asking if Chou had any regrets about the way it was handled. "You can reflect on the past, without regrets," Chou said.

Chapter Eleven

Across the Deep Pacific Ocean

Crossing the Ocean for the Children's Education

In 1973, concerned for his children's academic prospects, Steve decided to send them to the United States for their education. Taiwan had created an economic miracle, emerging in a short time as one of the Four Asian Tigers, and making tremendous improvements in its education system all the while. However, education in Taiwan still suffered from many problems. The college entrance examination system imposed a significant hurdle to the pursuit of higher education, with only a small number of university places available to an ever-growing number of aspirants, putting tremendous pressure on high school students.

I Left My Heart in San Francisco

The resulting exam-oriented education system put wealthy families in an unfairly advantageous position as they could hire private tutors to give their children a critical edge over the competition. The area south of Taipei Station became a hub of cram schools dedicated to giving their tuition-paying students a leg up. Under these circumstances, many qualified and intelligent students were excluded from higher education, severely hindering their future professional prospects.

1967: Steve and Tina accompany a group of ROC representatives to the 50th anniversary celebration of the International Lions Club in Chicago.

It was in this context that Steve decided to send his children to the United States for education. He chose the US over other possible destinations (Canada, the UK, France, etc.) because of the deep affinity he had developed for the United States during the War of Resistance against the Japanese. "The United States and the Chinese fought side by side during Second World War and defeated Japan," he said. "After the end of the war, the United States enjoyed tremendous global prestige and respect."

In addition, the United States was not only the world's most advanced country in terms of science and technology, but also in terms of business education, which held special appeal to a man of commerce such as himself.

Why San Francisco? In 1967, Steve and his wife had accompanied a ROC Lions Club delegation to Chicago to celebrate that organization's 50th anniversary. At that time, the Tsai family had many friends in New York and Los Angeles, but most of their friends were in San Francisco.

There are also geographical considerations. "New York is too far away from Taiwan. San Francisco is the gateway to the east from the United States. From Taiwan to the United States, you will reach

San Francisco in one stop. If you go to New York, it's an extra five or six hours by plane. Also, I like San Francisco. San Francisco has mountains and lovely ocean views. It's a relatively small city, and it is easy to find people. The weather is also better, the east is too cold. The air quality in San Francisco is excellent. Los Angeles is too big, and the climate and air are not as good as Northern California, so I chose San Francisco."

Steve with his eldest daughter, Tenny.

Steve, Tina, and their four children together in Taipei.

Steve, Tina, and their four children.

Steve's four children when they were young.

He decided to move the whole family to San Francisco to keep them all together. "Young international students are in a bad situation," he said. "Many families in Taiwan would send their children to the United States when they are teenagers - it's too young an age for them to be on their own. The environment in the United States is too free. These students arrived like immature trees being transplanted in unfamiliar soil. Their roots aren't set deep enough and its easy for them to fall over."

In 1973, Steve's eldest daughter Tenny was studying at Chinese Culture University in Taipei, while his second daughter Elizabeth had just graduated from Taipei American School, and his son Solomon was studying at St. Stephen's College in Hong Kong. At the age of 13, Solomon transferred to a high school in the United States where he acclimated easily due to his intensive training in English in Hong Kong. The headmaster at St. Stephens was British, and Solomon did not return to Taiwan for his school breaks, rather staying with the headmaster in Hong Kong. The youngest daughter Vivien was studying at Taiwan's Sacred Heart Girls High School.

At Chinese Culture University, Tenny had studied biology, and later transferred to the University of California San Francisco where she continued in biology. She also studied computer science. However, she found her greatest interest was in real estate, and has since made a successful career. Upon arriving in the US, Elizabeth studied at San Francisco State University and Syracuse University, studying marketing and management. In 1999, she completed her EMBA at Stanford University, and has spent the majority of her career managing the Tsai family hotel business. Solomon completed middle school in Hong Kong, and then attended Washington High School in San Francisco. He then went on to SFSU where he studied finance for two years, and then transferred to Syracuse to study finance and marketing, later joining the family firm to manage the hotels as COO. Vivian first studied art at SFSU, and then took a master's degree in accounting before studying for a year at Harvard

University's Kennedy School of Government. She also ended up working in real estate. The Tsai family children thus emerged from school ready to take on the business world, in no small measure due to the careful guidance of their father. After graduating from college, at his father's advice, Solomon pursued a career first in banking and then in insurance.

Family MBA Training Program

"To do business, it's best to start in finance because every businessman needs access to capital. It also provides a professional environment which is conducive to developing close relationships with all kinds of businessmen through developing a detailed understanding of their businesses. Therefore, finance is the best entry into the industrial and commercial sector."

"First, you will develop a good understanding of the characteristics and trends of various industries along with a clear picture of their changes over time. Second, you will meet many different kinds of people, make friends from all walks of life, broaden your knowledge, and build a foundation for future entrepreneurship. Third, financial institutions have to watch their accounts very closely. If the books are off by fifty cents at the end of the day, everyone has to stay behind until it's accounted for. This provides excellent training for business."

"So, what you need to do in business is to grasp market changes, make useful connections, and learn to work with caution. With these things, you have laid the foundation for success."

Early on, Steve began a special course of education for his children, which he humorously referred to as an "MBA training program." At the time, the children were still small. During the day, Steve was outside conducting business and, when he came home, he would have extensive discussions with his children about the events of the day. With his children seated around him in the living room he would ask them, "What are the main considerations in this business situation? To make a decision, there are two or three options to consider, but I don't know which one is the best. I would also tell my children how to approach such a decision. Then I'd give them two or three days to consider, and then come back with their thoughts or suggestions. For example, I'd talk to them about developing shopping malls and help them understand the background of such developments and teach them how to make relevant decisions. They'd come back with a recommendation to go ahead or withdraw from the deal and explain their reasoning."

Imagine if you will: several kids, sitting on small stools in the living room, listening to their father, "attending a class." This may have been the only program of its kind in the world.

His daughter Vivien remembered these lessons well: "I was the best behaved - my older brother and sisters would get fidgety, but I always appreciated my father taking the effort to talk to us about these things. Even though I really didn't understand what he was talking about, I enjoyed having his attention, so I made sure to make him feel like I was paying close attention."

Steve's philosophy for his children's education was as follows: First, they should have a strong foundational understanding in Chinese culture. Thus, it was best for them to graduate from a university in Taiwan, or at least to finish high school before going abroad for college. Children should only go abroad for education at a younger age as a last resort or due to special circumstances. Second, children should be sent to study abroad to pursue personal and professional development and to learn innovation skills and be exposed to new ideas. Third, make it your goal to integrate into Western society, cultivate in yourself a good civic education, and base your life on inherently peaceful and benevolent Chinese ethics. In short, Steve emphasized that a basic moral education rooted in Chinese culture will help develop a strong foundation, while professional education in American universities is good for professional development. The combination of Chinese and Western education will provide a unique advantage for Chinese students.

The Tsai family opened a trading company in San Francisco located in the World Trade Center near the Embarcadero. They also purchased a home at the same time.

However, Steve's professional focus at the time was still on Taiwan. After setting up his family in the United States, he did not stay, but rather returned to Taiwan to continue his financial and real estate businesses and volunteered to serve as the standing supervisor and director of a business organization, while his wife stayed in the United States to look after the children. This marked a new chapter in his family's life.

I left my heart in San Francisco.

Establishing a Hotel Group in the United States

Solomon recalls the day of March 25, 1976. He was representing his father Steve in purchasing the Best Western Hotel in San Mateo outside of San Francisco. This was the Tsai family's first hotel purchase in the United States, but as of the writing of this book in 2014, the Tsai family have expanded their holdings to include a total of six hotels, with the group's flagship Crowne Plaza Hotel located in Foster City near San Francisco International Airport. At the time of the purchase, this property had been a Holiday Inn, but was upgraded by the subsequent renovation and expansion.

Crossing the River by Feeling the Stones

In 1976 when Solomon closed the Best Western deal, he was still a high school student. Today, he manages many of the family's hotels and has served as the director of two major international hotel chains. He spent six years as a director for the Hilton Garden Inn Company, and eight years on the board of Holiday Inn.

Steve noted that having his young son handle these important business contracts on behalf of the family was designed to integrate him into the family operations as early as possible. Steve said, "We wanted to get him experience early on in buying real estate and managing real estate."

When the Tsai family immigrated to the United States, they mainly operated through trading companies, focused on importing Christmas lights and other products to the United States. However, the family's most successful ventures in the US have been their hotels.

Steve's business experience in the United States left him with a great deal of respect for the business practices and foreign trade strengths of the American Jewish community. In the face of this community's united front, it was difficult for outsiders to make solid inroads. "We have to know both ourselves and our adversaries clearly," he said. Facing a losing battle, he knew when to retreat from imports and focus his attention on real estate and hotels, capitalizing on his experience in Taiwan. His real estate experience extended from building his own house in Taipei to building that city's Hilton Hotel and developing commercial and residential properties. "I had a strong foundation in real estate in Taiwan, and hotels are a kind of real estate business with high cash flow."

Steve saw hotel development as a means of raising the value of entire areas. Hotels not only bring in visitors and income, but also provide employment opportunities and outsourcing to other businesses. A critical mass of quality hotels to attract domestic and foreign visitors can spur local industrial and commercial development and increase government revenue, thus many local and regional economic development plans often prioritize the development of new hotels.

From 1983 to 1986, Steve brought Solomon back to Taiwan to learn how to operate his businesses. Solomon served as a board member of the OCBC Bank, a board member of the Qiaofu Construction Management Company, and as an assistant manager in a property management company, serving under his father. Through these positions, Solomon accumulated useful experience at a time when Taiwanese politics was in turmoil. "When I left Taiwan in 1986 to return to the United States, I suggested to my father that we move forward by specializing in one industry. As it was, our efforts were spread out among different enterprises, but focusing on one particular business will bring greater chance of growth and success."

Solomon had bought the family's first hotel property in San Mateo seven years earlier. Part of the reason to buy an American business had been the foreign exchange controls in place in Taiwan at the time, forcing emigrants to use underground banks when sending money overseas. The official exchange rate was around NT$40 to US$1, but the rate for these underground banks was closer to NT$45. The fact that the income of an overseas hotel would be sourced overseas was part of the family's motivation to get into business in the United States, as a way of generating income outside of Taiwan, allowing them essentially to "buy a cow and produce their own milk". The hope was that the income from this hotel could cover the family's living expenses in the United States, along with the children's tuition, without having to rely on expensive remittances from Taiwan.

Despite a prime location next to the Marina Food Market and US Highway 101 , the Tsai family's hotel venture was not all smooth sailing at first. Steve's business focus was still on Taiwan at the time, and he had hired an American to serve as general manager. Solomon, meanwhile, was busy at school and, after graduation, he took his father's advice and went to work in banking and insurance, accumulating experience that would benefit him greatly later in life. Hired by Bank of America, he rose quickly from teller to manager.

United Pacific Hotel Group

While their family owns many hotels, the Tsai family children have each personally worked their way up through the business, starting from working at the front desk, carrying guest luggage, and housekeeping, up through managing food and beverage operations and finances. This experience has given each of them complete and rounded education in the hotel business.

Starting from the San Mateo property, the Tsai family's business operations gradually shifted to focus on the hospitality industry. In 1990 they bought the Foster City Holiday Inn. That year, Steve and his wife were in Hong Kong when they received a phone call from Tenny. Through unofficial market channels, she had learned that the newly constructed Holiday Inn in Foster City was for sale. Without hesitation, Steve told Tenny and Solomon to buy the property. Despite being thousands of miles away, Steve was absolutely confident in buying the property sight-unseen because he understood the inherent value of the hotel, due to its prime location at the intersection of the US 101 and California SR 92 highways, making it easily accessible to and from all directions, and only a ten-minute drive from San Francisco International Airport.

Tenny took charge, skillfully negotiating the purchase of the Holiday Inn, while Steve established the United Pacific Hotel Group, with himself as Chairman. The hotel at the time only had 240 high-end guest rooms. In 1996, the Tsai family added another 120 guest rooms. The expansion was completed in 1999, increasing the hotel's capacity by 50%, making it the largest hotel in Foster City up through the writing of this book.

This expansion proved well-timed as the US economy was

Steve and Tina at their Holiday Inn prior to its expansion and upgrading to a Crowne Plaza.

still in the process of recovering from the recession caused by the 1991 Gulf War and the resulting oil price spike. Solomon said: "I started the process of applying to expand the hotel in 1996 and spent two years getting the necessary approvals. Construction started in 1998 and was completed within one year. In 1999, we had added 120 new rooms and the expansion investment was earned back within a single year of full operations. In fact, most of our hotel properties earned back their purchases prices within a year to 18 months of operations. These kinds of margins are almost unheard of in the hotel industry." How was this achieved? Solomon noted that their move into the hotel business in the Bay Area coincided with the rapid development of the Internet industry in Silicon Valley, making hotels in the entire Bay Area very hot.

In 1997, the Tsai family bought a piece of land in San Mateo and built a Hilton Garden Inn with one hundred and fifty-six exquisite guest rooms, and the investment in this property was also recovered quickly due to the Internet boom.

However, there were also unforeseen circumstances. The

Steve and Tina welcome ROC President Ma Ying-jeou to the Crowne Plaza upon his second visit.

Steve, Tina and Elizabeth welcome ROC First Lady Christine Chow Ma for her third visit.

2004: Steve and Tina (left) and second daughter Elizabeth (3rd from left) greet US President George W. Bush to the Crowne Royal during one of his two visits.

September 11 attacks shocked the world and threw the tourism industry into turmoil. Solomon said: "Prior to September 11, business had been good. September 11 affected business negatively, but we had already recouped our investment, so we were not greatly impacted." There was another reason why the Tsai family hotels were able to weather this recession, namely because the properties were carrying unusually low levels of debt.

Holiday Inn, Crowne Plaza, Hilton, Marriott

The hotels were also an emotional investment for the family. Solomon remembered, "My father was very supportive when we decided to buy the Holiday Inn. I decided to focus my career on the hotel business. He supported me then and let me try my luck with this. Our family started with nothing, and then bought the first small hotel, and gradually expanded our holdings."

In 1990, the Tsai family bought the Holiday Inn in Foster City, and in 1998 upgraded the property to a Crowne Plaza. Within the Intercontinental Hotel Group, the Holiday Inn brand is relatively mid-range, while the Crowne Plaza brand is more high-end.

Of course, the upgrade involved much more than simply changing the name. Solomon said, "These two hotel brands have different requirements for room amenities and service standards. For example,

Crowne Plaza hotels provide room service, dedicated doormen, at least two restaurants and a formal bar, a large banquet hall and meeting facilities."

The service and facilities upgrade from Holiday Inn to Crowne Plaza represented a significant investment.

As noted, the Foster City Crowne Plaza was well situated along the North-South Route 101 and the East-West Route 92, making it very accessible in all directions, an ideal business location according to Chinese tradition. Only a ten-minute drive from San Francisco International Airport, it is one of the most popular hotels between San Francisco and San Jose. Notable guests from Taiwan have included Presidents Ma Ying-jeou and Chen Shui-bian, as well Premier Hao Po-tsun, President of the Legislative Yuan Wang Chin-ping, President of the Control Yuan Wang Chien-shien, General Chiang Wei-kuo and leaders of Taiwan's various political parties. US President George W. Bush has also stayed at the hotel twice, once before and once after his election.

In 2002, the Tsai family bought a parcel of land in Fairfield, next to the City Hall on Interstate 80, with plans to build another Hilton Garden Inn.

Premium Hotel Project in Napa Wine Country

Solomon took another big gamble in the hotel industry, and while the project didn't pan out as expected, it did have a happy result.

In 2001, Solomon bought a large piece of land in Napa County, planning on building a hotel. However, local zoning regulations prohibited hotel construction and the application process to change the zoning would be very difficult and possibly take as long as ten years without assurance of success. Due to the lengthy application time and difficulty, few investors were willing to try to build hotels in Napa.

For these reasons, Steve and Tenny were initially opposed to the idea, but Solomon pointed out the lack of high-quality hotels in Napa and the resulting demand. Despite the difficulties, he insisted that this parcel of land represented a rare opportunity to expand the family business.

Steve pointed out that the family would be required to put up 70% of the cost of the land purchase and construction in cash, which represented a substantial risk. Tenny had already spent years working in real estate and had accumulated considerable experience and expertise, and she cautioned that their likelihood of successfully having the land rezoned was low. Once the land was purchased, if the necessary permits could not be obtained, it would leave the family in a difficult situation. However, despite her reservations and those of her father, Solomon was successful at bringing the family around to his point of view.

Napa County records for 2014 show that Napa annually attracts over 4.7 million visitors a year, of whom more than 2.75 million stay overnight, while the remainder are day-trippers. In comparison, in 2012 Hawaii welcomed 7.86 million visitors. Napa County's population was only about 136,000 in 2010, while Hawaii in 2012 was home to nearly 1.4 million people. Napa County covers about 2,000 square kilometers, compared to Hawaii's 16,000 square kilometers. This comparison shows that Napa County is already a major tourist site. Of course, visitors to Hawaii generally stay longer, but one reason that visitors tend not to stay long in Napa is the lack of high-end hotels.

The land purchase went through around Christmas of 2001, and Solomon began the long process of developing local support for the development, getting to know local officials and ordinary residents, explaining the proposed hotel plan and how it would benefit the community. "I got to know every family living near the development site," remembers Solomon. "I met so many people I could probably run for mayor and win." At first, there was significant opposition, but the objections gradually diminished as the locals grew to appreciate the potential advantages the hotel would bring to the area.

Solomon explained that while the Napa wineries attract millions of visitors, the visitors do not stay overnight because of the lack of good hotels. These visitors end up taking their money elsewhere but keeping them in Napa would boost local tax revenue. The construction of the hotel would immediately increase the land values of nearby houses, thus directly benefiting their owners. Steve visited Solomon in Napa at this time and was thoroughly impressed by the efforts and success in lobbying local interests. "He is very optimistic and enterprising and very confident," Steve said.

The planned new hotel would have 351 rooms, a 25,000 square foot conference hall, four restaurants, and many other facilities. When completed, it would attract many companies and organizations to hold events at the hotel and would bring huge economic benefits to Napa. The hotel building was designed to integrate well with the built environment of downtown Napa along with the surrounding natural environment. The city council held a public hearing about the proposal, and more than 400 people attended, about half in support. The meeting began at 7pm and went on until well past midnight, with highly contentious debate. However, at about one in the morning, Solomon was greatly relieved when the city council voted to approve the hotel's construction.

Appointed as Board Member of Two International Hotel Groups

The plans to purchase the land were put together in 2000 and took five years of hard work to complete. Once Solomon had secured the building permits, a father and son from a different family in the hotel business came to Napa from Florida. These two were true hotel entrepreneurs with several dozen properties including two 5-star Ritz Carlton hotels. They wanted to buy the Napa site from Solomon in order to build a Ritz Carlton.

Solomon recalled: "They gave me an unbelievably good price; it was very hard to refuse. So, I sold the land." Based on his performance in the process of acquiring the land for the development of the new hotel, along with his experience steering the Crowne Plaza and Hilton Garden Inn properties, he secured board seats on two of the world's largest hotel chains, serving as a board member of Hilton Garden Inn for six years and Holiday Inn for eight, overseeing the hotel properties of these two chains all over the world. If his board membership was not term limited by corporate regulations, he would likely have stayed on longer.

Today, Solomon looks back on this time in his life as a time to serve and to learn. All the board members of these two hotel groups are leaders in the industry. "Each of these board members owned multiple hotels, some up to one hundred or more. How do they manage the hotels? How did they take their companies public? How do they do marketing? How do they go about developing new properties? Some started out as family-operated enterprises, but later brought in professional management and corporatized. Some hotel directors have their own management methods. Surrounding myself with such rich industry experience was very beneficial to me."

At the same time, Solomon never lost a chance to learn from other industries, and the network of friends he built over the years has served him well in his own career.

In 2011, Solomon purchased a 243-room Holiday Inn in Chicago in a deal brought to him by his sister Tenny.

Hilton Teams Up with Solomon to Develop Hotels in China

The Hilton Hotel Group was previously divided into two corporations, one focused on the American market (Hilton USA), and one focused on all other countries (Hilton International). Hilton International was headquartered in the UK and was completely separate from Hilton USA. At the end of 2006, the Blackstone Investment Group bought Hilton USA, and subsequently purchased Hilton International, merging the two companies into a single entity.

At this time, the Holiday Inn Hotel Group was operating nearly 60 hotels in mainland China, compared to only 12 for Hilton. Following the Hilton merger, the top priority of the new company was to expand into mainland China, seeking to catch up with its rival.

Before the merger, Stephen Bollenbach, co-chairman and CEO of Hilton USA, came to see Solomon, telling him, "Once the two Hilton companies are merged, you will have a mandate to open up the China market for us. We want to open 25 Hilton Garden Inn properties in China over the next five years. Are you interested?"

This was a rare opportunity. In 2006, Solomon already had 20 years of experience in the hotel business and had served on the board of directors of both the Hilton and Holiday Inn groups. He was well-known and respected in the industry, and thus the Hilton leadership placed great trust in him to accomplish important tasks. Solomon also felt that this was an opportunity to pursue new challenges, and he readily agreed.

Obstacles to Hilton's China Development Plan

After more than a year of preparation and negotiation, on

July 4th, 2007, Solomon, Bollenbach and other senior Hilton leadership met at Citibank's offices in Shanghai's Pudong District with representatives from Deutsche Bank and Asia Pacific Venture Capital to sign contracts and agreements to establish a preparatory office for Hilton's China expansion. With 100 million dollars in cash on hand (half from Deutsche Bank), the company was prepared to borrow another 150 million for a total of $250 million in working capital.

However, the situation in China was extremely fluid and unpredictable. Solomon remembers, "In 2007, when we went to China, the economic outlook was highly positive, but the following summer, Beijing would be hosting the Olympics, thus from January 1, 2008, all construction in Beijing was suspended. Following the conclusion of the August Olympics, it was time to restart construction, but the global financial crisis began to catch fire in the US. In January 2009, Deutsche Bank's investment arm wanted to divert their entire US$50 million investment from our project to save other investments." In 2013, the US was still emerging from the financial crisis. The hotel development project had planned for 25 new Hilton Garden Inns to be completed in China by that year, but by the end of 2013, only one had been built.

Solomon said, "It was really a pity - our hopes were completely dashed by this unforeseen financial crisis. I was very disappointed at the time, but looking back at it later, there was a positive aspect to it. I think that, if I had gone to China to work on this project, I would have lost myself there. Instead, I came back here to the Bay Area to focus on our operations here, thinking of our current and possible future hotels on SR 92 and US 101. Coming back here to focus my attention on these developments may have been best."

However, Solomon still had a "special mission" to perform for the Hilton Group in the Asia Pacific region: to participate in the establishment of a standard of operations for Hilton properties in the region including Taiwan, mainland China and India, a project to which he devoted his extensive understanding of Asian cultures and traditions.

While Solomon had left China with regrets, his prospects were looking up in the United States, in addition to his new Chicago acquisition in 2011.

In June 2013, the Foster City Council approved the Tsai family's plan to build a 121-room extended-stay hotel, with each guest room including an independent kitchen, making it an unusual facility in the Bay Area. The new hotel was slated to open in 2015.

In addition, the family planned to demolish the San Mateo Best Western, originally bought in 1976, and rebuild the property as a Hilton Hotel.

In June 2013, during an interview at his office at the Foster City Crowne Plaza Hotel, Solomon pointed out the window and said, "New tech companies are coming to Foster City every day, and this development brings tremendous opportunities for area hotels. Near the Crowne Plaza, the pharmaceutical giant Gilead Sciences was building a 1.6 million square-foot production facility located near the Crowne Plaza Hotel, while VISA was planning a 1.5 million square-foot headquarters building in the area.

The hotel industry in Foster City and the nearby areas benefits greatly from the continued northward expansion of Silicon Valley. As he looked out his office window, Solomon spoke like a general reviewing his war plans, full of confidence for his future development plans in the San Francisco Bay Area.

2001: American-Pacific Hotel Group CEO Solomon Tsai (second from right, son of Steve) receives the "Outstanding Development Award" from the US Hilton Hotel Group.

Chapter Twelve

Dr. Tsai 's Business Philosophy

Invigorating a Country through Commerce, Creating Prosperity Through Righteousness

Steve once said that you need to seek many beneficial friends in life. There are two kinds of beneficial friends. The first kind is superior in wisdom and can help you correct your path. The other is superior in strength and fortitude and can help you overcome difficult times.

Steve found a mentor who would have a great influence on his life, providing expert guidance that affected his entire outlook on life and success.

Shortly after Steve first arrived in Taiwan, Tsiang Ting-fu, then the Permanent Representative of the Republic of China to the United Nations, gave a public address in Taipei. Steve eagerly attended the lecture with his wife.

Today, few young people are familiar with the name Tsiang Ting-fu. Originally from Hunan, Chiang held a Ph.D. from Columbia University, and had achieved wide recognition in Chinese scholarly and diplomatic circles. He served as a professor at Nankai, Beijing and Qinghua Universities, and had served as chair of the history department and dean of the School of Humanities of Qinghua University. Tsiang was the author of a book, "Modern Chinese History" that formed the basis of his academic reputation. His diplomatic achievements included serving as ROC ambassador to the Soviet Union, the United States and the United Nations.

Steve had been out of school for a while, but was still consumed with a passion for learning, treating all of society as a school and life as an education. When he learned that Tsiang would be speaking, how could he pass up the opportunity?

Today, more than sixty years after that day, Steve still remembers the speech. Tsiang noted that the United States was the world's key superpower, and the country's prosperity was based on its excellence in business and commerce, led by a class of brokers who were dedicated to serving the interests of their clients, earning both respect and wealth. China, on the other hand, valued scholars and officials over merchants and businesspeople. Since ancient times, China has generally divided its social classes into "intellectuals, farmers, laborers, and merchants." Historically, Chinese society emphasized scholarship over commerce, with the best and brightest of each generation aspiring to perform well on Imperial civil service examinations. Many spent over a decade in constant preparation for the exams, and those who prevailed were celebrated as national heroes.

Tsiang noted that the social contribution of merchants is not necessarily lower than that of laborers or farmers. Merchants transport products from one place to another for consumption by local people, thereby improving the living standards of people everywhere, and are crucial to generating the livelihoods of laborers and farmers.

Tsiang was very familiar with the United States, and said that in the US government system, the President's cabinet includes a Secretary of Commerce, but there is no Secretary of Industry. Rather, industry is recognized as belonging under the purview of commerce. The American point of view places a particular importance on merchants. This mercantile outlook believes that sales should precede production, where production only occurs when there is demand in a market.

China, on the other hand, prioritizes production over marketing, and laborers and farmers generally speaking have little concept of the market economy. When they hear about a product that makes money, everyone will begin to produce that product, resulting in a glut that drives down prices. Due to insufficient information and an immature understanding of market forces, they end up producing an oversupply that can result in them actually losing money.

Nations must establish legal environments that encourage fair competition and protects the rights and interests of businessmen, encouraging them to promote business development. Only countries with a strong commercial tradition can become strong and prosperous. Modern businessmen are different from their ancient counterparts, and today's businessmen often have command of knowledge and expertise that rivals or even surpasses that of high-ranking officials. They need this knowledge to access and understand production and sales information from around the world, and to compare against historic conditions to elucidate current conditions and anticipate future trends for production and sales.

The United States idolizes successful businesspeople, and many of them go on to serve as high-ranking officials. Presidents George HW Bush and his son George W Bush both came out of the business world, and many of America's most influential cabinet secretaries also have strong business backgrounds. One good example is Michael Bloomberg, who served as mayor of New York City from 2001 to 2013. Working for a nominal annual salary of one dollar, during his 12-year tenure Bloomberg spent $640 million of his personal wealth during his time as mayor. His company, Bloomberg L.P. is one of the world's leading publishers of financial news and information. In 2014, Bloomberg's 88% holding in the company gave him a net worth of $34 billion.

Education and learning are the key to social advancement and improvement, and Tsiang's words had an electrifying impact on Steve- showing him the key role that business plays in a country's development and progress.

Prior to this, Steve had been well educated in the humanities, and took feverish notes during Tsiang's speech. Afterwards, at home, he and Tina compared notes and reconstructed his full remarks.

Seeing an Advantage, First Check if it is Righteousness. If Righteous, Take the Advantage.

Through the process of organizing the notes on Chiang's speech, Steve developed a more nuanced understanding of the Chinese concept of "commerce" (shang). He remembered how Sun Yat-sen's 1894 "Address to Li Hung-Chang" had mentioned "An important indicator of the quality of a country's governance is the degree to which people are able to make the best use of their talents, land is used to the greatest benefit, resources are used most appropriately, and goods flow maximally."

"Goods flow maximally when there are no obstacles to block their path, when commerce is protected by effective laws, and with easy access to transportation by ship and rail. Goods are produced by farmers and laborers and shipped by merchants. Merchants locate surpluses and transport goods to relieve shortages. The service provided by merchants is no less important than that provided by farmers and laborers. "

Steve recalled that during the Anti-Japanese War, he and his classmates collected donations for the war effort and supported the frontline. The majority of contributions often came from the merchant class.

Eventually, Steve came to the conclusion that China's traditional disdain for commerce may, in fact, have been a key factor in China's long-term weakness.

During Steve's time in mainland China, he worked as a teacher, a freelance writer, a newspaper editor and an editor-in-chief. After arriving in Taiwan, he became the editor-in-chief of a publishing house. For many years, he was engaged in education, journalism, and cultural work, and had little to do with business. Chiang Ting-fu's words brought him to a different understanding of the role of business in society, but he could hardly have suspected that he himself would one day venture into the world of business.

Later, he served as the special correspondent for the Philippine Xinmin Daily News in Taiwan, often writing reports about the ROC government's efforts to lure overseas Chinese investment to Taiwan, which was of considerable interest to the overseas Chinese community in the Philippines. Some wanted to invest in Taiwan but did not have a channel to invest. Steve's eldest brother and sister were in the Philippines, along with many other relatives. Steve was also good friends with Shih Hsing-shui, then chairman of the Manila Chinese Chamber of Commerce, which included many people interested in investing in Taiwan. Thus, they enlisted the help of Tsai Steve to improve bilateral ties. Leveraging Steve's knowledge of Taiwan and connections there, these investors made substantial returns with considerably less effort than such investments normally required.

The overseas Chinese in the Philippines would visit Steve in Taiwan, or ask him to visit them in the Philippines, appealing for his help and insight into Taiwan's investment environment. The government's desire to promote inward investment from the overseas Chinese community thus gradually introduced Steve into commerce through assisting overseas Chinese in the Philippines navigate Taiwan's investment opportunities. Throughout this period, he continued to work as a journalist until September 1972 when Philippine President Marcos declared martial law and closed all Chinese newspapers.

Entering the business world from the media changed Steve's identity but his commitment to the improvement of society remained unchanged. For example, at the time, the government had a policy of providing preferential treatment to overseas Chinese investors in developing Taiwan's insurance industry, with the intention of opening to domestic capital investment once the overseas Chinese funded insurance industry had stabilized. However, Steve saw how critical the insurance industry was to social and economic development and felt that the industry should be fully opened to all investment to accelerate the industry's development. Together with Shih Hsing-shui, President of the Philippine Chinese Chamber of Commerce, he lobbied President Chiang to reject this preferential policy and open the industry to all investment. They were eventually able to bring him around, leading to the full liberalization of Taiwan's insurance industry. Coming to business from a different background than most of his contemporaries gave Steve a different perspective on how business and industry should operate.

Another example is a piece of "garbage land" he jointly invested in with Yang Tsu-hua, the Philippine paper industry king, and Lin his-ching,. Following the Republic of China's withdrawal from the

United Nations in 1972, Yang and Lin were worried that the CCP might soon invade Taiwan. They thus wanted to sell the plot as quickly as possible. Steve, however, realized this "garbage land" as actually a treasure with unlimited future development, and he was skeptical that China would invade, so he resisted selling the land. In the partnership, any one partner could effectively veto the sale of the land. However, despite his reluctance to sell, Steve recognized his friends' anxiety and prized their continued friendship. He thus reluctantly agreed to sell in a story which has since become Taiwan industry lore (as detailed in Chapter 4). Confucian ethics emphasizes righteousness over profit and forms the core of Steve's approach to all things.

In the early 2000s, Steve was in Shanghai to attend the graduation of a nephew from the Fudan University Business School. When school officials discovered that the legendary Taiwanese businessman Steve would be in attendance, they invited him to deliver brief remarks at the ceremony. Speaking to the new graduates, Steve offered four suggestions:

First, production must be preceded by effective market research, unlike traditional Chinese practices of starting with production and following with development of sales channels. Second, corporate R&D is very important. Many well-known large companies are also essentially R&D companies. Institutions should allocate a certain percentage of their annual profits for research and development. "The amount of R&D funding often determines whether a company can continue to develop and progress," he said. Third, there are two modes of corporate decision-making, one is top-down, and the other is bottom-up. Chairman Tsai told business graduates that, based on his experience, he advocates bottom-up participation in decision-making at the grassroots level. A sense of participation will generate a sense of honor and responsibility among all personnel. Fourth, Steve emphasized the importance of social responsibility. While business exists to make money, it must be done in an ethical way.

At this moment, Steve recalled listening to Chiang Ting-fu's speech at the Taipei Armed Forces Stadium nearly half a century earlier. Over the years, Steve had acquired new insight and ideas about business. He saw that the government needed to establish policies that promoted business, and that businessmen should likewise seek to expand their knowledge of economics and professional ethics and seek to become modern businessmen with a sense of justice, integrity and social responsibility.

Recent years have seen a series of scandals involving food safety, with unethical businesses putting the public at risk in search of greater profits. While these misdeeds eventually came to light and the wrong doers were punished, people were still harmed, and the public's trust was eroded. However, if businessmen seek profits through righteousness, everyone wins, and their wealth will continue to grow.

2012: Steve and his eldest grandson Nathan accompany a US delegation to the London Olympics. Picture taken at a London airport.

{{ Part 5: Converging to Benevolence }}
Chapter Thirteen

Behind the Success

Behind Every Successful Man is a Good Wife

Men want trust and respect, while women want love. We each gave the other what they wanted.

-- Steve Tsai

Tina Tsai Hung was born in Xiamen, where her family owned more than 70 buildings.

"My grandfather Hung Wan-tsung was a wealthy businessman who made his fortune in Manila," she recalled. "He established a food factory and the famous Riguangbiao Soy Sauce Factory. His business was prosperous, and Δhe grew wealthy, but sent most of his fortune back to China to invest in commercial real estate on Xiamen's main commercial streets: Tatung Road, Siming Road, Chungshan Road, and Kaiyuan Road. At home, I really didn't think

Tina Tsai Hung

about money - I had everything I could want. At six or seven years old, I was in elementary school, and there was a boy servant who accompanied me to school every day. If it was raining or hot, he'd carry an umbrella for me. So I was always under the impression that money came easily and never understood why people got upset about money. I really didn't have any concept of money, and that's still true even today."

When Tina was studying in Chimei Middle School, she met Steve at the home of her friend, Lan, and later learned that Steve was the brother of her classmate Tsai Youcong. "Steve's family was also made up of overseas Chinese. His father was very famous. When I met him, I was only fifteen years old. He was five years older than me. When we first met, I really didn't think of him in terms of love - he was just a big brother figure for me. Over the next two or three years, I grew very fond of him, but it was just affection between friends. He was like a tutor to me, helping me with my schoolwork. He was the one who persuaded me to transfer to Quanzhou Peiying Girls' School. Quanzhou's academic approach is rather straightforward, and I made good progress after I transferred. It was during this time that my family developed a very good impression of him despite his work as a policeman - they saw him as a committed and serious young man."

Although Steve was in his twenties at the time, he was already well-known within the Xiamen police force as "Inspector Tsai," lead investigator on some bizarre cases.

1949 brought great changes to China, with the culmination of years of civil war resulting in the displacement of huge numbers of ordinary people. That year, Tina graduated from high school and traveled to Taiwan. She and Steve communicated by phone despite the exorbitant cost and inconvenience of making long-distance calls at the time. Their feelings for each other grew as the Communist army approached Xiamen, leaving her unable to return home.

Resolved to stay in Taiwan for at least for the time being, she urged Steve to follow her to Taiwan.

The siege of Xiamen left the city nearly cut off from land, sea and air. Tina asked her uncle to ask Yan Ling-feng, the mayor of Fuzhou, and Mei Ta-fu, the mayor of Taipei, to help obtain the Taiwan entry permits and sea passage for Steve's family, and to intervene with the Xiamen garrison to help the family safely get on board.

At the time, military and government personnel would choose to move to Taiwan with the government, but Steve had resigned from his position before the city came under siege. Without his connection with Tina, Steve might have not been able to go to Taiwan, and more likely would have reunited with his family in the Philippines by way of Hong Kong, resulting in a completely different life story for the Tsai family.

Reminiscing about this past, Tina said, "At the time, I was helping him as a friend. I really didn't expect to marry him in the future. I was only a teenager at that time, and I hadn't thought about getting married yet."

During the Kinmen Artillery Battle of 1958, Steve had registered to conduct onsite battlefield interviews, but when the Press Bureau called to let him know where to assemble for the trip, he was away from home and Tina answered the call. She told the Press Bureau that Steve would not be attending because the Mid-Autumn Festival fell on the following day. Steve was furious when he discovered that he'd lost his chance to conduct battlefield interviews. "I'd never lost my temper with my wife like that before," he said. Tina recalls: "But I didn't say anything. I was thinking, so you don't go to Kinmen. It's not such a big deal. You can yell all you want, but you'll stop sooner or later, and then I'll talk to you."

Two days later they learned that the ship the reporters were traveling on had been sunk by enemy fire, and nine of the eleven journalists died. The happenstance of Tina's answering that phone call may have inadvertently saved Steve's life.

Tina stood by Steve throughout his professional life in Taiwan as he moved from the media to banking, insurance, hotels, manufacturing and property development. She provided the support and reassurance he most needed throughout his decades of work to promote social welfare in Taiwan.

"My husband is very enthusiastic, especially in public affairs. He values his reputation far above money. He works hard and is generous with others, and these qualities are what attract so many friends to him. He simply decides the right course of action and takes on tasks and difficulties that others are reluctant to take on. He's still like this today at the age of ninety."

Steve's business career in Taiwan inevitably exposed him to the less savory side of Taiwan's business culture. Many of his friends and business associates kept mistresses and even second families. Though his acquaintances provided ample opportunity for Steve to indulge in such pleasures, he consistently held himself to higher standards of behavior. His focused his energy and attention on his professional pursuits and his family. "My wife trusts me. She knew I had to meet people in these places, and sometimes would even send me there herself. Men want trust and respect, while women want love. We each gave each other what they wanted."

In 1973, Tina first traveled to San Francisco to set up the trading company that would pave the way for the next stage of the Tsai family's businesses and the education of the next generation. However, the focus of Steve's career was still in Taiwan. Tina started a new life in San Francisco with her four children.

Building a new life in a new country was very difficult at the beginning. At first, Tina rented a bedroom from her classmate, rode the bus, ate TV dinners, and studied English. The trading company hired Peng Chongyuan as the general manager while Tina served as chairman of the board. She was working during her studies and learning from her work. Gradually the four Tsai children found their footing and were on track towards flourishing futures in the United States.

Tina took a relatively hands-off approach to parenting. "As long as they stayed within bounds, I let them find their own way, and didn't push them in one way or another. My four children are quite competitive. They were well behaved and didn't cause us trouble."

When Steve told Tina of his first love, she was open-minded and felt moved by curiosity to discover what kind of person her husband had formerly loved.

"I found it very strange that she was still in his heart after all this time. I wondered how beautiful she was. I decided to track her down. I found her in Quanzhou and went to see her without my husband's knowledge. It had been decades since they'd last met, and of course she had changed and grown old. But she was a very kind person. I brought her a suitcase full of clothes. "

"I like what he likes, including his friends" Tina said of her husband. "If you like someone, it stands to reason you'll have similar tastes. When I first met Steve's first love, I could see that she felt both awkward and grateful, but we got along very well. Later, for many years, for Steve's birthday, Tina brought her children from San Francisco to Xiamen where she invited Steve's former classmates, including Steve's first love, and their families. "At this stage of our lives, all that matters is being happy, so I've never felt jealous. I don't even know what jealousy means. This other woman is important to him, so I treat her well and buy things for her. He wondered – 'why aren't you jealous?' I said, 'There's nothing to be jealous of! I have a great deal of self-confidence."'

On January 4, 2013, Steve and Tina celebrated their 60th diamond anniversary. Hundreds of relatives and friends gathered at their Crowne Plaza hotel in Foster City to celebrate the most precious sixty years of their lives.

The celebrations included three pastors who had come to give the couple their blessings, and to officiate as the couple reaffirmed their vows in front of the assembled guests, along with their children and eight grandchildren, who had first made the wish that such an anniversary celebration could happen at the time of their golden anniversary ten years earlier. The children and grandchildren had spent months planning the event, which brought together friends and relatives from all over the United States, along with Taiwan and China.

Tenny said that it took a lot of thought to prepare. They designed the invitations and menus themselves. "Each table was named after a different place where our parents have lived," said Tenny. "Gulangyu Island is where they fell in love. Chihfeng Street is where their first tiny, dark Taipei apartment next to the railroad tracks that shook the walls.

Music was also an important part of the family and the night. The couple's second grandson Ethan started studying violin at the age of six and has since won many awards, including the 2004 Menuhin-Dowling Violin Competition Young Musician Award. In 2008, Ethan was selected to join the San Francisco Youth Symphony Orchestra.

The evening of the banquet, the grandchildren kicked off the festivities with Ethan playing the cheerful violin piece "Saut d'Amour" by Edward Elgar, followed by all eight grandchildren singing the classic Chinese pop songs "The Moon Represents My Heart" and "Sweet Secret." The grandchildren each offered their congratulations.

Their granddaughter Hsu En-hsin said that the love her grandparents had shared for 60 years had inspired their grandchildren to treasure life even more. At the banquet, a slide show accompanied by romantic music walked the guests through a gallery of the Tsai family's journey over the previous 60 years, produced by their grandson Wu Yi-tao. As the photos transitioned from black-and-white to color, the scenes grew brighter and ever more hopeful.

All eight grandchildren had played key roles in preparing and producing this diamond jubilee, and in the process had deepened their understanding of their family history and their joint bonds.

A Role Reversal in the Coming Life

A ten-piece band serenaded the guests. Though the music was from the 1950s and 1960s--when Steve and Tina were in their prime, the couple took to the dance floor with gusto, showing vigor and enthusiasm that belied their age.

Steve noted that a diamond wedding anniversary is also a betrothal in that it gives the couple a chance to commit to each other again in the next life. Tina said she would marry Steve again in the coming life, but only if she got to be the husband.

Steve expressed his fervent hope that they would meet and fall in love once again, when he was young again and before she found someone else to marry.

During the banquet, a guest asked what their secret was to maintaining their love over 60 years. Steve responded first by emphasizing the importance of mutual respect, and also quoted the bible: "Love is patient and kind; love does not envy or boast; it is not arrogant or rude. It does not insist on its own way; it is not irritable or resentful; it does not rejoice at wrongdoing but rather rejoices with the truth. Love bears all things, believes all things, hopes all things, endures all things. Love never ends."

Pressed for further wisdom, Steve finally revealed the secret to enduring marital harmony. "It's not enough to tolerate each other's shortcomings," he said. "Instead, you have to accept and appreciate them. There is no absolute right or wrong, and one must learn to appreciate and understand others through being humble and objective about oneself. Don't be hasty when discussing urgent matters. Put it off until later, and never speak in anger."

Calligraphy presented by ROC President Ma Ying-jeou to celebrate the couple's 60th anniversary.

Painting with calligraphy by Ou Hao-nian presented to Steve and Tina.

Calligraphy by Yu You-jen on the occasion of the wedding of Steve and Tina.

Steve and Tina celebrated their 50th wedding anniversary by dressing in imperial costumes.

Steve and Tina celebrate their diamond anniversary with a grandson playing violin.

Steve teaches three granddaughters the cha-cha.

Wedding portrait of Steve and Tina
from 60 years ago.

Steve and Tina married in Taipei in
1953, witnessed by Chief of Staff
Wang Shu-ming and General Hu
Wei-ke.

A big pileup to celebrate Tina's
birthday.

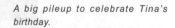

Steve celebrates Christmas
with two grandsons.

Steve marks his 90th birthday with his own calligraphy.

Steve's four children celebrate his birthday.

ROC San Francisco Office Economic and Cultural Attaché Fu Cheng-kang presents Steve with commemorative calligraphy from President Ma Ying-jeou.

January 4, 2013 60th Diamond Anniversary.

World Journal report of the diamond anniversary.

2013.1.4 蔡實鼎夫婦慶鑽石婚

婚禮照上的甜蜜60年不變　盼下輩子再結婚　馬英九賀詞「華堂偕老」

【本報佛斯特市訊】盧夢、溫情、親情，還有愛，在「愛你一生一世」的2013年1月4日，充滿在佛斯特市Crowne Plaza飯館中。灣區商界德望蔡實鼎和太太洪珍珍，當晚在自己家族的親朋中慶祝鑽石婚。60年前的婚禮照鋪放在宴會廳入口處，甜蜜情形彷彿昨日。

當晚由牧師作證，蔡實鼎和蔡洪珍珍重申當年結婚誓言。他們的孩子，女兒蔡懷香和蔡慧中、兒子蔡少鼎、女兒蔡慧雯，以及八名孫兒，以各種方式祝福兩老。蔡懷香說，十年前為父母慶祝金婚時，曾許願再十年後的慶祝，「因為神的恩典，十年後我們為父母慶祝鑽石婚。」

她透露，當晚客人有的來自美國其他城市，台灣和中國大陸。鑽石婚慶的一切，同由兒女和孫輩花了好幾個月籌備。「大家都非常用心，每一桌都有名字。『鼓浪嶼』是父母定情之處。『赤崁街』是父母在台北第一個住處的所在街道，那是一個很小很小的公寓。」

張紹或表演小提琴，或發表祝詞，八名孫兒並合唱「月亮代表我的心」。外孫女徐思心說，外公外婆感恩60載，激勵孫輩更加熱愛生命，也越來越充滿青春活力。

晚宴上，伴著浪漫的音樂，用幻燈片放映了60年前的結婚照，以及60年來一個家庭走過的路程。照片從黑白到彩色，展示出人生越來越燦爛。

私下說話時，蔡實鼎說，鑽石婚慶也是一場婚禮，是兩人下輩子再次結婚的婚禮。蔡太太說，下輩子她不嫁給蔡實鼎，兩人要在一起的話，她要做老公。88歲的蔡實鼎聞言哈哈大笑。晚宴上兩人並同切結婚蛋糕。

駐舊金山台北經濟文化辦事處副處長蔡強華出席晚宴，中華民國總統馬英九送來賀詞「華堂偕老」。副總統吳敦義的賀詞是「鴻案相莊」。中華民國全國商業總會理事長張平昭送來賀匾，內有「百年琴瑟」，頗於驚嘆。

蔡實鼎和蔡洪珍珍結婚60年，鶼鰈情深。
(本報記者攝影)

A leisurely afternoon.

Four generations at Lake Tahoe. From left: Steve, Elizabeth Tsai, Tina, and their 10-month old great granddaughter. (photo taken by granddaughter)

2014: Steve celebrates his 90th birthday in San Francisco.

A Wife's Phone Call Saves Her Husband's Life

August 1958 - Kinmen Artillery Battle

In August 1958, a fierce artillery battle broke out over Kinmen. Hundreds of Chinese and foreign reporters gathered in Taipei, hoping to report from the battlefield, with priority given to foreign reporters. As Steve was a special correspondent for the Philippines Xinmin Daily News, he was given a space on the boat.

Shen Chi, the head of the Central News Agency, held a pre-departure press conference for Chinese and foreign reporters, at which they presented the potential dangers of approaching the battle zone by various routes. The Kinmen airport was completely within PLA artillery range from Xiamen, making approaches highly hazardous, though successful landing would put passengers in close range to air-raid shelters. By ship, they could land at Liuluo Bay, on the east side of the island. However, the lack of port facilities meant that passengers would have to disembark in open waters and make the final approach in small landing craft, leaving them exposed to enemy artillery for an extended time. Both approaches were dangerous, but in different ways, and the military advised the journalists to choose for themselves. They were also each required to sign a waiver acknowledging the inherent risk of the landing and absolving the government and military of any liability for their potential injury or death.

Steve signed the waiver, choosing to travel by warship.

The Mid-Autumn Festival was coming up, and Steve was concerned that the Kinmen trip might mean he wouldn't be home with his family for the holiday. As such, he went out to buy moon cakes and other seasonal foods. But when he returned home, Tina told him that the Central News Agency had called to say that he should report to the Tsoying Naval Base the following morning to board his transport, but she had told them he wouldn't be attending due to the holiday.

Tina didn't want Steve to go to Kinmen. The whole family would be together for the holiday, and she was worried about his safety. "Five minutes after he left the house, the call came to say where they were assembling the following day. I told them he wasn't going, and they should give his spot to someone else."

When Steve returned home and learned what had happened, he called the Central News Agency and told them his wife had made a mistake and that he still wanted to go. However, his place had already been given away. "I've never been so angry with my wife as I was that day," he said. "Being a war correspondent is a tremendous honor. I was fuming all night long but resolved to try to get another opportunity at a later date."

In the face of Steve's anger, Tina recalled: "I didn't say anything. I was thinking, so you don't go to Kinmen. It's not such a big deal. You can yell all you want, but you'll stop sooner or later, and then I'll talk to you."

The following day, nine of the reporters who left Tsoying on the military transport were lost at sea when their landing craft

Overseas Chinese Insurance Corporation leaders Chiu Han-ping (2nd from right) and Steve (far right) on a trip to visit troops in Kinmen.

1958: Steve visits the front lines in Kinmen, visiting his close friend Kinmen Garrison commander Cheng Lee-chun.

蔡實鼎和太太洪珍珍。

B1 世界日報 World Journal
2008年8月23日 星期六
LOCAL NEWS
美西新聞

新聞提要
- 水星報顯美勿與中國搶比奧運 (B2)
- 聖縣11月選戰 參選人全確定 (B3)
- 亞洲婦女服務中心24周年慶 (B4)
- 金山庇護非法移民 掀訟 (B6)

生計 SHENGKEE BAKERY
三藩市／日落區
1447 IRVING ST. S. F. CA94122
TEL(415)753-1111 7AM-7PM
中城／奧斯福（三藩和都板街市南邊）
2004 S NORFOLK BLVD SAN MATEO,CA94403
TEL(650)341-8836 7AM-8PM
南區／庫柏蒂諾（東和超級市場內）
10122 C BANDLEN DR CUPERTINO,CA95014
TEL(408)255-9999 8AM-9PM
東灣／密爾必達（美洲銀行對面）
1842 N Milpitas Blvd Milpitas,CA95035
TEL.(408)262-3588

憶823砲戰 蔡實鼎感慨萬千

五十年前遭太太阻攔無緣到戰地採訪 卻因此撿回一條命

【本報記者劉問平舊金山報導】
「聽太太的話不會錯，」蔡實鼎對此 份有親切身的體驗。五十年前，因太太的阻攔，蔡實鼎無法前往發生「823砲戰」的金門戰場採訪，卻使他倖免於難。

「823砲戰」50週年前夕，蔡實鼎於22日接受採訪時表示，當時他是菲律賓「馬尼拉晨報」以及「新聞日報」駐台特派員，「823砲戰」發生後，當時在台灣的三、四百名國際媒體記者，紛紛申請前往金門採訪，「價多例少」新聞局跟難安排。外國記者優先，國內記者讓「客人」，蔡實鼎仍有希望排前往採訪。

蔡實鼎說，當時去金門有南側途徑，一些搭飛機，但機場遭到福建，供返航，和到金門抖湖搭機，後，由俗稱「水鴨子」的登陸船送上岸。儘管共軍砲火不斷對大陸，但登陸船駛向南岸時，仍可能遭共軍砲擊。

蔡實鼎申請搭船前往，臨行前一天，他想到中共特至，恐無法與家人共度中秋節，於是先上街採買用具等，回家後，太太洪珍珍對他說，國防部新聞局某官員，請務必左營南軍基地集合上船，但太太回答說，「中秋節快到了，不要了。」

蔡實鼎聽後，馬上打電話要求上船，但名單早被別人占去，他因此很不高興。「我過去對太太從來沒有發過這麼大的脾氣，戰地記者是我最高的榮譽，整個晚上一直非常鬱悶，只好下次再選了。」

第二天早上讀報，這艘船搶灘時遭共軍砲火轟中，除青年戰士報採訪主任嚴重倒外，其餘的人全部罹難。蔡實鼎對自己避過大難非常感激，「後來情勢改變那麼緊張，菲律賓華僑到金門勞軍，找也搶先去到金門了。」

稍後，蔡實鼎在台灣與剖辦華僑銀行、華僑人壽保險公司、華僑產物保險公司、九〇年代到美國發展。今年83歲的蔡實鼎壯心不已，現在隆有福斯特市的Crowne Plaza旅館、聖馬刁市和費爾蒙德市的兩處希爾頓Garden Inn旅館，在美國的第一家旅館是聖馬刁市的Great Western，現仍在其名下。他的最新計畫是在硅巴賬購地興建全新旅館。他在上海外灘也有開發項目。

was hit by PLA artillery fire. Among the group, only two reporters survived, including one from Japan's Kyodo News Agency. Reading reports of the disaster in the newspapers, Steve was overwhelmed by conflicting emotions - gratitude to be alive, but grief for his lost colleagues. Recalling how he'd lost his temper with his wife, he apologized to her and thanked her for saving his life.

Soon after, a delegation of overseas Chinese from the Philippines left for Kinmen, and Steve was invited to join them. From Taipei, their aircraft was forced to double back twice after radar showed PLA fighters approaching to intercept. Finally, the plane was able to land safely on its third attempt. Steve filed three reports from Kinmen, fulfilling his ambition of becoming a war correspondent.

Dedication of One Generation to the Next

With four generations of the Tsai family under one roof, the family was very close. For many years, the eldest daughter Tenny took the lead in caring for her grandmother who was suffering from Alzheimer's disease, an experience that led her to devote herself to related causes for many years.

The love of Steve's four children for their families has also been extended to the broader society through their participation in charity activities.

Tenny said, "My father often missed my grandparents, and from the things he told us it's clear that he is a dutiful and filial son. He passed on these ideals and concepts to us and to our children." Tina was an only child, and her mother lived with her both in Taiwan and in the United States. She and Steve were often busy taking care of business, leaving their children to spend time with their grandmother. Tenny said, "My grandmother was closest to me. In 1976, we began to notice a cognitive decline. She would forget things on the stove. We didn't know what was wrong." Later, she was diagnosed with Alzheimer's, and spent more than ten years in bed. Tenny took the lead in arranging caretaking responsibilities among the four siblings. One was responsible for feeding, another for washing, another for dressing, and another for taking her to medical appointments.

Later, Tenny learned that 10% of people over 65 in the United States suffer from Alzheimer's, rising to 1/3 of people over 85. Patients are prone to irritability and suspicion and are subject to violent outbursts. Understanding of Alzheimer's is low among the Chinese community, and many Chinese people assume it is a type of psychiatric illness and are reluctant to seek treatment.

Their grandmother died in 1991. Having spent a decade caring for her through her illness, Tenny took part in San Francisco Alzheimer's Association and Northern California Alzheimer's Associations as a volunteer, eventually assuming board positions and serving as Chairman of the Northern California organization, playing key roles for over two decades. From their decade's experience of caring for their grandmother suffering from Alzheimer's, the Tsai family has continued to play a role in supporting patients and their families throughout California and all over the United States.

The National Alzheimer's Association was established over 80 years ago and currently has 172 chapters throughout the country. Tenny served as chairman for the national organization for eight years, as the first Asian American woman to ever hold that position. "In my eight years as chairman, four years were focused

Steve and Tina taking part in an annual Golden Gate Walkathon in support of the Northern California Alzheimer's Association, with Daughter Tenny (center) who servs as a board member and chairperson.

on establishing the Diversity and Inclusion Committee, devoted to addressing the need of Alzheimer's patients and their families among minority communities, and poor rural areas. The establishment of this committee was more difficult than expected. While we received verbal support from many board members, they didn't follow up with concrete action. At times, it felt like I was pushing a boulder up a mountain, but we eventually prevailed."

Every two to three years, the Association's board would bring in new members, who would often take the opportunity to propose new committees or functions. "I proposed establishing the Diversity and Inclusiveness Committee as a permanent standing committee, with board membership in proportion to the populations they represented within the country as a whole. Thus, African Americans make up 15% of the population, and thus 15% of committee seats should be held by African-Americans. I also recommended that the committee include someone with early-onset Alzheimer's. The term of committee membership was set at one year, rather than two."

To honor her grandmother's memory, Tenny established a foundation in the Bay Area called the Asian Community Foundation (ACF). With initial funding of $100,000, the foundation promotes Alzheimer's awareness and support groups for patients and families, along with translating relevant information into Chinese.

The ACF sponsored an event at the San Francisco Medical Center, bringing together Chinese-speaking caregivers, doctors, nurses and community members to share information on the care for Alzheimer's patients.

"I was at an Alzheimer's support group meeting, when a young woman from San Francisco's Chinatown area broke down in tears recalling the ordeal she'd endured due to her father's Alzheimer's. She was recently married when her father started showing symptoms. Her family assumed it was some kind of mental illness, and her mother refused to speak to anyone about it. When her husband's family heard about it, they were afraid that the disease could be genetically transmitted to their future grandchildren and forced their son to divorce the young woman. They didn't understand what caused Alzheimer's and based their understanding only on what they could observe."

Mercury News report of Steve's eldest daughter Tenny receiving the Mike Murphy Award.

MERCURYNEWS.COM   SAN JOSE MERCURY NEWS   **TUESDAY, MARCH 7, 2006**

SPACES AND PLACES
JON ANN STEINMETZ

Broker honored by her peers for service to community

A San Jose-based commercial real estate broker who devotes much of her time to organizations for the elderly was recognized by her peers last week with their highest honor for community service.

Tenny Tsai of NAI BT Commercial "has managed to make a difference in our community locally and nationally," said Grubb & Ellis' Bill Hvidt, president of the Association of Silicon Valley Brokers, which presented her with the Mike Murphy Award at its annual awards dinner. "She exemplifies the spirit and activism this award is meant to honor."

Commercial real estate companies and individuals raised $102,000 at the charity event for three organizations: Senior Housing Solutions, HomeSafe and the San Jose Family Shelter.

"This is the first time that the ASVB has achieved the $100,000 contribution level," Hvidt said.

Tsai has done plenty of fundraising herself

World Journal San Francisco edition reports on Tenny's winning the Mike Murphy Award.

二〇〇六年三月八日 星期三 WEDNESDAY, MARCH 8, 2006   世界日報

蔡懷香 榮獲麥克莫非獎
延伸對外婆的愛 長期關懷老人及阿滋海默病患

Based on her personal experience in caring for Alzheimer's patients and her years of service to the broader Alzheimer's community, in March 2006, Tenny was honored with the Association of Silicon Valley Broker's Mike Murphy Award.

Thinking back to the birth of her son, Tenny to this day feels lament that her grandmother had a chance to hold him at the hospital but did not understand that this baby was her great-grandson. Tenny said, "I would be willing to give anything if I could get her real self back, even for a moment, and let her know that the baby she was holding was her own great-grandson."

Tenny's daughter has continued this family tradition of caring for the elderly. After graduating from Wellesley College, she continued, going on to earn a Masters in nursing from UCSF specializing in geriatrics and holistic nursing.

In 2005, Solomon, began to actively support the Peach Foundation, a Bay Area charitable group, founded by Ms. Cheng Tian-chin. In 2005, Cheng visited China's Yunnan Province, where she learned that many local children were unable to attend school due to their family's poverty. After returning to the United States, she sold a small hotel she owned, and began to devote herself to assisting these children in southwest China.

Solomon said, "The fathers of these young children are often alcoholics, and their mothers are sometimes sold as brides or into prostitution in Vietnam. These girls and boys sometimes get to third or fourth grade of elementary school before being pulled out of school to help their family work the land."

"Due to excessive drinking, the fathers of these children often die before they reach 40 or 50, and it's unusual for the grandparents to live to 50 years old as well. Everyone in the family is uneducated and illiterate. Ms. Cheng dedicated herself to helping these children, paying for their tuition and room and board so they could stay at school, where they receive three meals a day. The total annual cost to support a single student came to US$200."

On multiple occasions, Steve's son Solomon has taken his two sons to volunteer in schools in poverty-stricken areas of Yunnan Province.

"In the beginning, we were supporting between four and five hundred children, but today there are more than four thousand children, and the expenses have grown to US$250 per child. We also support local children who have the opportunity to go to college, and the annual budget for the program now exceeds US$1 million."

Solomon felt that the needs of these children went beyond money, but also to feel there was someone in the world who loved them and cared about them. "If no one else loves you, we do."

For two weeks a year for five years, Solomon took his two college-age sons to visit remote villages in China's southwest to assist in the Foundation's work in supporting these children.

"My sons were young teachers - coming to teach English to these children - but they ended up learning much more from their students. My sons were born and raised in the United States, and the time they spent working in China changed their outlook on life. Growing up, they had never wanted for anything, and here they got to observe a completely different way of living up close, and it helped them learn humility."

In China, poor families prioritize the schooling of sons over daughters. The Tsai's second daughter, Elizabeth, took part in the China Children and Teenagers Fund's Spring Bud Program, working with the Foundation's Bay Area director Ms. Chen Chin-ming in Gansu, Shaanxi and other areas in China to assist girls from poor families to continue their schooling.

She said, "I grew up in a family that is close to God, and this is the source of my concern for society for sharing the grace God has given me and my family."

In 1998 in Indonesia, anti-Chinese riots resulted in brutal massacres and the destruction of many Christian churches. Then, in 2004, the Indian Ocean earthquake and resulting tsunami hit more than a dozen countries, leaving more than 230,000 dead, with the majority of the casualties centered in Indonesia.

The youngest Tsai daughter, Vivien, was born into a Christian home and grew up in the church. But her greatest test came when she went to majority Muslim Indonesia, and she had to abandon her religious identity, carrying only unconditional love as the ideal international language. She and her husband established a non-profit organization to conduct philanthropic work in Indonesia, including drug rehabilitation, after-school counseling and crisis counseling for students, and investing in socially responsible companies. They raised funds to build a drug rehabilitation center in the mountains of Indonesia. This pristine and healthy environment is not only conducive to recovering from addition, but also attracts visitors from around the world.

Vivien said, "We are very grateful and have the honor and opportunity to create job training opportunities in these under-resourced areas that have been left behind by rapid economic development. Living in a global village, we are all connected. But our resources are limited, leaving us unable to serve in every area that requires assistance, so we work to enable and encourage local people to become self-sufficient."

Vivien and her husband actively sponsor micro-loan programs that lend to poor women in Indonesia. Each borrower receives up to US$100 to start a small business. "This small sum can change their lives. Once they start to make money, the borrowers pay back the loans, allowing us to help others. This is a form of permanent investment with a very high rate of return."

In just a single year, the program increased the number of women being served from 100 to more than 1,000. "Our goal is to extend the service to other regions once the total number of participants here in a single place reaches 5,000. We'll continue like this, expanding to new areas and countries." The couple have also created a website to recruit new supporters.

In 2003, Vivien spent a year auditing a course on non-governmental organizations at Harvard's Kennedy School of Government. The course helped her to realize that philanthropy is not something that only the wealthy can practice, nor is it just a way to minimize one's taxes. Rather, it is a faith that giving makes one richer than receiving. However, in many Asian countries, NGOs are in fact often directed by the government.

Vivien felt that, rather than rely on NGOs, a better solution is to focus on creating surplus resources through promoting economic development, and these resources can then be reinvested into society, creating a virtuous cycle.

The wealth gap in Taiwan has continued to grow, creating many social problems. The Hebron Life Care Center is a successful example of harnessing private efforts to address certain social problems. The Center assists marginal and disadvantaged people, including drug addicts, chronically indebted people, those suffering from mental illness, and ex-felons to get treatment and find their footing and begin life afresh in a half-way house type setting.

Vivien said, "It's been an honor for us to participate in this program, starting with just two or three people. Over the years, the Center has helped over 6000 marginalized individuals to re-enter society. Today, more than 300 people are living at the Center, which helps the government to care for young people, thus helping to resolve social problems. Representatives and delegations from many cities in China have come to Taiwan to observe the Center's operations, hoping to replicate this successful model on the mainland."

Vivien was born and raised in Taiwan and has a natural affection for the island. Years ago, she assisted in the development of the Christian evangelical "Good News" television station. This media outlet has extensive influence in Taiwan society and Vivien feels grateful for its success. "They have turned the church into a vibrant community through mass media, focusing attention on community needs and issues and helping people confront and overcome the challenges they face."

Vivien attributes her love of life and her dedication to helping young people to the influence of her father and grandfather. She hopes to spend her life continuously learning and innovating.

Family Album

But as for me and my household, we will serve the Lord.

— *Joshua 24: 15b*

Celebrating Steve's 97th birthday, 2022.

We are family!

Best Speaker in the House.

Steve and Tina celebrate their 50th wedding anniversary.

68th wedding anniversary.

69th wedding anniversary.

Tina and daughter Elizabeth.

Steve with five grandsons.

*Grandson Andrew and Shirlene's
wedding at Sun Moon Lake.*

Family celebrates grandparents' 60th wedding anniversary on a cruise

We are having fun!

A Happy couple on their balcony at home.

Celebrating Steve's 96th birthday at home 2021

Enjoying good food.

Tina's birthday.

Everyone in the family became an oil painter.

Concentrating on Practicing calligraphy.

Holding a 3D model of a residential project in San Francisco.

At home, before attending oldest daughter Tenny's wedding

Puo Puo meeting her great grandson Garrett for the first time.

Our beloved Puo Puo surrounded by friends and family, 1989.

Mother and Daughter.

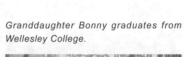

Granddaughter Bonny graduates from Wellesley College.

Grandson graduates from Cambridge University.

Granddaughter Bonny and Andrew's wedding, 2016.

Great granddaughter Kaylee kisses one week old baby sister Ari, the 5th great grandchild 2022.

Four generations, with daughter Tenny, grand children Garrett, Bonny & Andrew, great granddaughter Kaylee.

Kaylee's 3 year old birthday with great grandparents and 103 year old Tai-Puo.

Granddaughter Allison & Matthew's wedding 2012.

Zu Yei Yei spends time with oldest great granddaughter Hope.

Daughter Elizabeth, granddaughter Allison and grandchildren Hope & Hudson enjoy time with Zhu Yei Yei & Zhu Nai Nai.

*Through Peach Foundation, Solomon and
sons Nathan & Ethan volunteering in Yunnan*

Daughter in law Karen's birthday.

Steve and son Solomon.

Solomon's family, Karen, Nathan & Ethan.

Singing with granddaughter Ann.

Family celebrates Grandson Andrew and Shirlene's wedding at Sun Moon Lake 2018.

Rebecca Wang, Coco Wang, Shirlene Loi, Andrew Hsu and Chih Wang 2018.

Daughter Vivien and her granddaughter Ava.

Friends and relatives

Steve with niece A-bee at Tong Dong.

Steve with his youngest brother Yo Chong.

Steve's nephews and nieces.

Solomon visits Ambassador Lee of Republic of China to Vatican.

Joseph Kwok, Ambassador Matthew Lee, Dr. Samuel Chan and Solomon.

Director General Joseph Ma and Mrs. Ma visited Steve.

Grace, George, Steve, Yin Kee, Tina, godson Eric.

Tina with nephew George Chen.

Visit by Nanjing goddaughter Jenny.

Fan ma ma & Kitty.

Youngest good friend Yee Ong.

Yee Ong's three children.

Shuang Chiu and her husband Bob help translate "Modern Confucian Entrepreneur" from Chinese into English.

With old friend Ms. Cui Bing.

Childhood friend Guo Yin at Gulangyu island Xiamen home.

Dear friend Bee Hua visited from Manila.

Frank and Lorna Chang's family, dear friends and Neighbors.

Childhood friend Sho Gin.

Family with Pastor Peter & Liui Yang, and goddaughter Wendy.

Rev. Moody Yap, Steve, Elder Simon Lin, & Diana Lin and Pastor David Chu & Esther.

Church and charity

Solomon and wife Karen with their sons Nathan & Ethan join Golden Gate Walkathon for Self Help for the Elderly.

Autumn Glow 15th Anniversary Self Help for the Elderly.

Enjoying time under the sun during a break at a church retreat.

Annual Walk to End Alzheimer's 2021.

Steve & Tina attended summer retreat in 2019 with Pastor Chu & wife Esther.

Grace Gospel Christian Church Annual outdoor service, 2022.

Travel

A pair of fathers and sons play golf in Hawaii.

Steve with grandson Benjamin in Greece.

Visiting MaoKong, Taipei.

Remembering the old mail box in Taiwan.

Tenny & Eric accompany Steve and Tina to visit Mount Wu Yee.

Mount Wu Yee raft trip.

Riding yaks in Yunnan.

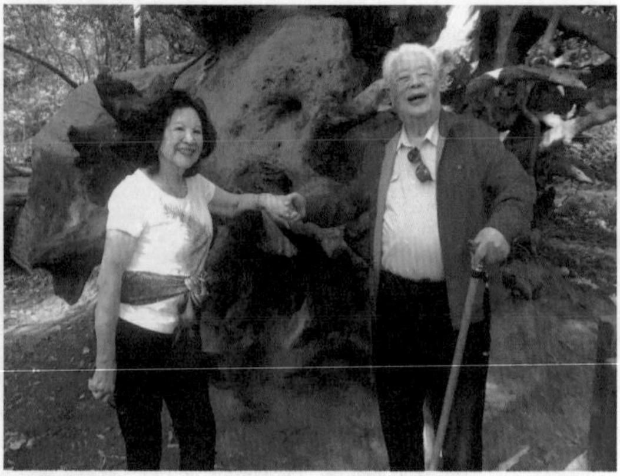

Hand in Hand in Redwood park.

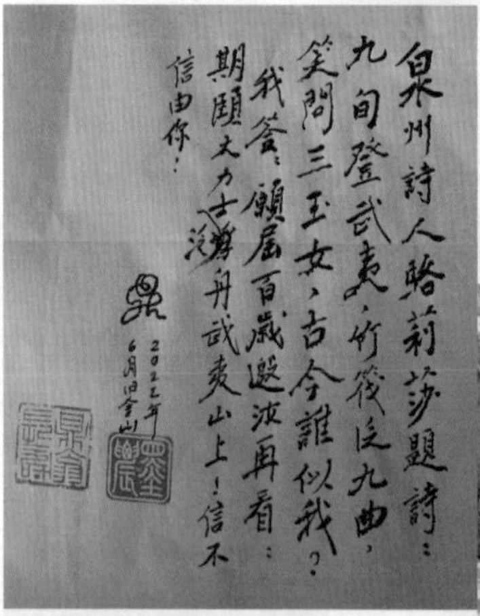
泉州詩人駱莉莎題詩：
九旬登武夷，竹筏泛九曲，
笑問三玉女，古今誰似我？
我答：願屆百歲遐波再看：
期頤大力士撐舟武夷山上！信不
信由你！
2022年
6月旧金山

Written by Lisha for Steve.

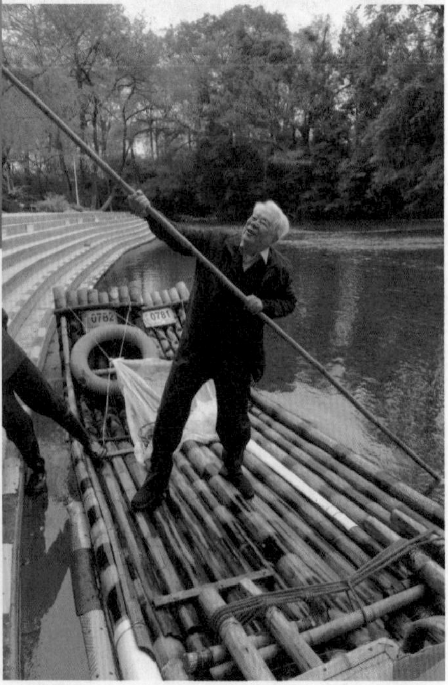

Work

Inspecting the progress of Construction Site of Hampton Inn and Suite, 2022.

In 2020, during the Covid pandemic, the family began the construction of a new hotel.

Steve getting a briefing on the construction progress.

Receiving the entitlement for a mixed-use project in San Francisco 12/03/2018.

Motto

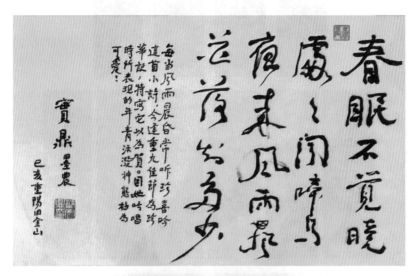

Calligraphy by Steve.

Chapter Fourteen

Homecoming

Rebuilding the Ancestral Home

Steve left home to study at the age of thirteen. After leaving Fujian for Taiwan in 1949, he often dreamed of returning to his hometown, but only finally came home to Tangdong Village for the first time in 1987.

His first priority was to rebuild the family's ancestral home.

After the family left the mainland for Taiwan in 1949, Steve's sister-in-law, alone with two young children, kept the house with little fuss for more than 60 years, up to her death. Steve's 1987 visit was in the latter part of those 60 years. Steve set to rebuilding the Ruyuan Pavilion, renaming it Huaixianglou (Huaixiang means "Nostalgia for one's Native Place") commemorating the history of the structure in an article named "About the Huaixianglou." Steve contributed all the funds needed for the renovation; but as it was the family's ancestral homestead, ownership of the property was equally divided between Steve and his three brothers.

While ownership of the newly refurbished three-story building was equally divided, a newly added additional half-story was not.

Steve's ancestral home, the Ruyuan Pavilion, was half-demolished by Japanese artillery. He demolished the original structure and replaced it with a new one named Huaixianglou. From right: Tina, Steve, nephew Jipin, and Jipin's daughter-in-law.

"The new half-story cannot be divided among the four families," said Steve. "If someday I retire here to my hometown, I'll take this half-story as my study, a place to read and write overlooking the sea."

Once the Ruyuan Pavilion was demolished and replaced by the even-larger Huaixianglou, Steve would sometimes stay overnight, reminiscing about the past.

Steve encouraged his children and his nieces and nephews to come from the United States, the Philippines, and Hong Kong to visit the old homestead, to ensure they would not forget their roots.

In 1996, Lifu Chen, a 96-year-old KMT veteran, presented two sets of calligraphic scrolls to be hung at the rebuilt Huaixianglou in commemoration of Steve's father Zhique.

The first set reads: *"Zhique may not have been able to read words, but he could read people and events, applying new thinking to old values."*

The second reads: *"Exhorting compassion for the poor, ethical behavior, benevolence and prosperity to rise above conflict for the benefit of the country and the people, thus leaving a lasting legacy for the future."*

Upon his return to Tangdong in 1987, Steve and his wife were invited to dinner with the Jindong School Management Committee. At the dinner, they heard about the deplorable state of the road connecting the village to the outside world. In rainy weather, the road was often impassable, but paving the road required funding. The villagers had unsuccessfully sought this funding from overseas Chinese.

Upon hearing this, Steve and his wife immediately decided to personally donate the needed funds. The villagers were delighted with the news. Steve's father, "Uncle Que," was still fondly remembered in the village for his devotion to improving the lives of the local people. Here, his son had returned home after being away for many decades, offering to pay for much-needed improvements. However, the surprised villagers were also concerned about whether Steve would be able to make good on his promise.

Three days later, a delegation of more than a dozen village representatives traveled to the Lujiang Hotel in Xiamen, bringing Steve the budget plan and the construction contract for the road. After careful review, Steve signed a commitment to provide the funds, finalizing the agreement with a handwritten couplet: "The splendid (Jin) landscape is unchanged, and now visitors from all directions (including from Dong) can come," and the words "Jindong Avenue." The village representatives were doubly impressed by Steve's financial and

After the construction of Huaixianglou, Kuomintang party stalwart Li-Fu Chen provided a couplet commemorating Steve's father.

calligraphic accomplishments.

The proposed road took more than a year to complete. Upon its completion, the grateful villagers proposed naming the road after Steve's father, Zhique, but Steve graciously declined, suggesting that the road be called "Jindong Avenue" (Jindong being an alternative name for Tangdong Village) to ensure that visitors would clearly understand where the road led. In addition, Steve and his second brother also made substantial scholarship contributions to the school in their hometown.

Steve attended the ribbon-cutting ceremony of Jindong Avenue with more than 20 members of his family, including his son, daughter-in-law, his second sister Binying, his sister-in-law Xie Shushun and her children. Schools let their students off for the day

1989: Steve arranged for the modernization of Jindong Avenue in his hometown, and widening it further 17 years later. From left: close friend Chen Xingwu, Steve, painter Zhang Renxi, Xiamen Daily News editor-in-chief Lin Wenyan.

2006: Jindong Avenue is expanded, strengthened, and widened, adding new gate pillars at both ends.

to mark the occasion, and the ceremony resonated with the sound of gongs and drums. The youngest generation of villagers, who had not previously understood the Tsai family's history and legacy, were amazed by the pageantry.

Steve built an archway on Tangdong Avenue, facing the village. Upon the arch was hung couplets in honor of his father. Facing the village, the couplet read, *"Support the poor in their desperation, and help a world in danger."* On the opposite side, a couplet read: *"The splendid (Jin) landscape is unchanged, and now visitors from all directions (including from Dong) can come."*

A marble stele was erected next to Jindong Avenue, engraved to commemorate the deeds of Tsai Zhique .

The stele's text read:

This avenue was built to commemorate Mr. Tsai Zhique, a sage of Tangdong (1884-1933). Born in turbulent times, he sought to preserve the peace, encourage filial piety, care for widows and orphans, and promote literacy. In 1925, he founded the Jindong School to raise up local students.

He was a man of fairness, benevolence, justice, and generosity, despite not coming from wealth. He urgently attended to the concerns of the people, especially in respect to morality. He dealt honestly in all affairs, mediating fairly in public disputes, and sought to shield the people from the ravages of war.

In a life of public good deeds, his greatest achievement was the establishment of the Xizi (a place name near Tangdong) Public Welfare Association which sought to placate disputes between people as well as disputes between villages. The affiliated Parents Association promoted moral virtue, with members pledging collective responsibility to ensure the honorable funeral rites for the older generation.

Jindong clan associations from around the world and the Jindong town association contributed to the erection of this stele, commemorating Steve's father at the entrance to Jindong Avenue.

In early 1933, he traveled to a neighboring village to mediate a public dispute, returning only late at night. He fell ill, and died soon after, only 49 years of age.

His funeral drew mourners from all directions, plaintively paying their respects.

Today, more than 50 years later, his many descendants have returned here from overseas to assist his hometown in its time of need, undertaking the construction of this road, sincerely reflecting the memory of his virtue.

Next to the stele about Tsai Zhique, the Jinjing Town Committee erected a stone monument, explaining the origin of Jindong Avenue and extolling Steve and his three brothers. The monument also explains that the four brothers, Shirong, Youhui, Steve and Youcong, built the road to commemorate the moral integrity of their parents, who generously contributed to build schools, bridges, and roads, and who spent much time and effort resolving disputes.

Tangdong Village is the mainland's frontline to Taiwan.

In 2006, a PLA military vehicle towing an artillery piece crashed into the memorial archway. Steve was overseas at the time, and the village committee members called and Steve immediately agreed to finance the reconstruction.

When it was built in early 1989, the road was constructed using the finest materials. But over 17 years, the road had suffered some wear and tear. "Rebuilding the arch was a trivial matter," said Steve. "Since we were rebuilding the archway, we decided we might as well rebuild the entire road. The new road would be wider and deeper, with an expanded drainage system to improve on the original one."

This time, rather than an archway, four large pillars were built at the road's entrance, built along the roadside and lacking an archway.

This would protect them from future mishaps. The two central pillars were wider in diameter and bore the original couplets, while the outer pillars were respectively inscribed with "Jindong Avenue" and "Steve Tsai, Chairman of the World Jindong Association."

The construction of the original road in 1989 was underwritten entirely by Steve, representing the four Tsai brothers to jointly honor their father.

The reconstruction in 2006 was a considerably larger and more expensive project, and Steve raised half of the funds from the children of his second brother. The other half was provided by Steve's four children. "Second brother's family and third brother's family split the cost".

He deliberately sought the assistance of his children and nephews to instill in the next generation his father's dedication to public service. A new stele commemorates their contribution, bearing the names of Steve's four children along with those of his second brother's two sons, Yiwen and Yiqi.

"Let them remember their ancestors and inherit their grandfather's sincerity and righteousness." At the time of their father's death, Steve, the second, and fourth brothers were all still young and the eldest brother, had taken on responsibility for all his father's debts. Before the mainland opened to the outside world, fourth brother took responsibility for maintaining the ancestral property. Therefore, the primary responsibility for the reconstruction of Jindong Avenue fell to the second and third siblings and their families. While Steve had taken on exclusive responsibility for the construction of the original road, Steve's children and the children of second brother each put up half of the funds for the 2006 reconstruction.

Alongside the road, they also built a pavilion for travelers to rest in. This Kindness Pavilion was dedicated to the memory of their mother, first brother and second brother.

Upon completion, Steve led his children and grandchildren to their ancestral hall to pay their respects. He knelt first before the ancestor tablets, followed by his entire family, all weeping together. "It was a very emotional moment," he recalled, "I was thinking of my father, my mother and so many family members who had passed away over the years."

Steve at the Jindong Avenue's Ci (Mother's Love) Pavilion, erected in memory of his mother and eldest brother, with an inscription from Kuomintang party stalwart Yu You-jen reading: In Mourning for a Loving Mother.

About the Huaixianglou

— Steve Tsai

The original name of this building is "Ruyuan Pavilion," a Western-style building erected in the 1920s. It survived more than seven decades of wind and rain and was repaired twice after being severely damaged by shelling by the Japanese navy. In 1987, after more than half a century away from home, I returned to find Ruyuan Pavilion completely disfigured. Touching the present and reminiscing about the past, I was filled with emotion. In memory of my father, we decided to build the much-needed Jindong Avenue, and then to rebuild the Ruyuan Pavilion.

My father, Zhique (1884-1933), was enthusiastically dedicated to public welfare, showed deep filial piety, and had boundless compassion for widows and orphans. His wife, Hongxiang (1893-1950), had four boys and six girls, and she taught them benevolence and righteousness. My father established the village's first school to bring literacy and education to the area.

He lived in troubled times, and there were frequent outbursts of violence. He established the Hsi-tsu Public Welfare Association to support the poor. He dedicated himself to mediating disputes, traveling long distances to keep the peace. Through the establishment of a Parents

Association, he promoted mutual aid in life and death.

On February 14, 1933, he traveled to a nearby village to mediate a dispute and did not return until the middle of the night, physically and mentally exhausted. The next morning, he could not be woken. It was as if a star had fallen, at the tragically young age of just 49, leaving his widow to keep the family together. Though his life was short, his legacy is far-reaching. To commemorate his virtue and achievements, we rebuilt the Ruyuan Pavilion. It is a terrible pity that my eldest and second brother did not live to see this rebirth of our ancestral homestead.

Today, nearly 200 members of my family live in the United States. To encourage them to carry on my love of our hometown and country, the new building was renamed "Huaixianglou" to reflect my feelings for my motherland. This building is a tribute to commemorate my estimable parents and my two dear brothers Shirong and Youhui.

1996, San Francisco, USA

Dreaming of Hometown

"The further I am from home, and the longer I stay away, the more deeply I miss my hometown," said Steve. "I often dream of the mountains and the ocean of my hometown and awake with fragments of memories."

Tangdong Style

Due to the political and military situation, after Steve arrived in Taiwan he was unable to return home for many years, and dreamed of his hometown every night, worrying about friends and students of his hometown. "I dreamt that one day I would return home, but no one would recognize me."

Impressions: He had once frequently traveled to the shrine of the sage Tsai Ding to pay tribute as a child. The funerary tablets of his mother and two brothers were now at the Xizi Rock Stone Buddha Temple.

But memories of his hometown lay heavy on his heart. "I would wonder what progress had been made on the reforestation projects covering Mt. Shigai and Mt. Fengzhi. The fields near the Shima Tomb where I herded goats were like a classroom for me, teaching me the ways of nature and agriculture when I was out of school."

The graves of Steve's father and other ancestors were erected on a hillside with a broad view of the sea. Before he was able to return to China, he entreated relatives in the village to maintain the graves and pay respects on his behalf. As China opened up, he would return every year to personally pay homage.

In Tangdong there is a pond called Longguang Pond, and Steve remembered the hubbub of villagers catching eels there, dozens of young men stripped naked, probing the muck at the bottom with spears, bringing the eels up to the surface where they could grab them with their hands. The eels would thrash and escape, only to be grabbed up again. Steve and the other children would gather by the waterside to watch this battle in progress, very nervous and excited, shouting encouragement to the young fishermen.

"When I was young, I went up the mountain to chop wood and herd goats with my friends. By noontime, we were hungry, and we went into the nearby fields to dig up some sweet potatoes. We roasted them over a fire and ate them peeled. They were delicious and fragrant. The war had made conditions very difficult for all of us, and if we found a way to feed ourselves up in the hills, it was one less mouth to feed at home."

After eating their fill, the boys would find pools in the mountains to swim in. Though small, these pools were deep and the boys would strip down and jump in, splashing and laughing. They would tread water and talk. Later in life, Steve thought that "If treading water were an Olympic sport, we would have all won gold."

At the time, it never occurred to Steve that this practice of treading water would come in handy later. At low tide, he and eight or nine other youths would haul a large net out into the sea, often treading water for hours at time against the wind and current, as a growing catch of fish would swim into the net, jumping and struggling, flashing in the late afternoon sun. "After we brought our catch on shore, I had to fight the temptation to eat them. Instead, we took them to the market to sell, bringing home some money for our family, along with the small or poor-looking fish nobody wanted to buy."

Steve often attended the Asian Games and other global sports competitions, either as a reporter or a spectator, with a particular interest in the swimming events. For the 2012 Olympic Games in London, the US hotel industry organized a delegation to attend, including Steve and his eldest grandson Nathan, staying at the Waldorf Hilton.

Nathan accompanied his grandfather to the events, often pushing him to the venue in a wheelchair. The swimming competitions brought back memories of treading water in these hills above his hometown. "If treading water were an event here, I would definitely win," he told Nathan. To his surprise, Nathanlearned this skill later.

Steve's home was close to the beach, with an ocean view from the second-floor bedroom, looking out over a long sandy beach, gleaming in the sun. To one side were the rough waves of the Pacific Ocean, while on the other side were tidal flats where stone slabs laid over the decades had turned into a thriving oyster colony. At low tide, oystermen walked the flats, collecting oysters and replacing the stones to raise the next generation, creating a sustainable cycle that benefits the whole community.

Later, in southern Taiwan, Steve saw oyster beds that were created with wooden boards, rather than the stone slabs of his hometown. Later still, he found large and expensive oysters in a famous seafood restaurant in San Francisco's Fisherman's Wharf. In New Orleans, he found street vendors selling oysters everywhere. In his extensive travels, Steve has sampled oysters all over the world but maintains that "The stone oysters in my hometown of Tangdong are the best in the world. They are the best I have ever eaten in my life. As to what they taste like, I'll keep that a secret. If you don't believe me, please come to Tangdong to try them for yourself."

When Steve was a child, he often played with children on the beaches of the bay, catching clams, small fish and shrimp. During the arduous years of the Anti-Japanese War, these were a precious source of food.

As a teenager, Steve would walk the 2km sandbank every morning, the receding tide having turned the beach into a free flea market.

One prized delicacy was horseshoe crabs. Shaped like a turtle shell with a long sharp tail, these delicious creatures would come up on the beach in mating pairs. Today, however, they're listed as a protected species and it's illegal to gather them.

Back then, however, there was competition for these prizes, including Steve's cousin A-ze. A-ze was only a few years younger than Steve, and although Steve was a bit taller, A-ze regularly won any fights the two had.

Later, A-ze joined the Chinese Communist People's Liberation Army and was captured by the Nationalist Army in the Battle of Kinmen. He subsequently switched sides and joined the Nationalist Army to serve in Taiwan. With this, Steve's former rival became a close relative, and A-ze stayed in Steve's home during leave from his military service. Once he had left the military and needed a job, Steve brought him into his own factory, despite his lack of experience, setting him up with a job and a place in the factory dormitory.

Despite A-ze's status as an employee in Steve's business, he kept a close eye on the other workers, telling them he was there to mind the shop on Steve's behalf. "The boss and I go way back," he would tell them, "So watch your step!"

Once, A-ze came to Steve's house in the middle of the night. "Do you remember our times on the sand bar back home," he asked. Steve smiled, patted him on the shoulder, and said, "Of course I remember, I may have lost all those fights, but I don't hold a grudge."

"Back then, we didn't understand anything," said A-ze. "Now, look at us. You're so successful, and I have nothing. I never could have dreamed that I would have arrived in Taiwan in chains, but really, it was a blessing in disguise because you took me in like this, and I don't know how to repay you." With this, A-ze burst into tears.

Finally, he composed himself and explained why he had come. He wanted to marry a woman who lived in the mountains and needed help with money. Steve and Tina immediately agreed, giving him the needed funds and their blessings.

Then, a few months later, A-ze reappeared unexpectedly, reporting that he'd been swindled by a matchmaker who'd promised him a bride in the mountains. He promised he'd learned his lesson and would be less trusting. He asked Steve to help him again with money. Steve and Tina were determined to see this through and sent him off with the needed funds. However, for some unknown reason, A-ze was still not successful in finding a bride.

In September 1987, President Chiang Ching-kuo began allowing veterans from Mainland China to return to the mainland to visit their relatives. A-ze took the opportunity to return to their hometown where he visited relatives, but also found a wife who he brought back with him to Taipei. Later, Steve's affairs took him away from Taiwan for increasingly long periods, and he lost touch with A-ze, only sadly learning two years ago that he had passed away in Taipei.

That sandbank had played a pivotal role in Steve's life. It was here that he and Miss H, his classmate from Dehua Normal School, first fell in love during that summer vacation she spent in Tangdong village. The two would take every opportunity to stroll the sandbank under the moonlight, listening to the waves crashing over the reef, joined in song.

On these summer nights, the villagers would lounge outside until late, enjoying the cool breeze. As the voices of the young couple carried over the waves, young people on shore would join in the song, serenading the village in the midsummer night.

In Steve's mind, part of him had never left his hometown, and would still stroll that golden beach in front of his house, surrounded by the mountains and rivers of his hometown.

§

A Truly Estimable Person

— Kaiping Liu

I had long been familiar with Mr. Steve Tsai and had interviewed him on the telephone several times before.

Kaiping Liu (right) congratulates Steve on his 90th birthday.

On January 1, 2009, California implemented a new law proposed by state Rep. Fiona Ma that explicitly allowed for a man to take his wife's surname after marriage. The next day, I called Mr. Tsai to get his view on the new law. He said that men should have the good grace to use their wives' surnames; women have a long history of taking their husband's surname after marriage, but it is not in line with equal rights between men and women; California's implementation of this new law is therefore a logical development in that it recognizes the equal status of women.

This is just one example of how Mr. Tsai's views are very forward-leaning.

The Bay Area Chinese community is very familiar with the Foster City Crowne Plaza Hotel and its owner, Mr. Steve Tsai. Thus, when

Ms. Chu Wan-ching called and asked me to help in writing Mr. Tsai's biography, I thought the story would focus on his success in the US hotel industry.

Then, I had a chance to finally meet Mr. Tsai in person, it quickly became apparent that his business success in the United States was the figurative tip of the iceberg, and that his life experience was in fact a treasure trove of extraordinary stories.

Mr. Tsai's time in Taiwan coincided with the development of an economic miracle that shocked the world, with average annual incomes rising from US$196 in 1952 to over $14,000 by the year 2000, a 72-fold increase in the space of barely five decades. Mr. Tsai stressed that Taiwan's economic development has been the result of the hard work of the Taiwanese people, and he only did his part. However, it became clear that Mr. Tsai actually played a unique and larger-than-life role in the Taiwan miracle.

What had initially seemed a small project with a limited scope quickly revealed itself as an epic story that needed to be told.

Several years ago, when we first started developing this book, Mr. Tsai was nearly 90 years old, but his mind was completely clear, and his memory was sharper than most young people. He effortlessly recalled events, both major and trivial, from previous decades, relating personal, institutional and national narratives in tremendous detail.

In addition, Mr. Tsai's command of current trends and technologies rivals that of even his grandchildren. He tracks the global events on his iPhone and iPad, firing off emails in response to information he teases from online newspapers reporting the latest developments in Taiwan and China. He retains his youthful passion for politics and world affairs, and his criticism of current affairs has lost none of its sting.

In fact, I found myself often surprised to remember Mr. Tsai's advanced age. The sharpness of his memory and tongue, and his love of fast cars and good food speak to an eternal sense of youthfulness.

Mr. Tsai mentioned that, upon retiring, he would like to return to his hometown in Tangdong Village, Fujian, where he would devote himself to reading in his rebuilt ancestral home Huaixianglou.

As I noted earlier, this book has been in the works for several years, and I am responsible for the delay. Despite this, Mr. Tsai has never been anything but gracious and kind-hearted, and I deeply appreciate his patience.

Making such an acquaintance is more valuable than power and wealth. The writing of this book has given me the opportunity to get to know a unique individual and a gentleman of great honor. It has been a great blessing in my life.

Kaiping Liu

June 2014

Special thanks to: Ms. Chu Wan-ching, Mr. Hung Tu, Ms. Ren Chia-yi, and Mr. Wang Yi-hsiang.

Appendix

The Life of Steve Tsai.

April 29, 1925 Born in Tangdong Village, Jinjing Town, Quanzhou City, Fujian Province, China.

1933 (age 9) Father dies of illness at age 49. From the age of 9 onwards, studied while working to support his mother and siblings.

1937 (age 12) Graduated from Jindong Elementary School. Participated in various anti-Japanese resistance activities.

1938 (age 13) Admitted to Quanzhou Peiyuan Middle School. Japanese army invades the Philippines, disrupting inward remittances from abroad. Dropped out of school to work, while studying on his own.

1939 (age 14) As part of the government's campaign to improve literacy, admitted to Provincial Dehua Normal School.

1941 (age 16) Graduated from Dehua Normal School, appointed headmaster of Elementary School. Hired as special correspondent to the Fujian News Agency.

1942 (age 17) Returns to teach at Jindong Elementary School, which is facing a financial crisis due to the war. Mistakenly arrested and imprisoned, refuses release without securing that of those arrested with him, securing the acquittal and release of over 100 people.

1943 (age 18) Recruited to the Xingquan Anti-Japanese Resistance Military Command Intelligence Unit, while also serving as chief correspondent for the Evening Times newspaper.

1945 (age 20) Japan surrenders. Assigned to the Xiamen Police Department to process repatriation of Japanese and investigate rape accusations.

1948 (age 23) Graduated among the first class of officers from the Xiamen Police Academy. Solved the murder involving the Xiamen Yitieling Company in which the owner murdered his younger brother.

1949 (age 24) Resigned from the police as the CCP enters Xiamen, leaves for Taiwan with his family.

1950 (age 25) His mother passes away in Taiwan at the age of 57. His siblings return to the Philippines, leaving the family scattered by the war.

1951 (age 26) Appointed chief editor of the Taipei National Culture Publishing House, publishing "*New Free China*".

1952 (age 27) Appointed Taiwan correspondent for the Philippines Xinmin Daily News, a post he would hold for over 20 years.

January 4, 1953 (age 28) Marries Tina Hung.

1953 Eldest daughter born.

1954 (age 29) Second daughter born.

1956 (age 31) Only son born.

1958 (age 33) Third daughter born.

1959 (age 34) Investigates the suspicious death of Yao Chia-chien at Taipei's Wuhan Hotel, finding against suicide. After fifteen years of investigation, the case was finally ruled a homicide.

1961 (age 36) Participated in efforts to lobby President Chiang to liberalize Taiwan's domestic insurance regulations. Refused special privileges for overseas Chinese investors, spearheading reforms that gave birth to a booming insurance industry. Established the Overseas Chinese Property Insurance Company (the first company that Steve established with overseas Chinese capital in Taiwan), serving as Executive Director and Deputy General Manager.

1963 (age 38) Establishes the Overseas Chinese Life Insurance Company (the second company that Steve established with overseas Chinese capital in Taiwan), serving as Executive Director, Deputy General Manager and General Manager.

1967 (age 42) Establishes the Huayang Development Corporation (the third company that Steve established with overseas Chinese capital in Taiwan), serving as Executive Director and Deputy General Manager. Responsible for the construction of Taiwan's then tallest building for Taiwan's first hotel in the Hilton Group, ushering in a new age of international tourism.

1968 (age 43) Established the Taishan Electric Industrial Corporation (the fourth company that Steve established with overseas Chinese capital in Taiwan), serving as General Manager. Established the Taiwan Decoration Bulbs & Light-Set Exporters Association, serving as Chairman of the board for 9 years, and Executive Supervisor for 38 years, spurring the development of Taiwan's "living room factory" business model, eventually providing employment for 150,000 residents of military dependents villages.

1973 (age 48) Elected Executive Director of the ROC National Chamber of Commerce, a post he would hold for 40 years, responsible for liaising between the ROC's Chamber of Commerce and its counterpart in other nations.

1976 (age 51) Appointed Chairman of the Board of the US Fangda Investment Corp.

1978 (age 53) United States and Canada end formal diplomatic relations with the Republic of China. Sent to the US and Canada to establish representative offices for the Republic of China Chamber of Commerce. Following the break in official ties, these two offices were the only institutions allowed to use the name "Republic of China". Led many delegations to visit counterpart institutions in Europe, the Americas, Australia, and Southeast Asia to promote commercial ties and diplomacy.

1980 (age 55) Baptized by Pastor Yeh Wen-yuan in San Francisco, officially begins his life as a Christian.

1982 (age 57) Elected as Managing Director of the OCBC, beginning 18 years of service, graduates with the 22nd class of the Revolutionary Practices Research Institute (later the National Research Development Institute).

1984 (age 59) Awarded an honorary Doctorate of Laws by Lincoln University, sharing the stage as California Secretary of State March Fong Eu received an honorary Doctorate of Education. Served as Managing Director of the Taiwan Paper Corp. beginning 11 years of service.

1985 (age 60) Served as Executive Director of the Republic of China Arbitration Association beginning 25 years of service.

1988 (age 63) Appointed Chairman of the Chiaofu Construction Management Company, a position he still held at the time this book was written.

1990 (age 65) Founded the US United Pacific Hotel Group.

1994 (age 69) Served as Chairman of the Republic of China Construction Management Association beginning 12 years of service.

2001 (age 76) Appointed to the Republic of China President's Advisory Committee on Economic Development.

Modern Confucian Entrepreneur

——Biography of Steve Tsai

The legendary life of the founder of the United Pacific Hotel Group

Written with Kaiping Liu

Translated by Jonathan Brody and Wang Shuang-chiu

First Published in Taiwan by Chung Hwa Book Company, Ltd., 29, April 2022

* The Traditional Chinese Edition of *Modern Confucian Entrepreneur*
was published by Chung Hwa Book Company, Ltd. in 2014.

COPYRIGHT © 2022 by

CHUNG HWA BOOK COMPANY, LTD.

For information of the publisher : 5F., No. 8, Ln. 181, Sec. 2, Jiuzong Rd., Neihu
Dist., Taipei, Taiwan (R.O.C.) / Telephone : 886 2 87978900 / Fax : 886 2 87978990
www.chunghwabook.com.tw

Book design by Chung Hwa Book Company, Ltd
Printed and bound in Taiwan by Herry Lithography Co.,Ltd.

Book No. G2032
ISBN 978-986-5512-90-3 (Paperback)

1912